HAUNTED CITY

THEATER: THEORY/TEXT/PERFORMANCE

Series Editors: David Krasner, Rebecca Schneider, and Harvey Young
Founding Editor: Enoch Brater

Recent Titles:

Haunted City

THREE CENTURIES OF RACIAL IMPERSONATION

IN PHILADELPHIA

Christian DuComb

UNIVERSITY OF MICHIGAN PRESS

Ann Arbor

Published in the United States of America by the
University of Michigan Press
Manufactured in the United States of America
⊗ Printed on acid-free paper

2020   2019   2018   2017   4   3   2   1

A CIP catalog record for this book is available from the British Library.

Library of Congress Cataloging-in-Publication data has been applied for.

ISBN 978-0-472-07358-0 (hardcover : alk. paper)
ISBN 978-0-472-05358-2 (paper : alk. paper)
ISBN 978-0-472-12301-8 (e-book)

For Caitlin, Madeleine, and Ezra

Acknowledgments

Haunted City never would have taken shape without my dissertation advisor, Rebecca Schneider, who nurtured this project from its larval stages to its present form. I also owe many thanks to the members of my dissertation committee—John Emigh, Patricia Ybarra, and Heather Nathans—who shared invaluable feedback on my research at crucial points in its development. LeAnn Fields, Christopher Dreyer, and Elizabeth Frazier at the University of Michigan Press—along with the anonymous readers of my manuscript—have suggested numerous improvements to the clarity and cogency of this book. Any errors in the evidence or imprecisions in the argument are entirely my own.

A number of generous grants and fortuitous affiliations have made the research for this book possible. As a graduate student, I received dissertation fellowships from Brown University and the American Society for Theatre Research (ASTR); a short-term research fellowship from the Winterthur Museum and Library; and an Andrew W. Mellon Research Fellowship from the Library Company of Philadelphia and the Historical Society of Pennsylvania. A courtesy appointment as a research associate at the McNeil Center for Early American Studies allowed me to access the University of Pennsylvania Libraries while completing my dissertation. Writing retreats sponsored by the Central New York Humanities Corridor and the Helen Weinberger Center for the Study of Drama and Playwriting at the University of Cincinnati afforded me time and space to revise my dissertation into a book manuscript. The Colgate University Research Council supported both a publication subvention and a stipend for my research assistant, Jessica Benmen, who helped attain permissions for many of the images in *Haunted City*.

Over the course of my research, I have benefited tremendously from the help and insight of a number of librarians, including Rosemary Cullen at the John Hay Library, Brown University; Rosemary Krill and Emily Guthrie at the Winterthur Library; and James Green and Phillip Lapsansky at the Library Company of Philadelphia. I also have had the pleasure of performing in the Philadelphia Mummers Parade, and I thank Hillary Rea, Tip

Flannery, Sonja Trauss, Jay Roselius, the Vaudevillains New Year's Brigade, the Murray Comic Club, and all the mummers I have spoken with over the years for welcoming me into their community.

Many superb teachers and mentors have contributed to my intellectual and professional development in the long journey toward publication of this book. As an undergraduate, Mark Lord, Paul Walsh, and Maud McInerney inspired me to pursue a life in theater and a career in academia. As a graduate student, Spencer Golub, Karen Shimakawa, Rey Chow, and Seth Rockman pushed me to expand my theoretical and historical imagination. Since joining the faculty of Colgate University, Adrian Giurgea, April Sweeney, Jane Pinchin, Constance Harsh, Margaret Maurer, and many of my senior colleagues in the Theater and English Departments have offered their wise counsel and generous mentorship.

Parts of the first and fifth chapter of this book were published, in earlier form, in the collection *Utopia in Performance* (London: Seagull Books, 2017), and I thank editors Rachel Bowditch, Pegge Vissicaro, and Mariellen Sandford for their incisive feedback. A host of friends and colleagues have read and offered comments on portions of this book (or closely related materials), and I am grateful to Paige McGinley, Pannill Camp, Elise Morrison, Michelle Liu Carriger, Christine Mok, Emily Sahakian, Katherine Zien, Peter Reed, Robin Bernstein, Kimberly Benston, Brian Connolly, Nimanthi Rajasingham, John Connor, Mary Simonson, Amanda Eubanks Winkler, Amy Holzapfel, and the members of the Carnival and Popular Fiesta working group at ASTR 2009 for their intellectual generosity. I am grateful also to the many friends who have endured my soliloquies about this project over the years, especially Andrew Daily, Aaron Tuller, Michael Winetsky, Alison D'Amato, Alena Smith, and Michelle Shafer. Thank you for your humbling intelligence and unwavering support.

My parents, Anthony DuComb and Robin Isenberg, were my first teachers, and I owe much of what I have accomplished in life to them. My father encouraged my interests in theater and history from the beginning, and my mother started teaching me to think critically and write clearly as soon as I could hold a pen. My children, Madeleine and Ezra Nye-DuComb, have taught me to balance work with play (and reminded me that work can be a form of play, if you open your mind to it). My sister, Adrienne DuComb, and my parents-in-law, Risa and Bruce Nye, have been tireless cheerleaders. And my wife, Caitlin Nye, has shared over fifteen years of adventure with me, from California to Kerala to Philadelphia to Providence to upstate New York (and many points in between). Without her love, wit, and wisdom, I never would have made it.

Contents

HAUNTED CITY

ONE | Haunted City

There is no place that is not haunted by many different
spirits hidden there in silence, spirits one can "invoke" or
not. Haunted places are the only ones people can live in.
—Michel de Certeau

In 2002 my wife, Caitlin, and I rented a one-bedroom row house on a treeless
alley near the corner of Seventh and Wharton Streets in South Philadelphia.
Two blocks from us, the city stopped. Vacant lots strewn with rubble stretched
eastward along Wharton from Fifth Street to Moyamensing Avenue, where
rows of houses suddenly sprang up again. This was Pennsport, a tradition-
ally Irish Catholic neighborhood with neat, lace-curtain homes (most of them
tiny, like ours) and a cluster of venerated mummers' clubhouses along Second Street. To an erstwhile Californian like me, this was a mysterious landscape. What used to occupy the empty blocks around Fifth and Wharton?
And if this corner and its environs were abandoned (for so they seemed to
me at first), how had Pennsport—a two-block-wide sliver of a neighborhood
between Moyamensing and Interstate 95—remained intact?

On warm weekend afternoons, I would walk past the old Italian man
selling loose cigarettes on our corner, past the Vietnamese and Cambodian
grocery stores on Sixth Street, past the sagging chain-link fences that pre-
tended to guard the vacant lots along Wharton between Fifth and Moyamensing, and then down Second Street, where groups of middle-aged men
gathered in front of mummers' clubhouses to laugh, drink beer, and play
music together on banjoes and saxophones. I loved living in South Philadelphia. I loved this walk. And before long, roaming these streets, I came to
believe that the places around me were haunted.

MUMMING AND RACIAL IMPERSONATION IN PHILADELPHIA

This book is rooted in my longstanding interest in the Philadelphia Mummers Parade, an annual, New Year's Day event with a complex and trou-

bled history of racial impersonation. Jill Lane and Marcial Godoy-Anativia argue that,

> While impersonation is at the very heart of theatrical practice, *racial impersonation* leads us to a dense social terrain shaped by struggles over power, nation, labor, and identity. Including practices as varied as blackface, passing, and ventriloquism, racial impersonation always involves drawing, crossing, and traversing a line of racial difference. While it may sometimes blur or contest that line, more often than not such impersonation serves to mark and police the boundaries that organize sociality along the axis of race, forcefully defining who can and cannot occupy what racial positions.[1]

In this chapter and the pages that follow, I explore blackface masking and other forms of racial impersonation in Philadelphia—as realized in street performance, festivity, theater, and graphic art—from the late eighteenth century through the present day. Given the interdisciplinary character and wide historical scope of my research, I do not attempt to offer a comprehensive history of racial impersonation in Philadelphia. Rather, I focus on select historical moments when local performances of racial impersonation—in whatever medium—inflected regional, national, transnational, and global formations of race, gender, class, and ethnicity. As such, this project draws on and contributes to scholarship on the history of street performance in the urban United States, the history of blackface minstrelsy, and performance studies research on racial formations in the Atlantic world. Although my arguments move across time and space, across media, and across academic disciplines, I remain focused throughout on local practices of racial impersonation, mostly (but not exclusively) in Philadelphia.

In early modern Europe—especially France, Britain, Ireland, Germany, and Scandinavia—groups of disguised mummers roved from house to house during the Christmas season, performing brief, comic sketches and expecting food, drink, or a small tip in return. As early as the seventeenth century, immigrants from England and Sweden introduced mumming to colonial Pennsylvania. In a diary entry from December 24, 1686, Englishman Richard Pennyworth, who was visiting family in Philadelphia, recalled "a great noise of bagpipes, and the door being opened, in comes a party of mummers alle decked out in a most fantastick manner."[2] During the winter holidays in 1780–81, Philadelphian Christopher Marshall wrote in his diary of men "firing guns in the night" and "before day sundry kinds of music, I presume, paraded the Streets."[3]

In both Europe and North America, mummers sometimes wore black-face makeup, a common disguise in early modern popular performance. Natalie Zemon Davis argues that blackface and male-to-female transvestism frequently appeared together in France, Britain, and Ireland in the seventeenth and eighteenth centuries, when men blacked up and dressed in women's clothes to protest abuses of power by the nobility, to license the transgression of class and gender roles, and to enforce sexual mores through charivari and "rough music"—ritual performances devised to shame infertile couples, adulterers, and husbands dominated by their wives.[4] Bryan Palmer finds a similar symbolic vocabulary at work in numerous instances of North American charivari (or *shivaree*, its Anglicized equivalent) from seventeenth-century Quebec to nineteenth-century Pennsylvania.[5] Blackface masking and burlesque performances of class and gender carried a wide-ranging set of resonances in these shivarees, but I am skeptical of the claim, advanced by Dale Cockrell, that practices of "nonracial folk blackface" took root in British North America and the early United States.[6] What is clear, as scholars like Robert C. Toll, Eric Lott, and David R. Roediger have demonstrated, is that blackface emerged as powerful technology of racialization by the early nineteenth century, deployed in both street and stage performances to construct working-class, white, male identity through the putative imitation of black speech, music, and dance.[7]

In Philadelphia and elsewhere in eastern Pennsylvania, Christmas blackface persisted from the colonial period well into the nineteenth century. German immigrants to the region brought with them the tradition of *belsnickling* (a term derived from the German *Pelz-nickle*, or "St. Nicholas in Fur"), which Philadelphia's *Pennsylvania Gazette* described as follows in 1827:

> Mr. Bellschniggle is a visible personage—Ebony in appearance, but Topaz in spirit. He is the precursor of the jolly old elf "Christkindle," or "St. Nicholas," and makes his personal appearance, dressed in [animal] skins or old clothes, his face black, [with] a bell, a whip, and a pocket full of cakes or nuts; and either the cakes or the whip are bestowed upon those around, as may seem meet to his sable majesty.[8]

Unlike the benevolent Santa Claus who sneaks down the chimney unseen on Christmas Eve, the *belsnickle* was "performed by real people—generally men of the lower orders," who did not hesitate to dispense punishment. As Stephen Nissenbaum suggests, "it was a thin line—and probably more of a terminological distinction than an historical one—that divided a belsnickle from a mummer" in antebellum Pennsylvania.[9]

By the mid-nineteenth century, the term *belsnickling* applied almost exclusively to Christmas revels in small, eastern Pennsylvania cities like Pottstown, Lancaster, and Reading. Meanwhile, the term *mumming* became popular in Philadelphia, although local newspapers often reported on Christmas mummers in the past tense. In 1857 the *Philadelphia Sunday Dispatch* published a derisive article on the "gangs of young fellows" who used to parade through the streets on Christmas Eve:

> With their shirts outside of their lower garments and their faces blackened over, they would visit homes, and, after going through a series of "mumming," as it was called, they would put the master of the place under contribution for money or drink, and then go somewhere else to go through the same foolery. . . . The Mummers were finally voted a nuisance, and all doors being shut against them, [they] metamorphosed into Calithumpians, and these noisy Christmas-keepers now go about at night creating all sorts of discord, and making night hideous with their yells.[10]

Claire Sponsler reads this account as an attempt to recast Philadelphia's Christmas revelry as an Anglo-Saxon tradition, rooted in British holiday customs like house visiting and mummers' plays, which then gradually "metamorphosed" into Calithumpian disorder.[11]

Although the term *mummers* was rarely used to describe holiday street performers in Philadelphia before the mid-nineteenth century, there is scattered evidence of mumming in the early United States. Federalist politician Samuel Breck left a sneering account of the "Anticks" he encountered during his childhood in Boston in the late eighteenth century, which describes a performance closely resembling a mummers' play:

> I forget on what holiday it was that the Anticks . . . used to perambulate the town. They have ceased to do it now [ca. 1830], but I remember them as late as 1782. They were a set of the lowest blackguards, who, disguised in filthy clothes and ofttimes with masked faces, went from house to house in large companies, and *bon gré, mal gré*, obtruding themselves everywhere, particularly into the rooms that were occupied by parties of ladies and gentlemen, would demean themselves with great insolence. . . . The only way to get rid of them was to give them money, and listen patiently to a foolish dialogue between two or more of them. One of them would cry out, "Ladies and gentlemen sitting by the fire, put your hands in your pockets

and give us our desire." When this was done and they had received some money, a kind of acting took place. One fellow was knocked down, and lay sprawling on the carpet, while another bellowed out,

> See, there he lies,
> But ere he dies
> A doctor must be had.

He calls for a doctor, who soon appears, and enacts the part so well that the wounded man revives. In this way they would continue for half an hour; and it happened not infrequently that the house would be filled by another gang when these had departed. There was no refusing admittance. Custom had licensed these vagabonds to enter even by force any place they chose. What would we say to such intruders now? Our manners would not brook such usage [for] a moment.[12]

Breck's account follows the general pattern of a mummers' play of the "hero-combat" variety, in which an important religious or political figure dies at the hands of an antagonist—often a Turkish or Egyptian knight—and is then revived by a doctor. According to Herbert Halpert, most hero-combat mummers' plays also include one or more devils and an assortment of "historical characters, figures from popular tradition or chap-books, and contemporary notables" who "shift and combine in bewildering ways."[13]

The extant descriptions of mumming in eighteenth-century Pennsylvania are neither as detailed nor as reliable as Breck's account. In their exhaustive *History of Philadelphia*, J. Thomas Scharf and Thompson Westcott quote the recollections of a "correspondent" on local mumming practices in the early national period:

It was considered the proper thing in those days to give the leading mummers a few pence as a dole. . . . It was also regarded as the right thing to do to invite them into the house and regale them with mulled cider, or small beer, and homemade cakes. It was considered a great breach of etiquette to address or otherwise recognize the mummer by any other name than that of the character he was assuming.[14]

Whatever the accuracy of this account, the 1857 *Sunday Dispatch* article and Breck's reminiscences show that nineteenth-century manners had rendered interclass house visiting and the performance of mummers' plays unfashionable and obsolete. Often masked in chimney soot and grease, Christmas revelers offended Philadelphia's bourgeoisie, who feared and resented the licensed incursion of brash, blackfaced men into their homes—regardless of whether they called these men mummers, anticks, *belsnickles*, or Calithumpians.

Given the rowdy and sometimes violent tenor of Christmas celebrations in Philadelphia, it comes as no surprise that "respectable Philadelphians condemned Christmas as a disgrace" for most of the nineteenth century.[15] From the 1830s through the 1880s, unruly bands of poor, young, white men—sometimes cross-dressed and often in blackface—roamed the streets on Christmas Eve, threatening and occasionally attacking recent immigrants, free blacks, and "respectable Philadelphians," both black and white. "By creating hilarity through the delineation of deviant characteristics (blackface, women's dress)," Susan G. Davis argues, these groups of young men "laughingly drew their social circle tighter."[16] After the consolidation of the city and county of Philadelphia in 1854, the city's new, central police force gradually imposed "organized crowd control" on holiday revelers and "shift[ed] the theater of disorder from holy Christmas Eve to secular New Year's Eve and eventually to New Year's Day."[17] In 1901 the city ensured its jurisdiction over holiday street festivities by sponsoring the first annual Mummers Parade, a publicly sanctioned procession up Broad Street, the major thoroughfare connecting the working-class neighborhoods of South Philadelphia to the city center. Although the route of the Mummers Parade has varied over the years, City Hall has always served as the symbolic focus of the parade. On January 2, 1901, the *Philadelphia Public Ledger* reported that "three thousand men and boys in outlandish garb frolicked, cavorted, grimaced, and whooped" in the first Mummers Parade "while the Mayor and members of Councils, Judges, and other officials, State and municipal, looked on." Clearly, "the city had put its official seal upon mummery," and city government has attempted to regulate the parade ever since.[18]

Both participation and attendance at the Mummers Parade have declined since the 1980s, but roughly eight thousand marchers and fifty thousand spectators still crowd the parade route each New Year's Day, and hundreds of thousands of viewers in greater Philadelphia watch the parade on local television.[19] Most marchers participate through licensed mummers clubs, which compete in one of five categories:

1. The comic division, which focuses on satire and clowning.
2. The wench brigade division, which emphasizes a traditional, burlesque performance style.

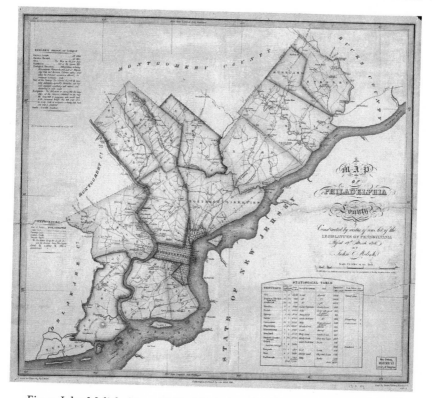

Fig. 1. John Melish, *Map of Philadelphia County*, 1819. This map shows the original boundaries of the city of Philadelphia, along with the outlying districts consolidated with the city in 1854. Courtesy Library of Congress.

3. The string band division, which features live music by large ensembles of banjoes and brass.
4. The fancy club division, which prizes elaborate costume design.
5. The fancy brigade division, which concentrates on Broadway-style staging and choreography.

Comic and fancy clubs are subdivided into smaller groups and brigades whose performances are professionally judged in front of City Hall, contributing to the overall score of the parent club.[20] Until the financial crisis of 2008, the city of Philadelphia offered close to $400,000 in cash prizes to be divided among all but the lowest-scoring groups in the competition. The five "traditional" mummers divisions still compete before the judges, and in 2016 the city added the Philadelphia Division, a noncompetitive branch of the Mummers Parade designed to encourage participation by African American, Asian American, Hispanic, and LGBT performance groups.[21]

Until the city banned blackface makeup from the Mummers Parade following civil rights protests in 1964, many comics, wenches, and string bands marched in blackface. At first the mummers fiercely opposed the blackface ban, but by 1965 nearly everyone in the parade agreed to put the aside the burnt cork and greasepaint on New Year's Day. Although a few marchers in blackface still appear in the parade each year, the mummers as a whole have grown considerably more diverse and inclusive since the 1964 blackface controversy. In the 1970s most mummers clubs in the comic, string band, fancy club, and fancy brigade divisions began admitting women. In 1984 the Goodtimers Comic Club, with an African American president and hundreds of minority members, started competing in the parade.[22] And in 1992 a group of Cambodian American artists and students teamed up with the venerable Golden Sunrise Fancy Brigade to stage a Khmer dance drama as part of the mummers' annual procession up Broad Street.[23]

As a devoted mummers fan since 2003, I have noted with enthusiasm that many new, nontraditional mummers groups have sprouted up over the past fourteen years. In 2009 I joined one of these groups: the Vaudevillains, a comic brigade established in 2007 at the Space 1026 arts collective in Chinatown. Sonja Trauss, a cofounder of the Vaudevillains, describes the group as anticapitalist, and the Vaudevillains' parade performances have confronted global warming, nuclear proliferation, big agriculture, student loan debt, and hydraulic fracturing (or "fracking") in rural Pennsylvania.[24] But despite the emergence of the Goodtimers, the Golden Sunrise/Khmer collaboration, the Vaudevillains, and other diverse, progressive mummers groups, the twenty-first-century Mummers Parade remains predominantly a white, male affair. And despite the apparent success of the blackface ban, other forms of racial impersonation in the parade continue to flourish unchecked. This book endeavors to unpack both the historical roots and the contemporary resonances of racial impersonation in the Philadelphia Mummers Parade.

FROM THE MESCHIANZA TO THE MUMMERS PARADE

Many of the groups that participate in the contemporary Mummers Parade rehearse along my old walking route through South Philadelphia, whether in clubhouses on Second Street or in parking lots under Interstate 95. To the east, just beyond the interstate, runs the Delaware River and a few blocks to the west, somewhere near the intersection of Fifth and Wharton, lie the remains of Walnut Grove, an eighteenth-century estate owned by the Wharton family (Wharton Street is named for them). On May 18, 1778, during the British Army's occupation of Philadelphia, Walnut Grove hosted an elaborate fete called the Meschianza, which theater historian Jared Brown singles out as "the most lavishly theatrical of all the entertainments presented in America during the Revolution."[25] The Meschianza included a regatta, a jousting tournament, fireworks, dining, and dancing, all of which unfolded along the Delaware River and on the plain between the river and Walnut Grove. "The location then was perfectly rural," wrote Charles Durang in 1854, "but now . . . it is converted into a busy manufactury, surrounded by rows of dwellings."[26] By 2002 (and probably long before) this bustling, nineteenth-century neighborhood had vanished—although new homes began sprouting up on the vacant lots around Fifth and Wharton just before my wife, Caitlin, and I moved away from the neighborhood in 2005.

At the Meschianza, the young, marriageable daughters of Philadelphia's colonial elite appeared in Turkish costumes, and black slaves in turbans and sashes waited on the guests. In chapter 2 I draw on descriptions of the Meschianza from newspapers, journals, and city histories to reconstruct the performances of racial impersonation staged at the event. I also engage an eclectic selection of texts and performances that sheds light on the significance of racial impersonation at the Meschianza, including Miguel de Cervantes Saavedra's *Don Quixote* (one of the most popular novels in the eighteenth-century Anglo-Atlantic) and Susanna Rowson's play *Slaves in Algiers*.

The racial impersonations staged at the Meschianza presaged some remarkably similar racial impersonations that appeared almost two centuries later in the Mummers Parade—many of them rehearsed on Second Street or under Interstate 95, on the same small parcel of land once occupied by Walnut Grove. In the first fourteen years of the mummers' fancy brigade competition (1950–64), half of the first-place performances featured elaborately costumed skits with oriental or African themes: "Congo Ceremony" (1952), "The Harem" (1953), "African Voodoo Warriors" (1954), "Persian Market" (1957), "Oriental Fans" (1959), "Javanese Temple Dancers" (1960), and "Jungle Madness" (1961).[27] Even today, racial impersonation is common—and surprisingly uncontroversial—among fancy clubs, whose entries in the 2013 Mummers Parade included "Echoes of Ancient Egypt," "King Tut and Strut," "Whispers of the Orient," "Aladdin's Flying Carpet," "Arabian Nights," "Lawrence of Arabia," "The Gypsy," "Pride of Africa,"

"The Glory That Was Africa," "Voodoo Man from Zulu Land," "Zulu Warrior," "African Princess," "Native American Spirit," "Tiki Dancers," "Polynesian Volcano Dancers," "Latin Rhythm and Dance," "Mexican Hat Dance," and "Brazilian Holiday."[28] Given that most fancy brigade and fancy club members are white men, themes such as these require many of the performers to assume racial, gendered, and historical positions other than their own.

In the 1990s scholars of racial impersonation like Joseph Roach and W. T. Lhamon Jr. broadened the historiography of blackface performance in the United States from a national to an Atlantic frame.[29] By thinking outside the epistemological limits of national culture, Roach and Lhamon uncovered the importance of gender, class, and diasporic conceptions of race and ethnicity to the politics of the nineteenth-century blackface mask. However, Shannon Steen critiques Lhamon (though not Roach) for neglecting other forms of racial impersonation in his analysis: "In the scholarship . . . on the racial dynamics of blackface . . . there has been a casual assumption that yellowface, brownface, redface, and so forth operate with the same racial and cultural effects that blackface produces." Following Steen's lead, I treat oriental impersonation and blackface impersonation as distinct phenomena, rhizomatically connected by orientalist constructions of blackness in the Atlantic world—an overlooked aspect of Atlantic racial formations in the eighteenth and nineteenth centuries.[30]

In his influential book *Cities of the Dead: Circum-Atlantic Performance*, Roach argues,

> Circum-Atlantic societies, confronted with revolutionary circumstances for which few precedents existed, have invented themselves by performing their pasts in the presence of others. They could not perform themselves, however, unless they also performed what and who they thought they were not. By defining themselves in opposition to others, they produced mutual representations from encomiums to caricatures, sometimes in each another's presence, at other times behind each other's backs.[31]

Roach's case studies, which range from Alexander Pope's poem "Windsor Forest" to the performance practices of the Mardi Gras Indians in twentieth-century New Orleans, tend to focus on triangular encounters "between and among red, white, and black peoples."[32] For Roach, these charged and often violent scenes of crossracial mimesis suggest "an alternative historical narrative of American literature and culture" resistant to the reductive racial binary of black and white.[33] But as John Kuo Wei Tchen argues, orientalism and oriental impersonation have been "intrinsic to American social, economic, and political life" since the Revolutionary War.[34] Throughout this book I explore the coarticulation of blackness and orientalism through performances of racial impersonation in Philadelphia and ask why such performances so often play out either across women's bodies or in conjunction with male-to-female transvestism.

Philadelphia's famous inwardness makes it an unlikely site through which to study oceanic and transnational constructions of race and gender. In 1834 Massachusetts politician Charles Francis Adams commended Philadelphia for having "something solid and comfortable about it, something which shows *permanency*"—in contradistinction to the "display" of New York City, the "upstart" of Baltimore, the "fashion and politics" of Washington, and the "unbending rigidity" of Boston.[35] While residing in Philadelphia in 1889, Lafcadio Hearn complained, "I do not know what has been going on anywhere. . . . Philadelphia is a city very peculiar—isolated by custom antique. . . . No echo from New York enters here—nor from anywhere else."[36] For Henry James, writing in the first decade of the twentieth century, Philadelphia was a place that "went back," that "had its history behind it." James commented wryly (but with affection) on the "intensity and ubiquity of the local tone," comparing the city to "a closed circle that would find itself happy . . . if only it could remain closed enough."[37]

Despite these accounts of its stolid provincialism (which resonate with my experience of the city today), Philadelphia in the eighteenth century was among the most tolerant and cosmopolitan cities in the Atlantic world. In his 1701 Charter of Privileges, William Penn—the Quaker founder of both Philadelphia and Pennsylvania—granted religious freedom to all settlers in the colony, provided that they worshipped "One almighty God."[38] In the wake of Penn's charter, Catholics, Jews, and members of persecuted Protestant sects (Amish, Moravian, Mennonite) sought refuge in and around Philadelphia, and "Quakers quickly found themselves a statistical minority in the Quaker City."[39] Nonetheless, Philadelphia's Society of Friends mustered enough political support to push an Act for the Gradual Abolition of Slavery through the state legislature in 1780, making Pennsylvania the first state in the country to adopt such a law.[40]

As a result of both gradual abolition and the in-migration of African Americans from the coastal South, early national Philadelphia emerged as "the largest and most important center of free black life in the United States."[41] Beginning in the 1820s, native-born white Philadelphians grew increasingly hostile toward both free blacks and Irish Catholics as more and more migrants crowded into fast-growing slums like Moyamensing. Recounting a visit to Philadelphia in 1841, the English abolitionist Joseph Sturge expressed shock at the racial discrimination he witnessed in the city:

> The prejudice against colour prevailing here [is] much stronger than in the slave States. . . . Philadelphia appears to be the metropolis of this odious prejudice. . . . There is probably no city in the known world, where dislike, amounting to hatred of the coloured population, prevails more than in the city of brotherly love![42]

Among the most virulent perpetrators of this "prejudice against colour" was graphic artist Edward Williams Clay (1799–1857), whose popular series of racial caricatures, *Life in Philadelphia*, made the city's black middle class into "the butt of an international joke."[43] In chapter 3 I argue that Clay's dalliance with French orientalism early in his career inflected his cruel depiction of African Americans in *Life in Philadelphia*. I also explore the interanimation of Clay's racial caricatures and performances of racial impersonation onstage in the early nineteenth century, both of which contributed to the production of popular blackface characters like Jim Crow and Coal Black Rose.

In the summer of 1832, T. D. Rice (1808–60), the renowned Jim Crow dancer, brought his blackface act to Philadelphia for the first time.[44] The following year, when the city's first horse-drawn omnibus began operation, "[it] was called the 'Jim Crow,' after Thomas D. Rice, the famous minstrel, whose picture was painted in the panels on each side of the coach."[45] At about the same time, Clay issued an engraving, *Mr. T. Rice as the Original Jim Crow*, which became popular as a sheet music illustration for blackface songs.[46] Later in the 1830s, Clay's engraving sometimes appeared on the playbill when Rice performed in Philadelphia, completing Jim Crow's passage from stage to bus advertisement to print—and finally back to the theater.[47] This rapid circulation across cultural forms exemplifies what Susan G. Davis, following Raymond Williams, calls "the unprecedented fluidity . . . [of] media genres" in the early nineteenth century.[48]

Jim Crow's repeated slippage from one medium to another complicates Diana Taylor's distinction between "the archive" and "the repertoire"—a distinction that has played an important role in recent scholarship on the performance history of the Americas. For Taylor, archival memory consists of "documents, maps, literary texts, letters, archaeological remains, bones, videos, films, CDs, all those items supposedly resistant to change."[49] The repertoire, by contrast, transmits memory through embodied practices:

"performances, gestures, orality, movement, dance, singing—in short, all those acts usually thought of as ephemeral."[50] The repertoire, Taylor argues, does not disappear from history; rather, it persists through "non-archival systems of transfer."[51] And because it cannot be fully captured by the technologies of the archive (writing, mapping, excavating, recording), "the repertoire allows for an alternative perspective on historical processes of transnational contact, [which] invites a remapping of the Americas . . . following traditions of embodied practice."[52] Although Taylor mobilizes the archive/repertoire distinction to great effect in her research on Latin America, the media-hopping construction of Jim Crow in the early 1830s resists explanation in terms of the archived versus the embodied or the recorded versus the performed. As such, I am not convinced that "the archive exceeds the live . . . insofar as it constitutes materials that seem to endure," nor am I convinced that the repertoire "cannot be housed or contained in the archive."[53] In the case of Jim Crow, it is through repeated transmission *between* archival and embodied forms that Rice's blackface character comes to have real, political effects, traceable today not only in Philadelphia's vast archives but also—and perhaps more so—in the performances staged each year in the Mummers Parade.

Nonetheless, Taylor's accent on embodied practices as sites of collective memory resonates with Michel Foucault's work on genealogy and Roach's work on circum-Atlantic performance—two threads of scholarship that deeply inform this book's methodology. In a famous essay on Nietzsche, Foucault theorizes genealogy as an approach to the past opposed to the search for purity of origin:

> If the genealogist refuses to extend his faith in metaphysics, if he listens to history, he finds that there is "something altogether different" behind things: not a timeless and essential secret, but the secret that they have no essence or that their essence was fabricated in a piecemeal fashion from alien forms. . . . What is found at the historical beginning of things is not the inviolable identity of their origin; it is the dissension of other things. It is disparity.[54]

If Europeans and their descendants in North America invented and performed their whiteness by donning blackface, then the history of racial impersonation in the Atlantic world demands genealogical thinking to unmask the dissension at the taproot of modern theories of race. But because Foucault situates genealogy "within the articulation of the body and history," Roach adapts Foucault's abstract treatment of embodied practices to develop a more precise tool for the study of racial impersonation (or "surrogation," to use Roach's term).[55] "Genealogies of performance," Roach argues, "attend not only to 'the body,' as Foucault suggests, but also to bodies—to the reciprocal reflections they make on one another's surfaces as they foreground their capacities for interaction."[56]

In 1825 a burlesque militia parade in Philadelphia transformed a diminutive man named John Pluck from an object of neighborhood mockery into an icon of working-class resistance and disorder. Chapter 4 follows Pluck's unlikely ascent from street performer to theatrical celebrity and traces the gradual blackening of images of Pluck in antebellum visual culture. To understand Pluck's parade performances as they circulate across media, I develop a theory of "parade time," which posits inherent distinctions in the temporal experience of the parade for participants, street-side spectators, and remote voyeurs. This formal argument serves as a framework to help unpack Pluck's transformation into a blackface figure—a transformation that suggests the proximity of blackness, ethnic whiteness, and working-class labor in the antebellum imagination. The chapter closes by excavating the afterlife of this historical constellation in the minstrel-show performances staged at Philadelphia's Eleventh Street Opera House from 1855 through 1911.

Chapter 5 traces a performance genealogy of the "wench," one of the most enduringly popular figures in both the minstrel show and the Mummers Parade. Frank Dougherty and Ron Goldwyn, who spent decades reporting on the mummers for the *Philadelphia Daily News*, describe the wench as "the most traditional, outrageous, and politically incorrect of all mummers. Basically, it's a guy in a dress. The hairier the legs, the longer the braids, the colder the beer, the better."[57] Until 1964 wenches almost always wore blackface, suggesting a genealogical connection between the mummers wench and the "wench act" of the early 1840s: a burlesque form of gender impersonation performed onstage by white men in blackface, often in the context of the antebellum minstrel show. This chapter situates the wench act as an important precedent to the performance style of the mummers wench and explores several other strands in the performance genealogy of blackface gender impersonation in the Mummers Parade: Philadelphia's African American brass band tradition, which dates to the War of 1812; the dress reform movement of the 1850s, which appropriated "oriental" fashions in the service of women's rights; and the cakewalk, an antebellum plantation dance popularized in the cities of the Atlantic rim at the turn of the twentieth century.

Taken together, these five chapters unlock some of the "counter-memories" secreted in the Mummers Parade—patterns of performance engaged in "the multiplication of meaning through the practice of vigilant repetitions" across bodies and across time.[58] Roach defines *counter-memories* (another term he borrows from Foucault) as "the disparities between history as it is discursively transmitted and memory as it is publicly enacted by the bodies that bear its consequences."[59] Charles E. Welch Jr., Andrea Ignatoff Rothberg, Patricia Anne Masters, E. A. Kennedy III, and Corey Elizabeth Leighton have produced illuminating studies of Philadelphia's mummers, and I build on their work by linking the counter-memories of racial impersonation that haunt the twenty-first-century Mummers Parade to practices of racial impersonation in both the United States and the broader Atlantic world.[60]

HAUNTED CITY

On December 16, 1987, twenty-five years after the ban on blackface in the Mummers Parade, a juried exhibit called *Mummery* opened at City Hall, the focal point of the mummers' New Year's Day celebration. Municipal workers supervised by Oliver Franklin, the city's deputy representative for arts and culture, installed glass display cases filled with costumes, photographs, and other artifacts of the Mummers Parade outside both the mayor's office and the chambers of city council.[61] After the opening reception for the exhibit, Mayor W. Wilson Goode ordered Franklin to remove three black-and-white photographs from the display case in front of his office because they appeared to show mummers in blackface. Goode, Philadelphia's first African American mayor, told the Associated Press that "[the photos] don't belong anywhere in City Hall. . . . They are an insult to black people and should be removed."[62] Franklin complied with Goode's order but then immediately rehung the photographs in the display case outside city council chambers. A number of council members objected, though none more so than Augusta Clark, who told the *Philadelphia Tribune*—the city's principal African American newspaper—that "we do not need a resurrection of this shameful episode in [the mummers'] history."[63] Shortly thereafter, Council President Joseph Coleman asked Franklin to deaccession the photographs from the *Mummery* exhibit.

In a letter to the *Tribune*, James Conroy, the artist behind the controversial pictures, explained that his photographs show mummers engaged in "a celebration, a unique parade . . . in white face, blue face, red, yellow, green, and purple face"—but not in blackface. Conroy further noted that he

Fig. 2. James F. Conroy, *Laughing Mummers*, 1984. Courtesy Joan Conroy.

was the third artist in as many years to have his work censored by Mayor Goode and the city council after it had been accepted for display in City Hall.[64] Goode's administration did not hesitate to repress dissent, whether through censorship or force. In 1985 city authorities surrounded a house in West Philadelphia occupied by MOVE, a black liberation and animal rights group, whose loudspeaker broadcasts of political manifestos had become a nuisance to the neighborhood. When MOVE refused to evacuate the house, a police helicopter dropped explosives onto the roof; two city blocks burned to the ground and eleven people (including five children) died in the ensuing conflagration.[65] African American poet Sonia Sanchez memorialized the bombing in "elegy (for MOVE and Philadelphia)," a poem that situates the Mummers Parade as one of the local institutions camouflaging the horrors of police violence:

> beyond edicts and commandments . . .
> beyond concerts and football
> and mummers strutting their
> sequined processionals.
> there is this earth. this country. this city.
> this people.
> collecting skeletons from waiting rooms
> lying in wait. for honor and peace.
> one day.[66]

Conroy and Sanchez clearly disagree about the meaning of the Mummers Parade, but they both lament the city government's disregard for freedom of expression. The "summary removal" of Conroy's photographs from City Hall also disturbed the curators of the *Mummery* exhibit, who argued that the "blue and green facial makeup" worn by Conroy's subjects would be "innocuous" in a color photograph.[67] The sudden popularity of dark-colored makeup in the Mummers Parade in the wake of the 1964 blackface ban troubles the curators' claim that blueface and greenface masking are "innocuous" modes of performance. Shortly before the 1964 Mummers Parade, a columnist for the *Tribune* quipped that it would take a spectrograph to enforce the blackface ban on New Year's Day.[68] According to the judges' notes from the 1965 parade, the Purul Comic Club marched in dark blue makeup, with some members painting black streaks on their faces as they processed up Broad Street. The Liberty Clowns, another comic club, paraded in dark blue makeup and kinky wigs.[69] Leighton theorizes performances like these as "strategically invisible" forms of blackface.[70] To paraphrase Richard Schechner—who writes that an actor playing Hamlet is "not Hamlet" but also "not not Hamlet"—mummers in dark blue makeup are not in blackface, but they also are not not in blackface. Their performances oscillate between the strategic disavowal of racial impersonation and the sly use of blueface as a licit vehicle for the illicit practice of blackface masking.[71] As Leighton argues in her analysis of contemporary mummers who don dark-colored makeup, "the invisibility of blackface will not disappear" from the Mummers Parade.[72]

By displacing dark blues, purples, and greens into the tonal spectrum of black-and-white photography, Conroy's images peel back the mummers' "innocuous" makeup to reveal the ghost of blackface underneath. In other words, blackface—seemingly past and gone—erupts into the present through photography, the medium that Walter Benjamin recognized eighty years ago as the gateway to the "optical unconscious." "It is another nature which speaks to the camera rather than to the eye," writes Benjamin, and this "other nature" reveals the secrets "which dwell in the smallest things—meaningful yet covert enough to find a hiding place" from unmediated vision.[73] In the shimmering appearance and disappearance of blackface in both contemporary mummers' performances and Conroy's photographs, I feel the presence—the real presence—of a haunting. As Avery F. Gordon argues, "haunting is a constituent element of modern social life" through which the presence of a *specific* absence "makes its mark by being there and not there at the same time." For Gordon, ghosts cajole the living "to reconsider . . . the very distinctions between there and not there, past and present."[74]

Invocations of ghosts and haunting appear frequently in theater and performance studies scholarship. For Herbert Blau, the enduring problem of theater, "that people are pretending to be what they're not," makes theatrical performance into a ghostly enterprise that "subverts all systems of value. Even its own."[75] In a different vein, Marvin Carlson argues that theater's recycling of materials—including texts, actors, and the physical elements of production—endows the stage with a uniquely haunted quality.[76] Drawing on Blau (and *pace* Carlson), Alice Rayner suggests that haunting inheres in theatrical practice because "a fully materialized reality" onstage is always haunted "by its own negation."[77] In other words, the material conditions of theater—its penchant for crafting illusions from real bodies in three-dimensional space—situate stage performance between "to be and not to be," challenging the distinctions between reality and illusion, visibility and invisibility, appearance and disappearance.

Responding to Peggy Phelan's influential claim that "performance . . . becomes itself through disappearance," Rebecca Schneider suggests an alternative approach to performance "not as that which disappears . . . but as both the *act* of remaining and a means of re-appearance." By engaging "chiasmically" with disappearance, performance can be "resiliently eruptive, remaining . . . like so many ghosts at the door marked 'disappeared.'"[78] In the case of Conroy's photographs, the eruption of blackface from the optical unconscious serves as a remainder (and reminder) of past performance practice. To quote Rayner—with echoes of Roach's work on race, memory, and surrogation—performance "does not inter the past so much as raise the dead."[79] Conroy's photographs challenge the boundary between photography and performance by exposing strategically invisible flashes of blackface masking in a moment of live encounter, the moment when one looks at the photographs. As Schneider asks, "Is the stilled image a call toward a future live moment when the image will be re-encountered . . . ? And if so, is it not live—taking place in time in the scene of its reception?"[80] Following Schneider, I view Conroy's photographs as taking place live whenever and wherever they are encountered, including in the pages of this book.

Hauntologies of performance run the risk of appearing vague and arbitrary, but they also hold promise for the disclosure of unexpected affinities between putatively discrete phenomena—such as orientalism and blackface, or the practice of racial impersonation and the politics of racial struggle. As such, attending to ghosts can unfold the layers of meaning secreted in a place like Philadelphia's City Hall, where specific performance histories both shape and index changing social relations in the city, the nation, and the broader Atlantic world. City Hall profoundly inflected the reception of Conroy's photographs as an inappropriate resurrection of the disappeared practice of mummers blackface. The current City Hall building sits atop Center Square, named for its location in the middle of Penn's original plan for the layout of Philadelphia. Penn intended Center Square as a site for "houses of Publick affairs, [such] as a Meeting-house . . . Assembly, or State-House."[81] According to Scharf and Westcott, "an act was passed [in 1838] authorizing the mayor, aldermen, and citizens of Philadelphia to erect a city hall" at Center Square, but political hurdles and the Civil War delayed the project for over thirty years. Construction crews finally broke ground in 1871, and City Hall took another thirty years to complete.[82] Designed by John McArthur Jr. and modeled on Parisian civic architecture (especially the Palais des Tuileries and the Louvre), the plans for City Hall featured a 548-foot clock tower topped off by an enormous statue of Penn. From 1901 to 1909 it was the tallest occupied building in the world, and it remained the tallest building in Philadelphia until 1987. To this day, it is among the largest municipal buildings in North America.[83]

Before the construction of City Hall, Center Square did not feel quite so central to Philadelphia's civic life. The city's urban development—concentrated along the Delaware River, 1½ miles to the east—did not reach Center Square until well into the nineteenth century. According to Susan G. Davis, the square served as an unenclosed commons "with recreational and symbolic uses" in the colonial and early national periods, boasting "a tavern, a race course, and a militia parade ground." Until the outbreak of the Revolutionary War, Center Square hosted Philadelphia's semiannual fair, as well as public hangings, "a potter's field, a burial ground for black and white paupers, and . . . a spot for slaves' festive dances."[84] Shortly after independence, the city enclosed and landscaped the square, adding trees, a fountain, and a short-lived pump house for the newly constructed water-works on the Schuylkill River, 1½ miles to the west.[85] But despite these improvements, public hangings in Center Square continued until 1837, and parts of the square served as unofficial "burial grounds and offal dumps" into the early nineteenth century—uses that city leaders suppressed in their effort to clear the square for the construction of City Hall.[86]

As the symbolic and geographic center of Philadelphia—situated, para-doxically, at the margin of the city's everyday social and economic life—Center Square became a gathering place for public holiday celebrations after independence. Through its dual position at both the center and the margin of the city, the square came to fit a spatial pattern theorized much later by Ro-land Barthes. In Barthes's view, the city center, which he calls the "empty focal point" of urban life, functions as "the space where subversive forces, forces of rupture, ludic forces, act and meet."[87] By 1823 the subversion, rup-ture, and *ludi* unleashed in Center Square on Independence Day had grown so disruptive that Mayor Robert Wharton issued a proclamation condemn-ing "the scenes of debauchery, gambling, and drunkenness, with many other acts of excess and riots, which annually take place on the Fourth of July, in and about the booths, tents, and other unlawful restaurants" set up at the square.[88] Wharton banned all July Fourth festivities except for military and militia parades within city limits, but according to Scharf and Westcott, "the liquor sellers and gamblers removed [from Center Square] to Bush Hill"—just north of the city, in the present-day Fairmount neighborhood—"where they soon became more objectionable than ever."[89]

In Philadelphia as in other northern cities, the Fourth of July inspired abolitionist activism in the late eighteenth and early nineteenth centuries. "And why should not Afric's sons be happy too [sic]?" asked Reverend Wil-liam Rogers in an oration delivered in Philadelphia on July 4, 1789.[90] As David Waldstreicher argues, white abolitionists like Rogers "were hardly the only [people] to notice the whiteness of the rites, as well as of the rights, of American liberty. . . . Free blacks made the point themselves through their persistent presence at the margins" at public Fourth of July celebra-tions.[91] As Susan G. Davis notes, blacks in early national Philadelphia usu-ally staged freedom parades on July Fifth rather than July Fourth, not only "to avoid the wrath of white crowds" but also "to make a temporal and kinesic distinction underscoring their separate but unequal status."[92] On July 5, 1804, the year Haiti won its independence from France, the *New York Evening Post* reported that a group of several hundred black men marched through the streets of Philadelphia, "damning the whites and saying they would shew them St. Domingo."[93] The Pennsylvania Abolition Society, the first and arguably the most conservative antislavery organization in the United States, exhorted black Philadelphians to refrain from such displays of racial antagonism, and the focus of organized black protest in the city soon shifted from raucous marches on July Fifth to more sedate, oratorical performances on New Year's Day.[94]

On January 1, 1808, Absalom Jones, a black Philadelphia clergyman and founder of the African Episcopal Church of St. Thomas, delivered a powerful sermon marking the fourth anniversary of Haitian independence and the first effective date of the Act Prohibiting the Importation of Slaves, which the U.S. Congress enacted in 1807. Jones called for "the first of January" to "be set apart in every year, as a day of publick thanksgiving," and Gary B. Nash argues that these words ushered in "the appropriation of New Year's Day as the black Fourth of July" in Philadelphia.[95] The emergence of New Year's as a specifically African American holiday coincided with the deepening exclusion of blacks from white-dominated festivities in the streets. In 1813 James Forten, a prominent black sailmaker, complained bitterly about the hostile conduct of his white neighbors on the Fourth of July:

> It is a well known fact, that black people, upon certain days of public jubilee, dare not be seen after twelve o'clock in the day, upon the field to enjoy the times; for no sooner do the fumes of that potent devil, Liquor, mount into the brain, than the poor black is assailed. . . . I allude particularly to the *Fourth of July!*—Is it not wonderful, that the day set apart for the festival of liberty, should be abused by the advocates of freedom, in endeavoring to sully what they profess to adore.[96]

Forten and his contemporaries no doubt experienced racially motivated harassment not only on July Fourth but also at other times of the year. However, the visual archive suggests that Philadelphia's boisterous street life had an interracial character in the first two decades of the nineteenth century, before frequent, organized violence against blacks overtook the city in the 1820s. For example, the paintings of the Fourth of July at Center Square in 1812 and 1819 by John Lewis Krimmel show black children at liberty in the midst of holiday celebrations. They do not appear to be slaves or servants, nor are they depicted in caricature. These figures exemplify the familiar contact between black and white Philadelphians that recurs throughout Krimmel's oeuvre, but do these interracial scenes accurately

Fig. 3. John Lewis Krimmel, *Fourth of July Celebration in Center Square,*
1819. Courtesy Large Graphics Collection, Historical Society of Pennsylvania.

represent the street life of early nineteenth-century Philadelphia? Krimmel's painting *Return from Market* (1819) shows a black boy in the foreground holding the reins of a horse, but in two preparatory sketches for the
painting, the boy appears to be white, suggesting that Krimmel chose to
darken the boy's skin in the final composition.[97] In view of this example, it
would be rash to conclude that Krimmel's paintings of Center Square index
free black participation in Fourth of July festivities. But given that Krimmel
was a critically acclaimed (if commercially unsuccessful) artist who regularly exhibited his paintings at the Pennsylvania Academy of Fine Arts and
the Boston Athenaeum, the idealization of interracial sociability in his work
must have resonated with museum patrons and other tastemakers in the
early United States.[98]

All these ghosts of Philadelphia's racial history still haunt Center
Square, present through their absence, weighing on the Mummers Parade
as it makes its annual circuit around City Hall on New Year's Day—a holiday once associated with black freedom and interracial revelry rather than
with racial impersonation. According to Al Heller, a longtime comic club
member and amateur mummers historian, "There is a feeling of great ambivalence [for the mummers] that you made it to the City Hall. That you've
reached the pinnacle of the city's power, and you were actually able to

stand there without being whisked away."[99] Heller's ambivalent experience of "goin' round the hall" (to borrow a mummers idiom) resonates with the contradictory histories of discipline and license at Center Square—of hangings and festivals, monuments and offal dumps, the center and the margin.

On October 6, 2011, Occupy Philadelphia opened a new chapter in this history when seven hundred protestors formed an encampment at Dilworth Plaza, outside the western entrance to City Hall.[100] Inspired by Occupy Wall Street, which had begun three weeks earlier, the Philadelphia branch of the global Occupy movement differed from its New York counterpart in one important respect: it occupied a public space rather than a privately owned park. As W. J. T. Mitchell argues,

> [Occupation] is not only a visual and physical presence in a space but a discourse and rhetorical operation. It is directly linked to the trope of *occupatio*, the tactic of anticipating an adversary's arguments by preempting them. . . . In the context of the rhetoric of public space, *occupatio* is, as the original meaning of the word reveals, the seizure of an empty place, one that is supposed to be *res nullius*, not owned by anyone, not private property. . . . But the demand of *occupatio* is made in the full knowledge that public space is, in fact, *pre-occupied* by the state and the police, that its pacified and democratic character, apparently open to all, is sustained by the ever-present possibility of violent eviction.[101]

Just as in New York, Oakland, and a number of other cities across the country, the police in Philadelphia ultimately cleared the Occupy encampment, but only after most of the occupiers had left of their own accord to make way for a planned, $50 million renovation of Dilworth Plaza that promised to create hundreds of unionized construction jobs.[102] Ahuyiva Harel, one of the occupiers who refused to leave until the police forced him, objected to the city's agreement to lease Dilworth Plaza to the Center City District—the merchants' group footing the bill for the renovation—for one dollar a year, privatizing a space that had been "*res nullius*" since William Penn's initial plan for Philadelphia.[103]

The gathering and dispersal of Occupy Philadelphia captures the tension between state and corporate power, on the one hand, and the people's right to free assembly and expression, on the other. On New Year's Day this tension transforms the street in front of City Hall into a stage where the mummers can transgress their everyday identities—where they have license to play, however briefly, before the seat of power. As Barthes puts it, the city center is "always experienced . . . as the privileged place where the other is and where we ourselves are other, as the place where we play the other."[104] For the mummers, the *jouissance* of goin' round the hall is bound up not only in clowning, dancing, and making music for the judges and the crowd but also in the practice of strutting up to the gates of City Hall in masquerade. "You get up there [in front of City Hall]," remarks mummer Jack Walsh,

> and you say, "in four minutes, it's over," but for those four minutes you can be Eddie Cantor, you can be Jimmy Durante, you can be the greatest soprano that ever sang at the Metropolitan Opera. And you get the whole judging area to perform. And if you want to be the best bird on Broad Street, the greatest Indian chief, whatever you want to be, you have that opportunity. You have it there, and it's up to you to do it.[105]

Here, Walsh captures the ecstatic entry into alterity facilitated by the impersonation of another race, another gender, another species than one's own. But he does not take account of the privileged (though by no means exclusive) access enjoyed by white men to the public pleasure of pretending to be someone or something else in the Mummers Parade.

SPATIAL HISTORY

The ghosts that haunt Walnut Grove, Moyamensing, and Center Square matter to the historiography of the Mummers Parade, but not necessarily because a traceable line of descent (Foucault) or a concatenated series of substitutions (Roach) links the Meschianza, the minstrel show, or Fourth of July festivities to contemporary mumming. In *Cities of the Dead* Roach posits New Orleans as a "ludic space . . . for the rest of the nation" by pointing up the proximity of three local landmarks that epitomize "the performance genealogy of the North American traffic in money and flesh": the St. Louis Exchange, an ornate rotunda that hosted the city's antebellum slave auctions; Storyville, the turn-of-the-century red light district where slavery was "explicitly and officially sexualized . . . in the development of legally sanctioned prostitution"; and the Louisiana Superdome, home of the New Orleans Saints, which displays "immensely valuable black bodies sweating for white people who still unblinkingly call themselves owners."[106] Roach wrote these words before Hurricane Katrina struck New Orleans in 2005, leaving more than twenty thousand people—most of them poor and African American—to take refuge in the Superdome, where they lived in abysmal conditions for days with almost no help from the local, state, or federal governments. He also wrote these words before the Saints' Super Bowl victory in 2010, which inspired New Orleans's historically segregated carnival krewes to parade together in front of the Superdome in a rare display of interracial solidarity.[107] However, I am less interested in the evolving racial symbolism of the Superdome than I am in a surprising turn in Roach's argument, when he interprets the ludic wedge of central New Orleans bounded by the St. Louis Exchange, Storyville, and the Superdome as evidence of "a line of descent from the past into the future" in circum-Atlantic racial history.[108]

Roach's generative remapping of New Orleans suggests more than he is willing to claim: a *spatial* history—to borrow a phrase from theater historian Rosemarie K. Bank—that reads historically resonant spaces as "collected in but not wholly governed by time."[109] Bank's approach to the historiography of antebellum theater and performance furnishes a bracing antidote to the linear-temporal bias of performance genealogy, sending me back to Center Square with a question: what would it mean to conceive of the cemeteries, public hangings, slave festivals, Fourth of July celebrations, monumental architecture, Mummers Parade performances, and Occupy Philadelphia encampment at Center Square as happening not only in the *same place* but at the *same time*—or, more precisely, at a series of times, copresent to one another through the social life of haunting? "Places are fragmentary and inward-turning histories," writes philosopher Michel de Certeau, "accumulated times that can be unfolded . . . symbolization encysted in the pain or pleasure of the body."[110] De Certeau views the body as an affective theater of history and memory, a palimpsest that makes multiple times accumulated in a given site simultaneously present, moving across the body as the body walks, dances, or parades through a haunted place. Choreographer Tere O'Connor theorizes dance as the practice of "spraying dust on invisible possibilities—or histories" in a specific place, much as a mummers fancy club rehearing in oriental costumes under Interstate 95 sprays dust on the Meschianza, making this long-past event shimmer in the haze of memories secreted in the pockmarked cityscape of my old South Philadelphia neighborhood.[111] Ghosts can and do appear through performance, erupting into the here and now, materializing and re-presenting those aspects of the past that remain stubbornly *in place*. The chapters that follow move between Atlantic performance genealogies and local, spatial histories in an endeavor to spray dust on practices of racial impersonation in Philadelphia, making visible the embodied presence of seemingly absent pasts in the performative life of the city.

TWO

Orientalism, Blackness, and
Femininity in the Meschianza
and *Slaves in Algiers*

On the afternoon of May 18, 1778, four hundred British officers and elite
Philadelphians embarked on a grand regatta down the Delaware River to
Walnut Grove, an estate just south of the city. This aquatic procession
kicked off the Meschianza, an extravagant, all-night party given to honor
General William Howe and his brother, Admiral Richard Howe, on their
departure from North America. At the Meschianza (which derives its name
from *mescolanza*, the Italian word for "mixture" or "medley"), the young,
marriageable daughters of Philadelphia's colonial elite appeared in Turkish costumes, and black slaves in turbans and sashes waited on the guests.

This chapter explores the co-construction of orientalism, blackness, and
femininity at the Meschianza and three other performances in late
eighteenth-century Philadelphia. The first section argues that the Meschianza triangulated orientalism, blackness, and femininity to project British
imperial power, a symbolically successful project belied by the weakness of
General Howe's military position. On July 4, 1778, after the Continental
Army had retaken control of Philadelphia, a blackface street performance
mocked the hairstyles of the women in attendance at the Meschianza. Six-
teen years later, a decade after the end of the Revolutionary War, Susanna
Rowson's play *Slaves in Algiers* (1794) rescripted the relationship between
orientalism, blackness, and femininity for an early national audience. The
hybrid iterations of race and gender in *Slaves in Algiers* emerge most explicitly through the character of Fetnah, a British-born Jew who cross-dresses
as a man, almost marries an American soldier, and is repeatedly mistaken
for a Moor. The final performance discussed in this chapter is Rowson's
cross-dressed hornpipe dance at Ricketts's Circus in Philadelphia, which
enacted a Fetnah-esque vision of racial and gendered hybridity.

The Meschianza, the July 4, 1778, street burlesque, *Slaves in Algiers*, and
Rowson's dance performance traverse three distinct historical moments in

Philadelphia: the British occupation of the city, its liberation by the Continental Army, and its engagement with racial and gendered questions of national belonging after the Revolutionary War. As such, the tissue connecting these various performances is better understood as a web of mutual hauntings than as a continuous line of genealogical descent. For example, the Meschianza and *Slaves in Algiers* haunt each other not only through their related co-constructions of orientalism, blackness, and femininity but also through their shared fascination with Miguel de Cervantes Saavedra's *Don Quixote* (1605–15), one of the most popular novels in the eighteenth-century Anglo-Atlantic. Descriptions of the Meschianza recorded in diaries and commonplace books refer again and again to *Don Quixote*, and the plot of *Slaves in Algiers* is based on an episode from the novel. To illuminate the Quixotic connection between these two performances, my argument takes a brief detour through Cervantes's text. And to map the shifting relationship between practices of oriental and blackface impersonation in the late eighteenth century, I include a compact analysis of Isaac Bickerstaffe's *The Padlock* (1768), a comic opera with a transatlantic production history that alternately blurs and parses the distinction between oriental and black.

THE MESCHIANZA

Major John André, the principal architect of the Meschianza, called it "the most splendid entertainment . . . ever given by an army to their general."[1] André's claim is exaggerated, but the spectacle of prominent Philadelphians hobnobbing with British officers in the middle of the Delaware was enough to attract a large audience, both in the river and on the shore. According to John Fanning Watson's *Annals of Philadelphia*, "Barges rowed on the flanks [of the regatta] . . . to keep off the multitude of boats that crowded from the city as beholders; and the houses, balconies, and wharves were filled with spectators all along the riverside."[2] After the guests disembarked, they proceeded to "a square lawn of 150 yards on each side, lined with troops, and properly prepared for the exhibition of a tilt and tournament, according to the customs and ordinances of ancient chivalry." Two pavilions lined the tournament ground, and "on the front seat of each . . . were placed seven of the principal young Ladies of the country, dressed in Turkish habits, and wearing in their turbans the favours with which they meant to reward the several Knights who were to contend in their honour."[3] There, the ladies and other assembled guests watched a mock battle between two groups of British officers, the Knights of the Blended Rose and the Knights of the Burning Mountain, dressed in medieval court costumes of fringed silk and satin.

André doubtless intended the troops lining the lawn to add to the grandeur of the tournament, but they also protected the knights and ladies of the Meschianza from "spectators not to be numbered [who] darked the whole plain around," posing a potential threat to the festivities.[4] For, as Paul Engle points out, the Meschianza took place "in what was technically a fortified camp in the midst of war."[5] General Howe's army had taken control of Philadelphia in September 1777, and while George Washington and his troops spent the winter of 1777–78 shivering and underprovisioned at Valley Forge, British and Hessian officers enjoyed "a season of gayety unprecedented" in the City of Brotherly Love.[6] By the spring, Britain's military prospects in Pennsylvania began to deteriorate, especially after news reached North America of the treaty of alliance between France and the United States. On June 18, 1778, precisely one month after the Meschianza, the British Army withdrew from Philadelphia under the command of General Howe's successor, General Henry Clinton. A letter from Valley Forge dated May 17 and reprinted in the *Pennsylvania Gazette* reported,

> By every intelligence from Philadelphia, the enemy are preparing to evacuate the city. Their ships are wooded and watered, their heavy cannon embarked, storage and provisions put on board their vessels, and stalls built in them for their horses, all which are striking circumstances of their departure.[7]

The letter made no mention of the preparations for the fete in honor of the Howe brothers that was to take place the next day.

The revolutionary press may have ignored the Meschianza, but given General Howe's lackluster military performance, his opulent send-off from North America provoked the ire of Tories on both sides of the Atlantic. In London, the colonial agent Israel Mauduit mocked the Meschianza as a "triumph upon leaving America unconquered," and the exiled loyalist Joseph Galloway quipped that General Howe preferred "the pleasures of indolence and dissipation to a discharge of his duty to his country."[8] In Philadelphia, Quaker diarist Elizabeth Drinker derided the Meschianza as "Scenes of Folly and Vanity," and Captain Johann Heinrichs, a Hessian mercenary, wrote that "Assemblies, Concerts, Comedies, Clubs and the like make us forget that there is any war, save that it is a capital joke."[9] In addition to the entertainments mentioned by Heinrichs, the culture of festivity in Philadelphia during the British occupation included gambling, cock-fighting, and thirteen double bills at the Southwark Theater, with scenery painted by André.

André is best remembered not for his theatrical endeavors but for his infamous plot with General Benedict Arnold of the Continental Army to seize the fort at West Point for the British. André's subsequent capture and execution elicited the sympathy of many Continental officers, and he became a divisive figure in the national imagination of the early United States. William Dunlap's play *André* (1798)—which depicts the British major as a tragic hero—sparked a fierce controversy when it premiered in New York, and Dunlap later bowdlerized the play into "a more overtly patriotic vehicle" called *The Glory of Columbia*, "which became a July Fourth staple for years afterwards."[10] In an ironic twist, Charles Durang reports that a pastoral drop scene at the Southwark Theater, painted by André, appeared in "a national play on the subject [of André's] capture and death" on July 4, 1807.[11]

Before André achieved notoriety as a spy, General Howe encouraged the young major's interest in theater, and André organized theater seasons in Boston, New York, and Philadelphia while serving with Howe's army.[12] Contrary to eighteenth-century Tories like Maduit, Galloway, Drinker, and Heinrichs, who read Howe's interest in staging plays as a frivolous distraction from military matters, I contend that Howe employed theater as a smart (if ultimately unsuccessful) tactic in a culture war. As Peter A. Davis argues, theater during the Revolution was "much more than an undesirable amusement; it was a political and social symbol of English oppression."[13] The 1774 resolution by the Continental Congress discouraging "shews [sic], plays, and other expensive diversions and entertainments" made producing theater and lavishly theatrical events like the Meschianza an excellent way for the British to thumb their noses at the rebels and display their putative cultural superiority.[14]

MESCHIANZA AND MASQUERADE

The new Pennsylvania Constitution of 1776 had rattled Philadelphia's colonial hierarchy by extending the franchise to nearly all taxpaying men and asserting "that government is, or ought to be, instituted for the common benefit, protection and security of the people."[15] On the eve of the British Army's withdrawal from Philadelphia, the conspicuous luxury of the Meschianza revealed the insensitivity of the city's upper class to the political aspirations and material deprivations of ordinary citizens caught in the middle of the Revolutionary War. David S. Shields and Fredrika J. Teute argue that, with the Meschianza, "Howe's cultural campaign had its dramatic climax." In honoring General Howe, André and his fellow officers "seemed to be campaigning on behalf of some more atavistic scheme, renovating the old ethic of valor, masculine prerogative, and elite familiarity"—an ethic that Shields and Teute describe as "neofeudal." This take on the Meschianza interprets the event as essentially a *private* affair, "a closing of the ranks" among a section of Philadelphia's elite.[16] But this private affair was made *public* through the Meschianza's regatta and tournament, witnessed by the crowds of spectators who gathered along the Delaware River and on the plain surrounding Walnut Grove.

Understanding the Meschianza as an elite gathering deliberately staged for an audience of ordinary people excluded from the festivities unsettles Shields and Teute's assertion that "dancing and dining in mixed company, not jousting, were the main events of the Meschianza."[17] Most contemporary accounts of the fete, by those who attended and by those who observed from a distance, devote far more attention to the regatta and tournament than to the dancing and dining that followed—at night, indoors, and out of view of the crowd.[18] In particular, André's descriptions of the Meschianza relate the costumes worn by the knights, ladies, and attendants at the afternoon tournament in exacting detail:

> [The Knights of the Blended Rose were] dressed in ancient habits of white and red silk, and mounted on grey horses, richly caparisoned in trappings of the same colours . . . [and] attended by their Esquires on foot, in suitable apparel. . . . Lord Cathcart, superbly mounted on a managed horse, appeared as chief of these Knights; two young black slaves, with sashes and drawers of blue and white silk, wearing large silver clasps round their necks and arms, their breasts and shoulders bare, held his stirrups.[19]

> [The Knights of the Burning Mountain] were in black Sattin contrasted with orange and laced with gold according to the stile of dress of the White Knights; Their Horses were black and likewise ornamented with black and orange. The Esquires were in orange coloured silk with black mantles and trimmings.[20]

> The Ladies selected from the foremost in youth, beauty, and fashion were habited in fancy dresses. They wore gauze Turbans spangled

Fig. 4. John André, frontispiece, *The Mischianza, Humbly Inscribed to Miss Peggy Chew*, 1778. Courtesy Cliveden of the National Trust.

and edged with gold or Silver, on the right Side a veil of the same kind hung as low as the waist and the left side of the Turban was enriched with pearl and tassels of gold or Silver & crested with a feather. The dress was of the polonaise Kind and of white Silk with long sleeves, the Sashes which were worn round the waist and were tied with a large bow on the left side hung very low and were trimmed, spangled, and fringed according to the Colours of the Knight.[21]

In his costume designs for the Meschianza, André mimicked the fashions popular at English masquerades, which pervaded English social life from the 1720s through the 1790s. For most of this period, Terry Castle argues, "the spirit of Orientalism suffused masquerade representation," with Persian, Chinese, and Turkish costumes proving especially popular.[22] According to Aileen Ribeiro, English and continental masqueraders also embraced "theatrically inspired tournaments" with "medieval themes" in the last quarter of the eighteenth century.[23] This neofeudal trend coincided with a rage for fêtes champêtres, or "country feasts"—outdoor, mock-pastoral entertainments embellished with opulent stagecraft and the fancy dress of a masquerade ball. General John Burgoyne, who led Britain's failed

Fig. 5. John André, sketch of a Meschianza costume, 1778. Courtesy Library Company of Philadelphia.

Saratoga Campaign against the Continental Army in 1777, organized an elaborate fête champêtre at the Oaks in Surrey, which he adapted into a comedy for the Theater Royal in Drury Lane in 1774.[24] With its stage Turks, country dances, and nostalgia for Agincourt, Burgoyne's *The Maid of the Oaks* served as a model for the neofeudal and orientalist aesthetic of the Meschianza.[25]

Edward W. Said famously claims that imaginative impersonations of oriental peoples in Western culture date to Aeschylus's *The Persians* (472 BC), although he also argues that modern orientalism, as a "corporate institution for dealing with the Orient," did not emerge until the Napoleonic expedition to Egypt (1798–1801), when European colonialism converged with an increasingly methodical discourse on Eastern languages and religions in Western academe.[26] *Pace* Said, *The Maid of the Oaks* and the Meschianza suggest that modern orientalism in Britain and British North America emerged by the 1770s. As a member of the House of Commons, Burgoyne oversaw an investigation of corruption in the British East India Company in 1772, and both he and André fought the American rebels to maintain Britain's Atlantic empire.[27] Daniel O'Quinn hypothesizes that "the trauma of the American war was handled indirectly through orientalist fantasies," and Burgoyne and André bear out this hypothesis, staging acts of oriental impersonation to project imperial power during a decade of economic and military vulnerability in British North America.[28]

This revised periodization of modern orientalism (at least in the British context) suggests that the oriental masquerade at the Meschianza was central to the meaning of the event. Linda Colley interprets the Meschianza costumes as "just one more manifestation of that taste for gothic romance and orientalism that was so prevalent in European polite culture" in the eighteenth century, and her reading of dress as "superficial" leads her to reduce the Meschianza to a wishful British reconstruction of the war with its North American colonies, "a splendid crusade fought according to the rules [of chivalry] by men of birth, and fought successfully."[29] In fact, the Meschianza tournament ended not in success for either side but in a draw, with the marshal of the field declaring

> the Fair Damsels of the Blended Rose and Burning Mountain [to be] perfectly satisfied with the proofs of love, and the signal feats of valour, given by their respective Knights; and command[ing] them, as they prized the future favours of their Mistresses . . . [to] instantly desist from further combat.[30]

Randall Fuller aptly labels this truce a "fairy tale of imperial benevolence, [in which] the bloody hostilities of the North American military campaign terminated at the special request of exotic others representing the colonies themselves."[31] Rather than staging a British military victory over the rebellion in North America, the Meschianza tournament staged the colonies' voluntary cultural submission to Britain by casting the colonists as oriental, feminine others to the knights' fulsome display of British, neofeudal masculinity.

Unsurprisingly, most of the women willing to participate in this imperial pageant had loyalist sympathies. André's companion, Peggy Chew (to whom he dedicated one of his written accounts of the Meschianza), suffered the humiliation of her father, Benjamin's imprisonment by Continental forces during the British occupation of Philadelphia.[32] Rebecca Franks, another of the Meschianza ladies, had a reputation for using her acerbic wit to mock the revolutionary cause. At a party on July 4, 1778, shortly after the British withdrawal from Philadelphia, Lieutenant Colonel Jack Steward of Maryland approached Franks dressed in "a handsome suit of scarlet" and attempted to flirt with her in terms borrowed from the Meschianza:

> "I have adopted your colours, my Princess, the better to secure a courteous reception—deign to smile on a true Knight." To this speech Miss Franks made no reply; but turning to the company who surrounded her, exclaimed—"How the Ass glories in the Lion's skin."[33]

In 1780 Franks left Philadelphia for New York with her father, David, a Jewish merchant who had twice been arrested for treason by the Continental Congress. Two years later she married Sir Henry Johnson, a wealthy Englishman whom she met at the Meschianza.[34]

THE QUIXOTE CONNECTION

The Meschianza not only attracted a large audience, it also spawned many commentaries, a surprising number of which describe the tournament at Walnut Grove through references to Miguel de Cervantes Saavedra's seventeenth-century novel *Don Quixote*. A favorable account "by one of the Company" repeatedly refers to the ladies of the Meschianza as "Dulcineas."[35] Captain Friedrich von Muenchhausen, Howe's aide-de-camp, writes approvingly in his diary of the contest between the Knights of the Blended Rose and the Knights of the Burning Mountain, who "fought with lances and swords in the style of Don Quixot and Sanchopancha [sic], their Dulcineas, sitting on elevated thrones, watching the knights who fought for them."[36] And Whig poetess Hannah Griffitts, in a scathing verse on the Meschianza, ridiculed the jousting British officer-knights as "Don Quixotes made of wonders."[37]

Don Quixote was the second-best-selling novel in British North America between 1750 and 1800, and it had a large English-language readership from the publication of Thomas Shelton's translation in 1612 until well into the nineteenth century.[38] The Quixotic comments on the Meschianza reflect not only the transnational popularity of Cervantes's novel but also a politicized split in the British reception of Don Quixote. As Ronald Paulson argues, Don Quixote was "for the Tories a symbol of the unbridled imagination" and "for the Whigs a symbol of outmoded chivalric assumptions."[39] Building on Paulson's analysis, Sarah F. Wood documents the frequent appropriation of Don Quixote by North American colonists during the political and military antagonism of the Revolutionary War:

> Used by the colonists to signify a self-deluded fool, an ineffectual figure of fun, [Don Quixote] became an easy means of sending up a pompous and incompetent enemy. . . . Colonial charges of British Quixoticism were particularly effective because they carried with them the assumption that Britain's defeat was inevitable, its military quest the final and ineffectual flailing of a bygone world, destined to be outmanoeuvred by a new republican reality, doomed to be as unsuccessful as Don Quixote's attempts to revive the fortunes of chivalric practice.[40]

Wood's cogent reading of the rhetorical uses of Don Quixote in revolutionary North America points up the potent derision implied in Griffitts's epithet for the Meschianza knights: "Don Quixotes made of wonders."

The Quixotic descriptions of the Meschianza tournament suggest the Quixotic nature of the Meschianza itself, with its insistence on staging a fantasy of British imperial splendor on the threshold of an impending military defeat. In contrast to the richly attired knights of the Meschianza, Cervantes's Don Quixote sets out on his first expedition equipped with "a rusty lance and worm-eaten target" and dressed in "an old suit of armour, which had belonged to some of his ancestors, and which . . . [was] quite covered over with mouldiness and rust."[41] When his ancestral helmet is destroyed in battle on his second expedition, he replaces it with a barber's basin that he believes to be the helmet of Mambrino, a legendary Moorish king whose solid-gold headpiece rendered its wearer invulnerable. And when Sancho, Don Quixote's squire, laughs at his master's folly, the ridiculously habited knight rebukes him with an elaborate rationalization:

> "Why truly, Sancho," said he, "I imagine that this very individual inchanted helmet, by some strange accident or other, must have fallen into the hands of some body who did not know its inestimable value, but, seeing it was made of the purest gold, melted down one half of it for sale, and left the other in this shape, resembling, as thou sayest, a barber's bason: but, be that as it may, since I am satisfied of its real worth and identity, the transmutation is of small consequence; for, I will order it to be repaired . . . [and] mean while, I will wear it in this manner; for it is still better than nothing at all" (138).

In this passage, like so many others in Cervantes's novel, Don Quixote attempts to remake himself and his perceptions in the likeness of his fantasy — and the material world refuses to cooperate. The barber's basin remains a barber's basin, whatever Don Quixote may say.

As a *hidalgo de la Mancha*, Don Quixote belongs to a low grade of *cristiano viejo* (or "old Christian") nobility in a region that served as a buffer zone between Christian and Islamic territories during the *Reconquista* (or "Reconquest") of modern-day Spain. As such, William Childers argues that Don Quixote's fascination with knight errantry has a geographically specific meaning:

> The arms Don Quixote dusts off and carries across the plains of la Mancha belonged *to his ancestors*, who would have used them to fight in the Reconquest and consequently would have been rewarded with the *hidalguía* and the lands he inherited, lands he sells to buy books of chivalry.[42]

When Don Quixote augments his ancestral arms with a barber's basin that he believes to be the helmet of Mambrino, his costume takes on a racially hybrid character, combining the rusty armor of the Reconquest with a helmet ostensibly captured from a Moorish king.

Although portrayed as an object of laughter, both for Sancho and for the reader, Don Quixote's hybrid costume mirrors the hybrid construction of the novel itself. Cervantes frames part 1 of *Don Quixote* as a translation from Cide Hamete Benengeli's Arabic manuscript, executed by a "morisco aljamiado" ("Spanish-speaking Moor") and retold by a Christian narrator who fashions himself "[el] padrasto de Don Quijote" ("the stepfather of Don Quixote").[43] The multiplication and displacement of narrative authority in the novel grows even more complex when Cervantes introduces a description of Cide Hamete as an "Arabian and Manchegan author" in the first sentence of the chapter immediately following Don Quixote's acquisition of the barber's basin (145). By depicting Cide Hamete as simultaneously "arábigo" and "manchego," Cervantes disrupts any connotation of racial or religious purity implied by the phrase de la Mancha appended to Don Quixote's name.[44] The mediation of Cide Hamete's manuscript through both a Moorish translator and a Christian narrator produces a thoroughly syncretic vision of Spanish identity, reflected in microcosm by Don Quixote's costume, with its blend of "old Christian" armor and a fantasy of a Moorish helmet.

Given the recurring images of racial hybridity in Don Quixote, Quixotic descriptions of the Meschianza—whether Whig or Tory in inclination—undermine the ethic of neofeudal masculinity staged through medieval and oriental impersonation in the mock tournament at Walnut Grove. The contrast between the medieval costumes of the Meschianza knights and the oriental costumes of the Meschianza ladies suggests a racial and gendered divide between the British and the North American colonists, which Shields and Teute view as a thinly veiled allegory of imperial domination:

> The Knights donned the court costume of Henry IV, the crusader king of France. The American women of both companies appeared in Turkish regalia—that is, in the guise of the Islamic "Other" of the Crusades. So, the costuming symbolized British/American enmity through gender difference and aestheticized it by substituting court clothes for uniforms and the crusades for the rebellion.[45]

Quixotic descriptions of the Meschianza trouble this allegory, reflexively subverting the neofeudal and imperial pretensions of the event by filtering it through Cervantes's racially syncretic text. Of course, written commentaries on the Meschianza, including André's two accounts of the fete, were set down after the fact. But the susceptibility of the Meschianza to discursive Quixoticization from across the political spectrum suggests that André's imperial allegory was more fragile than it first appears. The Quixotic discourse surrounding the Meschianza points to the inherent instability of the performances staged at Walnut Grove, an instability concealed in part— but only in part—by the stagecraft of André's spectacle.

FARCE AND THEATRICALITY

The discursive Quixoticization of the Meschianza, especially by Tory authors, presages a common tendency of post-Enlightenment colonial discourse, famously diagnosed by Homi K. Bhabha: "If colonialism takes
power in the name of history, it repeatedly exercises its authority through
figures of farce," producing texts "rich in the traditions of *trompe-l'oeil*,
irony, mimicry, and repetition."[46] Like Bhabha's examples of "authorita-
tive" texts on India produced by nineteenth-century British colonists, the
discourse surrounding the Meschianza ironizes itself, slipping into farce
even—or especially—when it endeavors to control and command.

At the conclusion of the Meschianza tournament, the knights, ladies,
and assembled guests processed through two triumphal arches—one for
each of the Howe brothers—into a spacious hall, where they enjoyed several hours of dancing. After the sun had set,

> the windows were thrown open, and a magnificent bouquet of rock-
> ets began the fire-works. . . . Towards the conclusion, the interior
> part of the [second] triumphal arch was illuminated amidst an unin-
> terrupted flight of rockets and bursting of balloons. . . . Fame ap-
> peared at top, spangled with stars, and from her trumpet blowing
> the following device in letters of light, *Tes Lauriers sont immortels*
> [these laurels are immortal].[47]

During this *feu d'artifice*, Captain Allen McLane of the Continental Army
set fire to the British breastworks just north of Philadelphia while his
company discharged their weapons in the direction of Walnut Grove. The
Meschianza knights, afraid the celebration might end in panic, persuaded
their ladies that the distant fire and gunshots were part of the festivities
and quietly sent a company of dragoons to pursue the rebels.[48] Meanwhile, the party continued uninterrupted, with Major Baurmeister (a
Hessian mercenary) going so far as to claim that "there was not the least
disorder nor any unfortunate incident" all evening.[49] Like Don Quixote,
Baurmeister and many of the other revelers at the Meschianza saw what
they wanted to see: a *feu d'artifice* glorifying the Howe brothers and Britain rather than the real fire of a revolutionary attack. The stagecraft of the
Meschianza tricked the perception of the guests, ironically concealing a
messy military skirmish behind the martial simulacra of flashing fireworks and bursting balloons. Both the fireworks and Baurmeister's insistence that "there was not the least disorder" sustain the illusion of colo-

nial authority, but McLane's attack punctures this illusion, threatening to turn colonial authority into farce.

The fireworks display and the riposte of McLane's arson and gunshots were the last public events of the Meschianza. "At twelve," writes André in one of his accounts, "supper was announced, and large folding doors, hitherto artfully concealed, being suddenly thrown open, discovered a magnificent saloon."[50] The knights, ladies, and other guests retired to the privacy of this temporary structure, "[which] was arched with Frame work and lined with Canvass painted and decorated in the manner of Scenes."[51] According to a loyalist newspaper, the *Royal Pennsylvania Gazette*, "A prodigious number of curiously ornamented mirrors were judiciously disposed [in the saloon] as to reflect to the greatest advantage the natural as well as the artificial beauties with which this splendid apartment was graced."[52] At the end of the hall, lined with trompe-l'oeil scenic painting redoubled in ornamented mirrors, the guests discovered "24 negroes in blue and white Turbans and sashes with bright bracelets & Collars bowing profoundly together" and "performing the submissive Grand Salam as the Ladies passed by."[53] Here, black slaves in oriental costumes paid homage to elite, Turkish-clad women under the voyeuristic gaze of Howe's officers and their invited guests—a spectacle that André labeled "a *coup d'oeil* beyond description magnificent."[54]

The phrase *coup d'oeil*, or "stroke of the eye," suggests an impression formed at a glance rather than through a sustained act of critical examination. Would the theatricality of André's saloon—the scenic painting, the mirrors, the Grand Salaam—have crumbled into semblance and farce under more careful scrutiny by the guests at the event? Thomas Postlewait and Tracy C. Davis warn that analyses of the theatricality of political spectacles like the Meschianza "must be careful not to settle into the familiar polarity that divides all things theatrical from all things natural and true."[55] Most of the participants in the Meschianza believed in the imperial ideology behind André's stagecraft, and as Greg Dening argues, awareness of theatrical illusion on the part of the actors does not necessarily disturb the realism of their understanding of the performance in which they are engaged.[56] Although André could not control the reception of the Meschianza by spectators situated outside the event, his stagecraft worked to recuperate farce and theatricality within the private enclosure of Walnut Grove, turning a coup d'oeil into a vision of "truthiness" (to borrow Stephen Colbert's famous neologism).

In a plenary paper delivered at the American Society for Theatre Research conference in 2012, Odai Johnson compared the Meschianza to President George W. Bush's 2003 "Mission Accomplished" speech announcing the end of major combat operations in Iraq, which Bush delivered after a dramatic landing on the aircraft carrier USS *Abraham Lincoln*.[57] Both the "Mission Accomplished" speech and the Meschianza used theatricality to hide the messiness of armed conflict, and the ongoing violence in Iraq belies Bush's triumphalism much as the outcome of the Revolutionary War belies the triumphalism of the Meschianza. In both of these examples, theatricality touches the other side of farce, betting wrongly on a victorious outcome that feels inevitable to the proponents of empire. In hindsight, it is easy to laugh off such displays, but in the moment, their projection of authority can seem powerfully truthful—at least to actors and audiences ideologically inclined to agree with the message of the performance.

LUXURY SLAVES AND ELITE WOMEN

None of the extant accounts of the Meschianza record the age or gender of the slaves arrayed in the Meschianza dining room, but André's description of their "blue and white Turbans and sashes" matches the costume worn by the bare-chested black boy who holds Lord Cathcart's stirrups in André's watercolor painting of the Meschianza tournament (figure 4). This exotic, erotic image emphasizes the boy's subservience, and Gary B. Nash argues that the Meschianza's conspicuous display of slaves as symbols of imperial power "caused great resentment among ordinary Philadelphians and came to haunt Philadelphia's aristocratic families after the British had left the city."[58]

Lavishly dressed black boys often served as markers of status for the eighteenth-century British elite. These "luxury slaves," as Monica L. Miller calls them, reflected the wealth of their owners through "the denial of [their] laboring power and potential." Appearing onstage, at fashionable parties, and in paintings and prints, black boys clad in oriental apparel began to proliferate in British performance and visual culture more than half a century before the Meschianza.[59] In 1710 a letter purportedly written by a luxury slave appeared in the London newspaper the *Tatler*: "I am a black-moor boy, and have, by my lady's order, been christened by the chaplain. . . . I desire to know whether, now [that] I am a Christian, I am obliged to dress like a Turk and wear a turban [sic]."[60] Along with oriental dress, luxury slaves like Cathcart's attendant often wore metal clasps around their necks and wrists, reinforcing the "representational prison" that obliged these young men to perform as ornamental adjuncts to their masters' status and power.[61]

Before the British occupation of Philadelphia in 1777–78, few people in the city had ever seen a luxury slave. Most of Philadelphia's several hundred enslaved people in the late colonial period labored as domestic servants or in semiskilled trades like sail making, baking, and tailoring.[62] After the first convention of the Continental Congress in 1774, "Philadelphia masters began to manumit significant numbers of slaves," not only because of abolitionist appeals to conscience but also because employing free laborers—who could be hired and fired at will—made more financial sense than slave ownership in the uncertain economic climate leading up to the Revolutionary War.[63] In 1775 Lord Dunmore, the royal governor of Virginia, shocked North American colonists by declaring "all indented Servants [and] Negroes appertaining to Rebels free," so long as they were "able and willing to bear Arms . . . [for] His Majesty's Troops."[64] Dunmore's proclamation accelerated the decline of Philadelphia's slave population as thousands of slaves from throughout the colonies ran away to join the British Army. But by the time General Howe reached Philadelphia in 1777, "the British had proved themselves less avid in their support of black freedom than American slaves had been led to expect."[65]

The shared attribute of oriental dress implies a metonymic link between the display of luxury slaves and the display of young, elite women at the Meschianza—although André's fete did not relegate the Ladies of the Blended Rose and the Burning Mountain to the "representational prison" that confined the black slaves performing a Grand Salaam to the dining room. On the contrary, Turkish costumes connoted women's independence in the late eighteenth century—albeit a peculiar sort of independence, achieved through disguise. In 1717 Lady Mary Wortley Montagu, wife of the British ambassador to Constantinople, wrote a letter to her sister in which she describes wearing a "Turkish habit" of drawers, smock, waistcoat, and veil. Lady Mary's letters were an instant sensation when they were finally published in 1763, and her remarks on Turkish attire reconfigured the meaning of oriental fancy dress at British masquerades. "'Tis very easy to see they [Turkish women] have more liberty than we [British women] have," wrote Lady Mary; "no woman of what rank soever [is] permitted to go in the streets without . . . cover[ing] her face. . . . This perpetual masquerade gives them entire liberty of following their inclinations without danger of discovery."[66] Like Lady Mary's veil, Turkish costumes conferred a measure of independence from "patriot strictures" on the female guests at the Meschianza.[67]

In addition to the explicit racial impersonation performed through their

Turkish costumes, the towering hairstyles worn by the ladies at the Meschianza also carried racialized undertones, at least in the Whig imagination (figure 5). In a pasquinade on General Howe's army that appeared a month before the Meschianza in the *New Jersey Gazette*, an anonymous correspondent wrote, "We hear that general orders have issued for having the *Royal African Regiment* shorn every three months; in order to supply the Ladies of the Court of Great-Britain with wool, sufficient for the present fashionable head-dress."[68] This passage mocked the women of the British court by racializing their coiffure, and it upended Dunmore's proclamation by reducing black loyalist soldiers to chattel whose hair could be harvested at Howe's whim and command. Considered alongside the Grand Salaam performed at the Meschianza, this excerpt from the *New Jersey Gazette* suggests another metonymic link between the elite women and the black slaves arrayed together in the dining room: in the eyes of Whig critics, the Meschianza ladies and the Meschianza slaves wore the same hair. Through the Grand Salaam, André and his fellow officers attempted to symbolically secure Britain's power in North America by staging an erotically charged encounter between two groups of people representing the spoils of empire. But as prefigured in the *New Jersey Gazette*, this mise-en-scène—like so many other theatrical displays at the Meschianza—carried with it two contradictory meanings: a theatrical affirmation of British authority and a farcical deflation of colonial power.

Both the luxury slaves and the elite women who participated in the Meschianza conformed to highly scripted roles as black, blackened, and/or orientalized "others," setting in relief the British officers' performances of neofeudal masculinity. André's staging restricted the agency of the colonial subjects cast in proscribed roles at the event, as attested by his fastidious control over the costumes at the Meschianza. But colonial authority frayed at the edges of the celebration, where private bled into public. Whigs and even some Tories openly criticized the Howe brothers' spectacular farewell bash, Continental soldiers attacked nearby British fortifications during the party, and troops had to be stationed to protect guests from the crowd that "darked the whole plain" around Walnut Grove. On the one hand, André and his compatriots employed the theatricality of the Meschianza to solidify their social and symbolic power among Philadelphia's elite. But on the other hand, the Knights of the Blended Rose and the Burning Mountain could not control the reception of their performances in a revolutionary public sphere about to be decolonized by the British Army's hasty withdrawal from Philadelphia.

INDEPENDENCE DAY BURLESQUE

On June 18, 1778, the British evacuation of Philadelphia officially began. Ten days later, in excruciating summer heat, Continental forces attacked the rear of the retreating British column near Monmouth Courthouse, in central New Jersey. In the ensuing battle, General Anthony Wayne, the revolutionary hero of the day, repulsed several British counterattacks. Writing to Richard Peters, secretary of the Board of War, Wayne quipped,

> Tell the Phil'a[delphia] ladies that the heavenly, sweet, pretty red Coats—the accomplished Gent'n of the Guards & Grenadiers, have humbled themselves on the plains of Monmouth. "The Knights of the Blended Rose" & "Burning Mount"—have resigned their Laurels to *Rebel* officers who will lay them at the feet of the Virtuous Daughters of America who cheerfully gave up ease and Affluence in a city for Liberty and peace of mind in a Cottage.[69]

Wayne's letter displays a close familiarity with both the form and content of the Meschianza. And he uses his knowledge of the event to feminize the British officer-knights through their association with "the Phil'a ladies," whom he contrasts with "the Virtuous Daughters of America"—a contrast that hinges on the meaning of the word *virtuous*.

Given that virtue derives from the Latin word *vir*, or "man," Wayne's use of the adjective *virtuous* to describe the *daughters* of America marks a profound transition in the gendered meaning of virtue. Historian Ruth H. Bloch contends that the definition of virtue transformed in the revolutionary and early national periods from "male public spirit" to "female private morality" and "female sexual prudence." "Throughout the revolutionary period," Bloch argues,

> virtue was the most valued quality defining individual commitment to the American republican cause. . . . If the virtues of heroic courage, glory, and fame were inherently male, the opposites—cowardice, idleness, luxury, dependence—were, not surprisingly, castigated as the "effeminate" weaknesses of unpatriotic men.[70]

As evinced in Wayne's letter, partisans of the revolution viewed the "heavenly, sweet, pretty red Coats" who organized the Meschianza as distinctly unvirtuous. The imperial fantasy staged in the mock tournament at Walnut

Grove subjected masculine courage, glory, and fame to the constraints of courtly romance, with the Meschianza ladies successfully petitioning their knights to resolve the battle in a draw, "reconciled by a happy compromise."[71] Wayne's letter reveled in the defeat of these milquetoast British warriors, and like many revolutionary critiques of effete fashion, it also aimed "to humiliate loyalist men and British soldiers on the social battlefield by attacking the characters of the women associated with them."[72]

Wayne's discursive attack on "the Phil'a ladies" proceeds indirectly. By opposing them to "the Virtuous Daughters of America," whom he relegates to "a Cottage," Wayne shores up the conventional exclusion of women from the public sphere by praising the virtue of female privacy and impugning the moral character of the women who appeared in public at the Meschianza. But as Bloch points out, "[women] who abstained from tea drinking, boycotted loyalist shops, made homespun clothing, and raised money in support of the revolutionary cause" exhibited private virtues—abstention, frugality, industriousness, charity—that differed little from the public virtues expected of patriotic men.[73] In other words, the gendered ambivalence of virtue in British North America troubled the gendered separation of the private and public spheres, contributing to a destabilization of social roles that allowed women to express their political views with unprecedented candor.

On July 4, 1778, in the immediate aftermath of the British withdrawal from Philadelphia, one anonymous woman performed a bold, public satire of elite sociability. The holiday festivities began with a public parade organized by General Benedict Arnold, the military commander of the city under Continental control. In the afternoon, upper-class guests, both Whig and Tory, gathered for a private supper and ball hosted by Arnold at the exclusive City Tavern. During his command in Philadelphia, Arnold, who famously sold military intelligence to John André later in the war, aligned himself with opponents of Pennsylvania's democratic constitution. In November 1778 the ardent revolutionary Joseph Reed complained that "treason, Disaffection to the interests of America, and even assistance to the British interest is called . . . Error of Judgment which candor and liberality of sentiment will overlook." Reed was particularly incensed that "not only Tory ladies, but the Wives and Daughters of Persons proscribed by the state" attended Arnold's frequent balls and assemblies.[74]

Arnold's extravagant fetes and his cozy relationship with the local elite angered both radical Whigs and ordinary citizens beset by hyperinflation and shortages of basic necessities after the British withdrawal from Philadelphia. On the afternoon of July 4, 1778, some of these citizens took their anger to the streets in a burlesque performance that mocked the towering hairstyles in vogue among Philadelphia's upper-class women. From her drawing room window, Elizabeth Drinker privately approved of the spectacle: "A very high Head dress was exhibited thro the Streets, this Afternoon on a very dirty Woman with a mob after her, with Drums & c. by way of ridiculing that very foolish fashion."[75] Elaborate hairdos adorned the heads of wealthy women at all manner of festivities in revolutionary Philadelphia, but the timing of this burlesque performance—six weeks after the Howe brothers' bash at Walnut Grove—suggests that the "dirty" woman's mimicry and mockery of elite fashion referred to the ladies of the Meschianza. The guests at Arnold's ball perceived the insult and responded in kind. The mother of one Meschianza belle christened the burlesque performer "Continella, or the Duchess of Independence," and Rebecca Franks quipped, "For though the style of her head is British, her shoes and stockings are in the genuine *Continental fashion*."[76]

In a letter sent from Philadelphia in August 1778, New Hampshire congressional delegate Josiah Bartlett claimed to find both Whig and Tory women in the city

wearing the most Enormouse High head Dresses after the manner of the Mistresses & Wh— —s of the Brittish officers; and at the anniversary of Independence they appeared in public Dressed in that way, and to mortify them, some Gentlemen purchased the most Etravgant [sic] high head Dress that Could be got and Dressed an old Negro wench with it, she appeared likewise in public, and was paraded about the city by the mob.[77]

Susan E. Klepp points out that Bartlett's letter is the only contemporary account of the July Fourth burlesque to identify the female protagonist as *black* rather than dirty or blackened, even though male writers employed "a veritable thesaurus of terms for degraded, sexualized femininity to describe the woman player . . . who quickly became the object of contempt rather than a representation of the contemptible." For Klepp,

the move from sexualized white woman to sexualized black women [in Bartlett's account] presaged the later course of racist thought in the country, and it was as "an old Negro wench," "a negro wench," and "a negress" that the woman satirist was remembered into the nineteenth century. A sexualized female could not be simply black-ened in the new nation; she must be black. And if black women were sullied, then white women must be virtuous.[78]

In light of this analysis, General Wayne's letter—penned a week after the July Fourth burlesque—can be read as implicitly distinguishing "the Virtu-ous Daughters of America" and "the Phil'a ladies" in racial and sexual terms, with the former presumed to be white and chaste and the latter pre-sumed to be black (or blackened) sluts.

ORIENTAL BLACKFACE

Klepp interprets the July Fourth burlesque as an instance of "rough mu-sic," likening the dirty, black, and/or blackened face of the woman with the high headdress to the use of blackface makeup in early modern European crowd actions designed to enforce social and sexual mores.[79] In E. P. Thompson's definition, rough music is the English version of a Europe-wide family of rituals, which used "a rude cacophony" to direct "mockery or hostility against individuals who offended against . . . community norms."[80] Like French charivari or North American shivaree, English rough music sometimes employed blackface makeup, although the performance genealogy of blackface in both of these traditions remains obscure. Dale Cockrell believes that "blackface masquerade among the common people of northern Europe might have first followed from direct contact with dark-skinned Moors (but probably did not)," whereas John Emigh specu-lates that European folk blackface may have derived from the black half-masks of comic servant and slave characters in Italian commedia dell'arte and Persian *ruhozi*.[81] Whatever one thinks of these theories, it seems clear that a multiplicity of sources, some of them unrecoverable, contributed to the use of blackface in early modern rituals of satire and shaming.

Whether or not there is an historical connection between *ruhozi* and rough music, blackface and blackening carried a subtle association with the Orient in the eighteenth century. In August 1778 a correspondent to the *Pennsylvania Packet*, a Whig newspaper, wrote that he

would not willingly purchase any article (except in a absolute neces-sity) of a Tory. To be asking always who are Whigs who have to sell, is troublesome, and, I am sorry to say, uncertain. I wish the same mark were put upon the houses of our well-known enemies, as the

Turks use to designate the residences of liars, that is, by painting them black.[82]

Commenting on this article in his diary, Lemuel Clift, a captain in the Continental Army, remarked,

This suggestion . . . does well enough as far as it goes, but we would propose a still more prominent designation of a Tory, that is, let the right side of the face and the right hand be dyed black, and if that don't answer, it will not be any great loss if the whole body be set to dying.[83]

Punning on the word *die,* Clift expands the ostensibly Turkish custom of blackening the houses of liars to suggest that the faces, hands, and bodies of Tories be dyed black. Was he kidding? Probably; but behind his comic tone, Clift seems to long for a sign painted on the skin by which to recognize his enemies and "set [them] to dying."

The alleged Turkish practice of blackening the houses of liars may well be fabricated, but regardless of its historical accuracy, it projects the Western association between blackness and deceit onto a non-Western culture. This rhetorical move naturalizes a Western understanding of the symbolism of blackness, drawing Turks closer to the West while pushing away objects and people discursively blackened for their treachery. In this scheme, Turks are racial others, but they are emphatically *not* black; instead, they are cast as agents of blackening—just like Europeans and Euro-Americans.

Given that British travel writers started drawing racial distinctions between "tawny Moors" and "black Moors" as early as 1600, the implicit distinction between Turks and blacks in the *Pennsylvania Packet* and Clift's diary comes as no surprise. But as Julie Ellison argues, these racial distinctions did not translate to the stage in Britain or the early United States, where "the notion that African stage characters had any historical referentiality whatsoever" did not emerge until the second quarter of the nineteenth century.[84] The changing styles of racial impersonation in Shakespeare's *Othello* ratify Ellison's point. In his 1827 acting manual *The Road to the Stage*, English actor Leman Thomas Rede notes that the custom of portraying Othello in blackface had fallen out of favor. Rede—who distinguishes among the pigments to be used for African, Arab, East Asian, and South Asian roles—advises that the Moor of Venice should be played in "Spanish brown" rather than "sable" makeup, and the five reprintings of his book in New

York between 1858 and 1868 suggest that plenty of actors and theater managers in the United States took his advice.[85]

The Road to the Stage appeared at a time when actors in the United States had begun to differentiate their representation of North African "Moors" from their portrayal of sub-Saharan and American "Negroes." As Heather S. Nathans argues, U.S. theater in the 1830s tended to endow Moorish Africans "with virtues of culture, learning, religion, and sentimental understanding"—virtues adamantly denied in stage depictions of Negro peoples.[86] The 1830s witnessed a spate of Moorish, Arab, and other oriental stage acts in London, Philadelphia, and other cities along the North Atlantic rim. In the summer and fall of 1836, T. D. Rice's blackface Jim Crow act alternated with a troupe of North African acrobats billed as "The Real Bedouin Arabs" at London's Royal Surrey Theater.[87] And in 1837–38 a pantomime ballet called *The Bedouin Arabs* was among the most successful productions of the Philadelphia theater season before touring to other cities throughout the United States.[88] W. T. Lhamon Jr. dismisses "The Real Bedouin Arabs" as a novelty act, but I view the orientalist stage entertainments of the 1830s as a recondite condition of possibility for the blackface minstrel show. Brownface Othellos, North African acrobats, and pantomiming stage Arabs siphoned off the oriental associations that accrued to the blackface mask in the late eighteenth and early nineteenth centuries, resignifying "sable" makeup as the exclusive property of protominstrels like Rice, Dan Emmett, and George Washington Dixon.

The commingling of black, oriental, and even Spanish overtones in the blackface stage makeup of the late eighteenth and early nineteenth centuries appears most clearly in Isaac Bickerstaffe's two-act comic opera *The Padlock*, which premiered at the Theater Royal in Drury Lane in 1768. Based on the Cervantes story "El celoso estremeño" (The jealous husband), *The Padlock*'s plot centers on an old man, Don Diego, obsessed with protecting the chastity of his young fiancée, Leonora (to whom he is already married in the Cervantes story). Diego's slave Mungo steals the show when he first appears near the end of act 1, talking back to his master in "an identifiable version of West Indian speech"—a first for the London stage.[89] Despite his caricatured dialect, Nathans points out that "Mungo also *feels* deeply," as the lyrics of his signature song attest:

> Dear heart, what a terrible life am I led!
> A dog has better, that's shelter'd and fed:
> Night and day, 'tis de same,

My pain is dere game [gain?]:
Me wish to de Lord me was dead.

Whate'ers to be done,
Poor blacky must run;
Mungo here, Mungo dere,
Mungo every where;
Above and below,
Sirrah, come; sirrah, go,
Do so, and do so.
Oh! oh!
Me wish to de Lord me was dead.[90]

Played in London by the actor Charles Dibdin, who later became famous for his Negro songs, Mungo appeared in a close-fitting striped suit
that contrasted sharply with the pathos of his condition as a slave. Dibdin's
Mungo defied the costuming conventions of eighteenth-century London
theater. David Garrick, manager of the Theater Royal, generally used one
of four styles to dress the panoply of characters that appeared on his stage:
costume à la turque for exotics, Spanish dress for villains, Old English dress
for Shakespearean characters, and Roman dress for heroes. As such, "the
character of Mungo, a black slave in a Spanish play, nominally a villain and
originally an exotic," presented Garrick with a costuming challenge.[91] Garrick's solution blended Turkish and Spanish conventions into an ensemble
not unlike the sumptuous livery worn by London's luxury slaves. And as
Rede points out, Dibdin played Mungo in the sable makeup used for both
black and oriental characters in the eighteenth century.[92]

As a hybrid impersonation—part black, part oriental, part Spanish, and
wholly imaginary—Mungo anticipated the hybrid impulse of Dibdin's
"readings and music" and "table entertainments," which he performed to
great acclaim from 1789 through 1805. In these monodramas, Dibdin served
as "speaker, singer, and accompanist" in impersonations of English sailors,
burlesque Irishmen, Italian singers, Jewish peddlers, and black slaves—all
without the aid of blackface or other pigmented makeup.[93] The tune "Kickaraboo" (1795), one of Dibdin's popular Negro songs from this era, begins
with these lines: "Poor Negro say one ting you no take offence / Black and
white he one colour a hundred year hence."[94] Hans Nathan interprets the
title "Kickaraboo" as "equivalent to the modern colloquialism 'kicking the
bucket,'" and the remainder of Dibdin's song focuses on the equality and

Fig. 6. Robert Sayer, *Mr. Dibden* [sic] *in the Character of Mungo in the Celebrated Opera of the Padlock*, ca. 1769. Courtesy Victoria and Albert Museum.

equivalency of black slaves and their white masters after death.[95] But the second line of the opening verse, quoted above, suggests not only the leveling effect of the grave but also the prospect of a racially hybrid future. After all, Dibdin named his eldest son Charles Isaac *Mungo* Dibdin, blurring the boundaries between himself, his most famous role, and his progeny—not to mention the boundaries between whiteness and its racialized others, collected in the figure of Mungo from Bickerstaffe's comic opera.

The Padlock had its North American premiere in 1769, with the Anglo-American actor Lewis Hallam Jr. as Mungo. The show was a huge success, and Hallam and his company performed *The Padlock* in New York, Philadelphia, Savannah, Charleston, Richmond, Baltimore, Boston, and Newport.[96] Jenna M. Gibbs argues that Hallam subverted *The Padlock*'s critique of slavery through "his portrayal of a clown-like Mungo . . . replete with 'black' dialect."[97] In New York, William Dunlap—an actor, playwright, theater manager, and abolitionist—praised Hallam for playing Mungo "with a truth derived from the study of the negro slave character, which Dibdin . . . could not have conceived." In Philadelphia, Durang offered a similar though more candid assessment: "Hallam was the originator of the negro character on the stage, and, having an opportunity of studying the genius of the African race in this country, was a better representative of the character than the English *Mungo*, who had probably never seen a negro."[98]

The Padlock is an obvious precursor of blackface minstrelsy, and as Felicity A. Nussbaum argues, it likely took on this meaning through Hallam's performance, which narrowed the hybrid construction of Dibdin's Mungo into a racial caricature.[99] But as the shifty lyrics of his song suggest ("Mungo here, Mungo dere / Mungo every where"), Mungo's meaning did not remain fixed for long. Nathans remarks that Mungo became "a byword for early abolitionists" in the United States, and Miller sees Mungo as a template for black dandies like Julius Soubise, a London luxury slave who emerged from "being stylized" by his master to claiming agency for himself through "self-stylization."[100] The nineteenth-century black actor Ira Aldridge "played Othello and Mungo occasionally on the same night in his natural skin," and T. D. Rice essayed the role in Louisville in 1830, where "he entered singing a *Kentucky corn song*."[101] In all of these examples, the hints of racial hybridity in Dibdin's Mungo—oriental and Spanish as well as black—recede into the background, leaving Mungo open to appropriation by both sides of the slavery debate. Abolitionists and self-styling black men like Soubise and Aldrige appropriated Mungo's aspirations to freedom, whereas Hallam and Rice appropriated Mungo as a comic slave, grist for minstrelsy's ever-churning mill of racial impersonation.

SLAVES IN ALGIERS

Susanna Rowson's play *Slaves in Algiers*, which premiered at Philadelphia's Chestnut Street Theater in June 1794, remixes the co-constructions of orientalism, blackness, and femininity in the Meschianza, the July 4, 1778, street burlesque, and *The Padlock*. Although no evidence survives to indicate the makeup and costuming techniques used to present the Algerian characters in the play, Peter P. Reed speculates that "the actors [at the Chestnut Street Theater] quite possibly donned the burnt cork . . . as they would for a more famous North African role, Othello."[102] Whether or not blackface makeup was used in the premiere of *Slaves in Algiers*, both the language and the action of the play associate blackness with the stereotypes of duplicity and licentiousness assigned to Muslims and other oriental peoples in eighteenth-century Anglo-Atlantic drama, before the profusion of sensitive stage Moors that emerged in the 1830s. And as with the Meschianza, the co-construction of race and gender in *Slaves in Algiers* comes into focus through a comparison with *Don Quixote*.

Rowson's play centers on an Anglo-American family separated during the Revolutionary War and reunited in Algiers, where they have all ended up as captives and where the entirety of the drama takes place. In the preface, Rowson notes that "some part of the plot is taken from the Story of the Captive, related by Cervantes, in his inimitable Romance of *Don Quixote*."[103] Although critics in the early national period tended to scoff at Cervantes's knight errant (much as they had during the revolution), *Don Quixote* remained a best seller in the early United States, just as it had been in the late colonial period.[104] Rowson probably knew *Don Quixote* through Tobias Smollett's 1755 translation, which was the definitive version of the novel for English-language readers in the United States well into the nineteenth century. Smollett's "Life of Cervantes," published with his translation of *Don Quixote*, "was the first biography [in English] to include an account of Cervantes's captivity in Algiers"—an experience that formed the basis of "The Captive's Tale."[105]

From the end of the Revolutionary War into the early nineteenth century, U.S. commercial interests faced a serious and persistent threat from North African piracy, which had long dogged European commerce in the Mediterranean. The pirates' habit of taking hostages from foreign vessels and holding them for ransom provoked widespread outrage in the United States, and the villainous Algerians and noble Anglo-American captives in *Slaves in Algiers* reflected popular opinion on the depredations of North African piracy. Elizabeth Maddock Dillon reads Rowson's play as symptomatic of the dependence of the U.S. national imaginary "upon peoples beyond the enclosure it seeks to make immanent," a point illustrated by the contrast between the sympathetic depiction of the play's Anglo-American characters and its largely negative portrayal of Algerians.[106]

Like "The Captive's Tale," *Slaves in Algiers* brims with images of racial hybridity. Near the end of the first volume of Cervantes's novel, a Christian soldier, who has recently escaped to his native Spain, relates the story of his captivity in Algiers to Don Quixote, Sancho, and an array of other characters at a rural inn. In this interpolated tale, the anonymous captive describes his first master, Uchali Fartax, as "a native of Calabria" and his second master, Azanaga, as "a Venetian" and "the most cruel renegado that ever was known" (286–87). Both Fartax and Azanaga practice Islam and hold high office in the local, Turkish-controlled regency. These characters are Cervantes's inventions, of course, but they reflect his familiarity with the swirling interculture of sixteenth- and seventeenth-century Algiers, where nearly half the inhabitants were either Christian captives or "renegades" from the northern shore of the Mediterranean who converted to Islam in order to participate in the city's lucrative pirate economy.[107]

Most of "The Captive's Tale" recounts the details of the captive's escape, which he effects with the help of Zorayda, the beautiful daughter of a wealthy Algerian Moor. Zorayda wants nothing more than to flee Algiers with the captive, marry him, and convert to Christianity. But despite (or perhaps because of) the force of these desires, Cervantes consistently paints Zorayda in racially and religiously ambiguous terms. When the captive first catches a glimpse of Zorayda through the latticework of her father's house, he sees only "a very white hand" holding "a small cross made of cane," leading him to the mistaken conclusion that "she must be one of those Christian renegades whom their masters frequently take to wife" (288). Zorayda then sends a secret letter to the captive—written in Arabic—which invokes both Allah and the Virgin Mary, whom Zorayda has revered since childhood, when "a woman slave . . . taught [her] the christian worship" (289). Her letter also warns the captive to "beware of the Moors, for, they are altogether deceitful" (290). Through a tortuous intrigue involving smuggled gold, a stolen key, a hijacked boat, and a band of renegades, the captive and Zorayda finally elope to Spain.

Rowson borrowed aspects of Cervantes's Zorayda to inform two of the female characters in *Slaves in Algiers*: Zoriana and Fetnah. But as Dillon observes, there is an important difference between "The Captive's Tale" and the plot of Rowson's play, in which "romances between Christian and Islamic characters do not ever result in marriage."[108] In *Slaves in*

Algiers, Zoriana, a Moorish princess, falls in love with Henry, a captive from the United States, and helps him to escape, but in the end, Henry's betrothal to Olivia, a woman from his own country, prevents him from marrying Zoriana.

More interestingly, Fetnah, whom Rowson identifies as "a Moriscan" (56), embodies and amplifies the racial and religious ambiguity of Zorayda from "The Captive's Tale." In the first scene of the play, Fetnah, sold by her father into the harem of the dey of Algiers, explains her refusal to sleep with her master to Selima, one of the dey's concubines:

> SELIMA: But how is it, Fetnah, that you have conceived such an
> aversion to the manners of a county where you were born?
> FETNAH: You are mistaken. I was not born in Algiers. I drew my first
> breath in England. My father, Ben Hassan, as he is now called,
> was a Jew. I can scarcely remember our arrival here, and have
> been educated in the Moorish religion, though I always had a
> natural antipathy to their manners (60).

Later, Fetnah is again mistaken for a Moor and again vents her distaste for Moorish people and customs, this time in explicitly racist terms. In a soliloquy on life in the harem, she complains,

> There's nobody here to look at one but great, black, goggle-eyed
> creatures, that are posted here and there to watch us. And when one
> speaks to them, they shake their frightful heads, and make such a
> horrid noise. Lord, I wish I could run away, but that's impossible. . . .
> I do wish some dear, sweet, Christian man would fall in love with
> me, break open the garden gates, and carry me off (72–73).

An American captive named Frederic overhears this speech and asks Fetnah, "You wish to leave this country, lovely Moor?" to which she replies, "Lord, I'm not a Moriscan. I hate 'em all. There is nothing I wish so much as to get away from them" (73).

Like Zorayda in "The Captive's Tale," Fetnah adopts Christianity early in life under the tutelage of a female slave in her father's house (in *Slaves in Algiers*, this slave is an Anglo-American captive named Rebecca, who also happens to be Olivia's mother). And in a further parallel with "The Captive's Tale," Fetnah—like Zorayda—distrusts and despises other Moors, even though the texts in which these two characters appear repeatedly identify them as Moorish. Fetnah's Jewish and English background complicates her putative "Moriscan" identity, but as Nathans points out, Rowson's portrayal of Jewish characters in *Slaves in Algiers* "owes much to the popular tendency to classify Jews with other 'Turks and infidels'" in the late eighteenth-century United States.[109] Indeed, Fetnah chooses to stay in Algiers at the end of the play to care for her disgraced, Jewish-turned-Muslim father rather than to marry Frederic and emigrate to the United States—an unexpected turn in the plot that supports Dillon's thesis that the racial logic of *Slaves in Algiers* cannot accommodate the marriage of a white, Christian man and a racially and religiously othered woman.

Fetnah's masquerade as a man earlier in the play further complicates both her racial and gendered identity. At the end of the second act, Fetnah disguises herself as the dey's son to escape the harem. She then flees to a seaside grotto where Henry, Frederic, and several other captives have gathered to plan a revolt against their masters. The captives mistake Fetnah for a spy and attack her, and "in her struggle, her turban falls off" (78). The revelation of Fetnah's female identity clears her of suspicion, and Henry and Frederic insist on hiding her "in an inner part of the grotto" while they stage their uprising:

FETNAH: What, shut me up? Do you take me for a coward?

HENRY: We respect you as a woman, and would shield you from danger.

FETNAH: A woman! Why, so I am. But in the cause of love or friendship, a woman can face danger with as much spirit, and as little fear, as the bravest man amongst you. Do lead the way; I'll follow to the end (79–80).

With this speech, Fetnah joins the revolt, no longer clad in her masculine disguise.

Rowson's stint as an actress in Philadelphia suggests that she felt an affinity for Fetnah's cross-dressed adventure and racially hybrid identity, even though she played Olivia, not Fetnah, in the premiere of *Slaves in Algiers*. Rowson had a varied career on both sides of the Atlantic as a novelist, actress, playwright, and teacher.[110] Between 1794 and 1796 she performed not only at the Chestnut Street Theater but also in John B. Ricketts's circus troupe, which operated in Philadelphia from 1795 to 1799. According to Charles Durang, "Mrs. Rowson used to dance a hornpipe . . . in the character of a sailor"—an act she likely learned from John Durang, Charles's father and a member of Ricketts's company famous for his dancing.[111] The hornpipe, a popular stage dance in the early United

States, featured the miming of shipboard labor to an up-tempo beat, with the high steps and bent knees and elbows of an Irish jig—a movement style that presaged the nineteenth-century Jim Crow dance. Peter Linebaugh and Marcus Rediker argue that seventeenth- and eighteenth-century sailing ships were the first places where working people from throughout the Atlantic world mixed, with "African, Briton, quashee, Irish, and American (not to mention Dutch, Portuguese, and lascar) sailors" laboring side by side.[112] As such, Rowson's cross-dressed hornpipe staged not only a gender reversal but also a class transgression, tinged with implications of racial hybridity. No wonder Durang fils complained that Rowson's "refinement" as an educated white woman should have dictated "better taste—or, rather, an omission of the spectacle."[113]

Rowson's sailor act aligns her with Fetnah in *Slaves in Algiers*, especially since Fetnah, more so than any other character in the play, embodies Rowson's protofeminist agenda. Rowson's support for women's rights comes across explicitly in the prologue delivered by actor James Fennell at the premiere of *Slaves in Algiers*:

> Some say the Comic muse, with watchful eye,
> Should catch the reigning *vices* as they fly,
> Our author boldly has reversed that plan,
> The reigning *virtues* she has dar'd to scan,
> And tho' a woman, pled the Right of Man (58).

The epilogue, which Rowson delivered, added bite to Fennell's words: "Women were born for universal sway / Men to adore, be silent, and obey" (94). These paratexts establish Rowson's claim for virtue in the public sphere as the unique prerogative of women, and Fetnah's actions live up to Rowson's rhetoric. The fact that Fetnah is also a Jew and a Moor hardly suggests that "race emerges as an aspect of gender construction" in the play, as Dillon contends, but rather that racial transgression licenses gender transgression.[114] Despite Rowson's radical politics, Fetnah's breach of racial and gendered norms requires her self-abnegation. Fetnah voices more explicitly racist lines than any other character in *Slaves in Algiers*; she stands by an abusive father, even after he sells her into sexual slavery; and she decides to remain in Algiers rather than emigrate to the United States at the end of the play. These words and actions rein in the power of Fetnah's liberated, interracial, and gender-bending womanhood, safely containing her transgressions of race and gender outside of the U.S. national imaginary.

Fetnah's character arc suggests that *Slaves in Algiers* does not limit its claim for women's public role to white women, even though the play's denouement excludes Fetnah from U.S. citizenship. With reference to eighteenth-century British drama, Michael Ragussis argues that the stage Jew "functioned as the limit . . . of the recuperation and empowerment of ethnic minorities" in the British national imaginary.[115] *Slaves in Algiers* reinscribes this limit in a U.S. context: as a Jew and a "Moriscan," Fetnah cannot marry Frederic and immigrate to the United States. But her virtuous and risky rejection of the dey's lust legitimizes her public role, as a woman, in the captives' rebellion.

The performances of race and gender staged at the Meschianza, the July 4, 1778, street burlesque, *Slaves in Algiers*, and Rowson's hornpipe each had different political effects, but they all partake in the co-construction of orientalism, blackness, and femininity that recurs in late eighteenth-century Philadelphia. These four performances appear at dangerous and historically discontinuous moments of war and captivity, moments that bear witness to the radical reconfiguration of local, national, and transnational hierarchies of power in the late eighteenth century. Through their overlapping symbolic vocabularies, deployed when the stakes are high, the ghosts of the Meschianza, the July Fourth street burlesque, *Slaves in Algiers*, and Rowson's hornpipe *all haunt each other* at one geographically specific site: the City of Brotherly Love. As Rosemarie K. Bank puts it, invoking a Native American (and de Certeauian) view of history, "what has happened in a place is always happening."[116] "Haunting is historical," writes Jacques Derrida, "but it is not *dated*, it is never docilely given a date in the chain of presents, day after day, according to the instituted order of a calendar."[117] As such, this chapter cuts across the revolutionary and early national periods to bring a broad constellation of ghosts to light. The next chapter takes up the subsistence of these ghosts in the racial caricatures of graphic art, popular theater, and street performance in early nineteenth-century Philadelphia.

THREE

Life in Philadelphia

Racial Caricature in Graphic Art and Performance

On January 3, 1799, Philadelphia diarist Elizabeth Drinker remarked on the fine clothes her two black servants had recently worn to a wedding:

> Jacob dress[ed] in a light cloth coat, white cashmere vest and britches, white silk Stockings and a new hat. Sarah, the bridesmaid, [dressed] in white muslin . . . with white ribbons from head to foot, yellow Morocco shoes with white bows, &c. They went in Benjamin Oliver's coach, [driven] by his white man. . . . They are both honest servants, but times [are] much altered with the black folk.[1]

As historians Shane White and Graham White argue, the "feelings of disquiet about free blacks" expressed by Drinker and her contemporaries "coalesced around the perceived lack of self-control African Americans exercised in the presentation of their bodies."[2] Writing in 1830, thirty-one years after Drinker, John Fanning Watson lamented the changing deportment of African Americans in Philadelphia:

> In the olden time dressy blacks and dandy *colour'd* beaux and belles . . . were quite unknown. Their aspirings and little vanities have been rapidly growing since they got those separate churches, and have received their entire exemption from slavery. Once they submitted to the appellation of servants, blacks, or negroes, but now they require to be called coloured people, and among themselves, their common call or salutation is—gentlemen and ladies. Twenty to thirty years ago, they were much humbler, more esteemed in their place, and more useful to themselves and others. As a whole they show an overweening fondness for display and vainglory—fondly imitating the whites in processions and banners, and in the pomp and pageantry of Masonic and Washington societies, &c.[3]

Richard Allen established Mother Bethel African Methodist Episcopal Church at Sixth and Lombard Streets in 1794, and by 1811 black Philadelphians had set up "schools, insurance companies, masonic lodges, and several additional churches within a few blocks of Bethel," forming an "identifiable [neighborhood] at the southern edge of the city."[4] Black Masons began parading publicly in Philadelphia in 1797, and in 1815 four black Masonic societies merged to form the First African Independent Grand Lodge under Absalom Jones, who also ministered to the congregation at the African Episcopal Church of St. Thomas.[5] Douglas A. Jones Jr. views the flourishing parade culture among black social organizations in the antebellum North as a performance of black presence, which "aimed to position African Americans as self-determined citizens and bearers of American possibility."[6] These aspirations, as expressed in parade performances, provoked fearful derision from whites—including Watson's racist screed and a caricature of a black Masonic procession by Philadelphia artist David Claypoole Johnston, to give just two examples.[7]

FICTIONS OF BLACKNESS

In 1819 James Thackera, another Philadelphia artist, produced an etching of two well-dressed white men scowling at a pair of black dandies they encounter on the street. In the background, a monkey perched on a windowsill holds a monocle to its eye, mimicking a gesture performed by one of the two flamboyantly dressed black men. In a note appended to this print, Thackera complains, "The black gentry . . . not only ape the dress of their masters, but also their cant terms, being well versed in the fashionable vocabulary."[8] Interestingly, Thackera's print laces its antiblack caricature with a barb aimed at rich whites. By drawing attention to the "cant terms" of the "masters" who employ Philadelphia's "black gentry," Thackera mocks not only blacks who imitate white fashions but also the very concept of fashion itself.

In his book on the literary history of Philadelphia, Samuel Otter analyzes the frequent appearance of "double parody" in antebellum racial caricature, arguing that works like Thackera's etching unmask "all social performance" as "mimicry" while also offering white viewers "the reassurance that their own [social] performances are more successful" than those of African Americans.[9] A decade after Thackera, Edward Williams Clay utilized double parody to great effect in Life in Philadelphia (1828–30), a series of fourteen aquatints lampooning the pretentious manners of both whites and blacks in the City of Brotherly Love. Four of these prints poke fun at upper-class white Philadelphians. In one, a dour Quaker couple exchange verses from the Song of Solomon in front of an extinguished fireplace.[10] In another, a young couple attend a "fancy ball" dressed in garish, pastoral attire.[11] However, the images in *Life in Philadelphia* that ridicule blacks employ a pointed style that makes Clay's mockery of affluent whites seem comparatively mild. Of the fourteen prints in the series, ten are racial caricatures, and eight focus solely on black fashion, speech, dance, music, and sociability—in short, the ensemble of practices through which upwardly mobile African Americans performed their individual and collective identities in antebellum Philadelphia.

Life in Philadelphia resonated with middle- and upper-class whites throughout the United States and the Atlantic world, despite the "double parody" that mocked the consumers of Clay's prints while simultaneously reassuring them of the relative efficacy of their own social performances. In a curator's note for an exhibition of Clay's work, Martha S. Jones recounts the major pathways of *Life in Philadelphia*'s national and transnational circulation in the early nineteenth century:

> The series [was sold] in print shops from Philadelphia and New York to Baltimore and New Orleans. It spawned a parallel series titled *Life in New York*. Clay's figures adorned sheet music and were mass-produced in miniatures. In London, they were incorporated into book illustrations and sold in elaborate, full-color reproductions. In Paris, Clay's images made their way into elite homes when they were incorporated into fine French wallpaper.[12]

Through its mass circulation, *Life in Philadelphia* constructed "a racial taxonomy of quotidian life" that stoked antiblack feeling throughout the Atlantic world, and Clay's later work contributed to mounting anxieties about abolition and amalgamation in the antebellum North.[13] This chapter traces the close connection between Clay's racial caricatures and blackface theater, focusing especially on performances of blackface gender impersonation. It also argues that the orientalism of Clay's early work shaped the obsession with race that drove him to construct increasingly vicious fictions of blackness later in his career.

In the 1830s Philadelphia's African American community consisted of "some 14,000 poor people juxtaposed to upwards of 1,000 economically 'substantial' black citizens," several of whom ranked among the wealthiest people in the city.[14] The scurrilous racial humor in *Life in Philadelphia* tended to focus on the less prosperous members of Philadelphia's black elite. In one print, an African American man dressed in a gold top hat and a bright green waistcoat presents his calling card to a maid at an open cellar door, asking, "Is Miss Dinah at home?" The maid responds that Miss Dinah is "bery pertickly engaged in washing de dishes," to which her gentleman suitor replies, "I'm sorry I can't have the honour to pay my devours to her."[15] The double parody in this print turns on the misappropriation of the French word *devoir*, a reflexive verb meaning to have a duty or obligation. In Clay's caricature of black speech, *devoir* becomes "devours," a jest that mocks both the use of French vocabulary by pretentious whites and the failed mimicry of this affectation by upwardly mobile blacks.

In addition, the pun on *devotion* and *devours* in this print anticipates the hysterical fear of black male sexuality that Clay exhibited later in his career, most notably in the six lithographs deriding "practical amalgamation" that he published in New York City in 1839. As Tavia Nyong'o remarks, Clay's antiamalgamation prints rely heavily on "the visual evidences of performance," with five of the six images in the series depicting some combination of interracial ceremony, music, theater, and dance.[16] Two of the prints show black men and white women socializing in erotically charged scenes that Clay imagines as the inevitable results of abolition. In *The Fruits of Amalgamation*, a white woman nurses an interracial baby beneath a framed image of Othello and Desdemona, and in *An Amalgamation Waltz*, pretty white women in ball gowns dance with caricatured black men in long-tail coats, while a white orchestra plays in the background.[17]

In both of these examples, Nyong'o argues, "racial equality [is] conflated with sexual intermingling," implying that "elevating blacks [can] only be accomplished by degrading whites."[18] However, it is not whites in general but white *men* in particular whom Clay pictures as degraded in his lithographs of practical amalgamation. As Elise Lemire observes, the white men in *An Amalgamation Waltz* "are relegated to working in the orchestra, at a great remove from the festivities"—a reversal of the custom at early nineteenth-century balls and cotillions in Philadelphia, where Francis Johnson, a "descendant of Africa," led the band at many of the most "fashionable" dances.[19] To Lemire, the "rude caricatures" of dandified black men in *An Amalgamation Waltz* look like they belong "on the covers of minstrel-show sheet music," whereas their white, female dance partners "seem to have stepped out of . . . a Currier and Ives print." In Clay's imagination, "the two different races belong to two different art forms"—or at least to two different genres of graphic art. Through the juxtaposition of

AN AMALGAMATION WALTZ.

Fig. 7. Edward Williams Clay, *An Amalgamation Waltz*, 1839. Courtesy American Antiquarian Society.

minstrelized black men and finely drawn white women, Lemire argues, Clay "strengthens the idea of racial difference" in *An Amalgamation Waltz*.[20]

I see a genealogical connection between the black men in *An Amalgamation Waltz* and the blackface stage character Long Tail Blue, who made his debut at New York City's Lafayette Theater in 1827, played by George Washington Dixon.[21] The lithograph illustrating many early editions of the song "Long Tail Blue" is not a caricature of a black dandy à la Clay but rather "an erect, refined, and respectable figure."[22] But as Monica L. Miller points out, "the blackface dandy's sartorial proximity to whiteness and wealth hardly effects his social equality. . . . Although the early minstrel show presents the dandy in different guises," it is "constant" in its association of dandies with "sexual threat."[23]

In the lyrics to his signature song, Long Tail Blue competes with Jim Crow for the affections of a "white gall" named "Sue," until "the watchman [comes] and [takes him] up / And [spoils his] long tail blue." A tailor mends Blue's coat, leading Blue to deliver this advice in the last verse of the song:

If you want to win the Ladie's hearts [*sic*],
I'll tell you what to do;

Fig. 8. G. Willig Jr., lithographer, *Long Tail Blue,* ca. 1837. Courtesy Library of Congress.

Go to a tip top Tailor's shop,
And buy a long tail blue.[24]

For Eric Lott, "Long Tail Blue" evokes the "bold swagger, irrepressible desire," and "sheer bodily display" that white observers associated with free
African American men in the cities of the antebellum North.[25] If Blue's
long-tail coat represents the white, male obsession with the black penis, as
Lott contends, then the prominent tails worn by the minstrelized black men
in *An Amalgamation Waltz* capture both the interracial desire and the fear of
sexual embarrassment that fueled white male anxieties about amalgamation.

The dual reliance of Clay's racial caricatures on African American social
performance and blackface theater appears not only in his practical amalgamation prints but also in *Life in Philadelphia*. As Nancy Reynolds Davison
argues, "the scenes in *Life in Philadelphia* strongly resemble scenes in a
play," both because of Clay's ventriloquism of black voices and also because of his consistent emphasis on black dress, dance, and deportment.[26]
White and White contend that the attainment of freedom in the North
"sparked an exuberant cultural display, as newly liberated blacks deliberately, consciously, and publicly tested the boundaries" of public behavior
through clothing, dance, and "the sociability of the street."[27] Clay no doubt
found these performances of black self-fashioning both attractive and re-
pulsive, and he probably studied them with care. But I am reluctant to follow Nyong'o in interpreting Clay's oeuvre as "one of the single largest archives of antebellum imagery of northern black Americans."[28] To take this
position is to assume that Clay glimpsed and captured fragments of real,
embodied black experience through the distorting lens of his fascination
and prejudice. I favor a more cautious approach, which grasps both the *fictions* of blackness portrayed in Clay's images and the *real* consequences of
these fictions in drawing and policing the color line that distinguished
black from white in the racial formation of the antebellum North.

CLAY'S CIRCULATIONS

In 1830, two years after the publication of the first prints in the *Life in Philadelphia* series, a highly derivative set of images called *Life in New York* began
to circulate.[29] Shortly thereafter the 1831 issue of the *New Comic Annual*, a
London magazine, cribbed images from both *Life in Philadelphia* and *Life in
New York* to illustrate a patronizing short story about the manumission of a

group of West Indian slaves.[30] This story then traveled back across the Atlantic two years later to be published serially in the *Saturday Evening Post*, a middlebrow Philadelphia magazine that had a national readership for much of the nineteenth century.[31] In a further twist, a lost play entitled *Life in Philadelphia; or, How They Do Go On* made up part of blackface performer T. D. Rice's repertory as early as 1833, and W. T. Lhamon Jr. speculates that at least one scene from Rice's play descended "verbatim" from Clay's graphic racial caricatures.[32] According to a notice about the play in the *New York Courier and Enquirer*, the cast impersonated "the Ethiopian Mobility of Philadelphia in all their glory—supper, champagne, bustle, and balls."[33] With a pun on *mobility* and *nobility*, this newspaper article imitated the malaprop-laden dialogue shared by both Clay's *Life in Philadelphia* and Rice's blackface stage performances, exemplifying the fluid circulation between graphic art, theater, and print in the antebellum period.

Through the centrifugal dissemination of Clay's images, *Life in Philadelphia* became "a stock phrase referring to fashions and manners in general and to the pretensions of blacks in particular."[34] Indeed, it would be difficult to overstate the ubiquity of Clay's *Life in Philadelphia* series and other graphic racial caricatures in local, national, and Atlantic popular culture in the 1830s and 1840s. In 1837 Hosea Easton, a free African American minister who preached in Connecticut and Massachusetts, complained that

> Cuts and placards descriptive of the negroe's [sic] deformity, are every where displayed . . . with corresponding broken lingo, the very character of which is marked with design. Many of the popular book stores, in commercial towns and cities, have their shop windows lined with them. The barrooms of the most popular public houses in the country, sometimes have their ceiling literally covered with them. This display of American civility is under the daily observation of every class of society.[35]

In 1841 Joseph Willson, a free southern black who migrated to the North, wrote a short book titled *Sketches of the Higher Classes of Colored Society in Philadelphia*. His preface warns that those "who like to see their neighbors' merits caricatured, and their faults distorted and exaggerated,—will expect burlesque representations . . . [but] they will find upon perusal [of this book], that they had indulged in a very erroneous impression."[36] Although Clay was far from the only graphic artist producing racial caricatures in the first half of the nineteenth century, Willson seems to be responding specifically to *Life in Philadelphia*, which had made his city's black elite into "the butt of an international joke."[37] Clay's images were still on display in Philadelphia as late as 1911, when historian Edward Raymond Turner saw an exhibit of "ridiculous colored prints by Charles Hunt and I. Harris," Clay's London publishers, "in the museum of Independence Hall." According to Turner's account, these prints mocked the "showiness and dress" of "the Negroes of Pennsylvania."[38]

Like his images, Clay himself circulated widely, and Davison argues that his three-year tour of Europe (ca. 1825–28) "sharpened his sensitivity to his native city and its people" when he returned to Philadelphia.[39] Clay's contemporary Nathaniel S. Wheaton (from Hartford, Connecticut) commented in his journal on the plethora of graphic art he saw while visiting London in 1823–24. "The print shops," wrote Wheaton, "furnish a never-failing source of amusement to the admirers of the imitative art. . . . Popular engravings, and particularly the caricature . . . meet the eye in almost every street."[40] When Clay arrived in London one or two years later, he encountered travesties of history paintings, prints ridiculing foreigners, caricatures of fashionable dress, and all manner of satirical engravings in the city's numerous print shops. Clay studied the work of English caricaturists like Thomas Rowlandson, George Cruikshank, and I. R. Cruikshank during his stay in London, later incorporating elements of these artists' techniques into *Life in Philadelphia*.[41] In particular, Clay's style borrowed from the Cruikshank brothers' illustrations for *Life in London* (1821), Pierce Egan's popular novel.[42] *Life in London* provided Clay with a primer in racial caricature, as well as an inspiration for the title of *Life in Philadelphia*. If Clay attended the theater in London, he likely saw one or more of the numerous dramatic adaptations of Egan's novel that proliferated in the city's "minor theaters and penny gaffs" throughout the 1820s.[43] He also might have seen Charles Mathews's *A Trip to America*, "a hybrid of travelogue lecture, ethnography, and comic monodrama" in which Mathews impersonated a variety of African American and Yankee characters.[44]

While abroad, Clay painted watercolors of the various social types he encountered in London, Paris, and aboard ship as he traveled from one destination to another. Over thirty of Clay's European paintings were sold at auction in 2006, most of them executed in Paris between 1826 and early 1828.[45] Like *Life in Philadelphia* and his practical amalgamation prints, Clay's European watercolors tend to foreground images of fashion, performance, and social life, such as a French dandy, a masquerade ball, and a perambulating serenade. Six of the paintings feature dancing and eight of them depict "oriental" scenes, reflecting the fascination with the East that Clay encountered in nineteenth-century French visual culture. Although Clay's contemporaries Eugène Delacroix and Honoré Daumier had not yet begun to produce orientalist paintings and prints when Clay visited Paris, Napoleon's 1798 military campaign in Egypt had already ushered in what French historian Edgar Quinet calls "La Renaissance Orientale."[46] As with Anglo-American orientalism, the term *Orient* in France encompassed a broad constellation of peoples. Victor Hugo, for one, described "hébraïques, turques, grecques, persanes, arabes, espagnoles même" (Hebrews, Turks, Greeks, Persians, Arabs, and even Spaniards) as oriental in the introduction to *Les Orientales*, a collection of his poems published in 1829.[47] The orientalist milieu in Paris probably inspired Clay to paint watercolors like *A Persian Lady*, *A Greek Lady in Her Walking Dress*, and *A Turkish Dancing Girl*, even though he himself had never traveled to the Orient.

BLACK(FACE) DANCE

Although Clay's orientalist phase abated upon his return to Philadelphia, his interest in dance remained strong, and careful attention to these two themes in Clay's art yields a nuanced understanding of the processes of racialization at work in *Life in Philadelphia*. Clay's best-known dance image is the lithograph *Mr. T. Rice as the Original Jim Crow*. In this pictorial interpretation of Rice's most famous blackface character, Jim Crow dances with one hip thrust out and his knees and elbows bent, a pattern of gestures that Lhamon traces to the dancing contests among enslaved blacks at New York City's Catherine Market at the turn of the nineteenth century.[48] In Lhamon's view, Rice—who grew up in the shadow of Catherine Market—absorbed the interracial culture of "saloons and brothels, groceries and commerce, bustle and performance" that overflowed onto the streets of his impoverished neighborhood.[49] Onstage, he appropriated this culture to create a performance style that appealed to a broad range of audiences, brought together through their shared identification with Rice's portrayal of blackface characters like Jim Crow and Long Tail Blue.[50] However, Clay's lithograph does not necessarily resemble how Rice performed Jim Crow on stage, and other images of Rice dancing Jim Crow—such as a print from London produced around 1840—show as much affinity for the straight-backed Irish jig as for the bending and twisting motions of African American dance.

The imbrication of black and Irish identities in the labor markets and performance cultures of the nineteenth-century United States has received a great deal of scholarly attention, and the next chapter takes up

Fig. 9. Edward Williams Clay, *Mr. T. Rice as the Original Jim Crow*, ca. 1827. Courtesy Lester S. Levy Collection of Sheet Music, Sheridan Libraries, Johns Hopkins University.

Fig. 10. *Jim Crow! The Celebrated Nigger Song, Sung by Mr. Rice*, London, ca. 1840. Courtesy Library Company of Philadelphia.

the co-construction of blackness and Irishness in more detail.[51] For now, one example must suffice. In 1869 Philadelphia publisher George W. Childs released a trade catalog entitled *Specimens of Theatrical Cuts*, advertising over five hundred poster images "for theatrical, variety, and circus business." One of these images, *Irishman in a Jim Crow Pose*, shows a figure of a white man dressed in a long-tail coat, his hip thrust out and his knees and elbows bent.[52] Crucially, he is not in blackface. This image implies that, even a few years after the Civil War, Jim Crow could plausibly represent Irish as well as black or blackface performance—an unthinkable elision in the post-Reconstruction era, when Jim Crow became a byword for racial segregation.

From the early 1830s through the mid-1840s, Rice played Jim Crow to crowded houses throughout the Anglophone Atlantic, no doubt modulating his blackface act to suit the tastes of local audiences by performing an adaptable mixture of racially and ethnically coded lyrics and gestures. Although his popularity waned in the years leading up to the Civil War, Rice's Jim Crow dance(s) catalyzed "the blackface lore cycle"—Lhamon's term for the haunted and haunting tendency of blackface performance to recur anywhere and everywhere, seeping "well beyond its masked variants" into U.S., Atlantic, and global popular culture.[53] If blackface lore is a *cycle* rather than a linear trajectory, as Lhamon suggests, then Clay's lithograph is not necessarily more "authentic" than the London print of Rice as Jim Crow or the image of an Irishman in a Jim Crow pose from *Specimens of Theatrical Cuts*. Clay's image of Rice caricatures the black rather than the Irish elements associated with the Jim Crow dance, even though Rice—unlike Clay—rarely used racial impersonation to mock African Americans. Indeed, the ever-changing lyrics of Rice's Jim Crow song featured instances of racial status inversion and abolitionist rhetoric that trouble the monolithic reading of blackface performance as invariably antiblack:

I am for Freedom
An for Union altogether
Aldough I'm a Black Man
De White is call'd my Broder . . .

Now my Broder Niggers
I do not tink it right
Dat you should laugh at dem
Who happen to be White.[54]

Fig. 11. *Irishman in a Jim Crow Pose,* in *Specimens of Theatrical Cuts,* plate 2031, ca. 1872–78. Courtesy Printed Book and Periodical Collection, Winterthur Library.

Given Clay's penchant for caricature—not only of black social performances but also of the fleeting antiracist impulses of the blackface stage—it
is surprising that his first publication upon his return from Europe to Philadelphia included an image of black dance relatively free of racializing dis-
tortion. The print, *Pat Juba: African Fancy Ball*, appears in *Lessons in Dancing,
Exemplified by Sketches from Real Life in the City of Philadelphia*, which was
published in 1828, the same year as the earliest prints in his *Life in Philadelphia* series.[55] This little-studied pamphlet, with eight illustrations of dancing couples, stands out in Clay's oeuvre for two reasons: it is the first complete set of prints he released after his European tour, and it is one of the
few works of his career that aims for verisimilitude rather than caricature.
Several of the prints in *Lessons in Dancing* show historical figures like Arthur Middleton (grandson of a signer of the Declaration of Independence),
Don Francisco Tacon (Spanish ambassador to the United States), and Mon-
sieur and Madame Hutin (French dancers who appeared briefly at Philadelphia's Chestnut Street Theater in 1828).[56] Other, more stereotypical images show a rural dance in New Jersey and an urban, working-class dance
in Moyamensing. Only one print, *Pat Juba*, depicts African American subjects—an inversion of the racial proportions in *Life in Philadelphia*, in which
ten out of fourteen images caricature blacks.

The fifth plate in *Life in Philadelphia*—published in 1828, the same year
as *Lessons in Dancing*—is an acerbic revision of *Pat Juba*. In *Pat Juba* the
dancing figures stand on their toes with their backs to one another, a stylish
composition that suggests a couple dancing as part of a quadrille. Their
color-coordinated costumes are brash but elegant, and with the exception
of the woman's lips, their faces and bodies are drawn in naturalistic pro-
portion. In contrast, the male figure in the *Life in Philadelphia* print wears a
blue, long-tail coat stretched along a diagonal line that crests at the top of
his unfortunate pompadour. His splayed feet make full contact with the
dance floor as he doffs his ugly, brimless hat to a large woman, whose
dancing feet are concealed beneath her loud, pink dress. "Shall I hab de
honour to dance de next quadrille wid you, Miss Minta?" the man asks.
"Tank you, Mr. Cato," the woman replies, "only I'm engaged for de nine
next set!" In this print Clay travesties his own work by ventriloquizing the
two black dancers and caricaturing their speech, clothing, and deportment.
"Minta's portly yet muscular physique" reveals the contrast between the
leisure she enjoys at the dance and her everyday physical labor, implying
that even ball-going black Philadelphians have not advanced beyond their
menial station.[57]

What accounts for the radical change in Clay's treatment of black ball-

Fig. 12. Edward Williams Clay, *Pat Juba: African Fancy Ball*, in *Lessons in Dancing*, 1828. Courtesy Rosenbach Museum and Library, Free Library of Philadelphia.

room dance in *Life in Philadelphia*, less than a year after he published *Lessons in Dancing*? Did sales of *Life in Philadelphia* improve when Clay shifted the emphasis of the series from gentle mockery of upper-class whites (plates 1, 2, 8, and 10) to satire of the aspiring black middle class (plates 3–7, 9, and 11–14)? Perhaps. But I also suspect that an African American ball held in Philadelphia on February 28, 1828, spurred Clay to heap derision on "Miss Minta" and "Mr. Cato" when he revised these figures for *Life in Philadelphia*. On February 29, 1828, the *Pennsylvania Gazette* reported,

Fig. 13. Edward Williams Clay, *Life in Philadelphia: "Shall I hab de honour to dance de next quadrille wid you, Miss Minta?,"* plate 5, 1828. Courtesy Library Company of Philadelphia.

A joke of no ordinary magnitude was enacted last night, by getting up a Coloured Fancy Ball. . . . At an early hour, carriages, in considerable numbers, arrived, with ladies and gentlemen of color, dressed in "character," in the most grotesque style, Grandees, Princesses, Shepherdesses, and so on. This excited the attention of boys and idlers, collected upon the spot, who, from mirth proceeded to mischief. All manner of noises were made; horses were frightened, and some of the ladies insulted, and their dresses torn.[58]

The harassment of black citizens by "boys and idlers," who were presumably poor and white, foreshadowed the scourge of racially motivated violence that plagued Philadelphia in the 1830s and the 1840s. *Freedom's Journal*, an African American newspaper in New York City, reprinted and contested the *Pennsylvania Gazette*'s account of the 1828 attack on black ballgoers in Philadelphia: "We do not deny that a plain subscription Ball took place at the Assembly Room in South Street; but we have [been] unable to learn that any part of the disturbances, which happened at the door, could be attributed to the company."[59]

Whether the ball in question was "fancy" or "plain" (i.e., uncostumed), its location is significant, since South Street marked the boundary between the heavily black neighborhood surrounding Mother Bethel Church and the heavily Irish Catholic districts of Southwark and Moyamensing. Although residential segregation was never complete in nineteenth-century Philadelphia, a correspondent to Frederick Douglass's *North Star* newspaper lamented the pervasive violence against blacks just a few blocks south of Mother Bethel. "Suffer me to live on South Street," he wrote, "and beat and stab me for walking on the next street below after 9 o'clock in the evening."[60] No newspapers reported serious injuries from the 1828 attack on the "Coloured Fancy Ball," but the perception that blacks had made whites into objects of imitation and subservience infuriated not only the "boys and idlers" on South Street but also the editors of the *Pennsylvania Gazette*, which concluded its account of the event with these portentous words: "It is worthy of remark, that many of the coaches containing these sable divinities, were attended by white coachmen and white footmen . . . and it may be well to inquire, if matters progress at this rate, how long it will be before masters and servants change places."[61]

This comment amplifies Elizabeth Drinker's subtle unease, at the end of the eighteenth century, about her two black servants riding to a wedding in a coach driven by a white man. The discursive, graphic, and physical assaults on black Philadelphians who imitated white manners or otherwise muddled the city's racial pecking order continued well into the twentieth century. But difference almost always inflected black social performances, even—or perhaps especially—when these performances appeared in the guise of borrowed European forms. As White and White argue, African Americans performed the steps of European dances like the quadrille differently than whites, "at different speeds, combined in different ways, and executed with different movements of the torso and limbs."[62]

In a stimulating book on racial impersonation in postwar Germany, Katrin Sieg diagnoses "the German actor's conceit of *universal performability*," through which "the white body [is able] to transcend its gendered and racial coordinates."[63] As Coco Fusco argues, following Richard Dyer, the racial category of whiteness in Western culture has consistently implied "the capacity to masquerade as a racial other without actually being one."[64] The black appropriation and revision of the quadrille in the antebellum United States posed a threat to the white conceit of universal performability, insofar as it allowed a black imitation—and a potential black parody—of a white social performance. The anxiety among whites provoked by black appropriation of ostensibly white cultural forms accounts for the biggest difference between Clay's *Pat Juba* print and his print of Miss Minta and Mr. Cato: in the latter example, Minta and Cato *are not dancing*. Indeed, they hardly look as though they could dance, with Minta's wide girth and Cato's big, flat feet lending an air of stasis to the composition.

COAL BLACK ROSE

Clay's portrayal of Miss Minta contributed to the rise of one of the most pervasive characters in early nineteenth-century blackface stage performance: Coal Black Rose. During a three-day period in July 1829, George Washington Dixon, the first actor to sing "Long Tail Blue," performed the song "Coal Black Rose" at three venues in New York City: the Bowery Theater, the Chatham Theater, and the Park Theater.[65] Although Dale Cockrell regards this triple-header as the moment of blackface minstrelsy's "mythical birth," J. Thomas Scharf and Thompson Westcott assert that "Coal Black Rose" premiered in Philadelphia before Dixon started singing the tune:

> "Coal Black Rose" . . . was first sung at the Walnut Street Theater in 1829, by William Kelly, and was afterward taken up by George Washington Dixon. . . . The air of this piece became immensely pop-

ular. It was sung in parlors, hummed in offices, whistled in the streets, and performed by bands. No single piece of music had ever been so treated.[66]

Even allowing for exaggeration, this account suggests that "Coal Black Rose" was an earlier (and perhaps bigger) hit in Philadelphia than in New York. A graphic of a black woman almost identical to Clay's Miss Minta, which appeared in at least one early edition of "Coal Black Rose," no doubt strengthened the song's link to Philadelphia for theater audiences on both sides of the Atlantic. This link had solidified by 1833, when an advertisement for a London printing of "Coal Black Rose" ran with "Love in Philadelphia" as its leading line.[67]

The eleven verses of "Coal Black Rose" tell a story rife with mischief, most of it of a sexual nature. At the beginning of the song, Sambo, a suitor to Coal Black Rose, calls on his beloved, singing and strumming his banjo. Rose puts him off for four verses, responding to his entreaties with the lines "yes I cum" and "I cum soon," whose sexual connotations landed just as squarely with early nineteenth-century audiences as they do today. While Sambo is "froze tiff as a poker" waiting out in the cold, Rose disguises Cuffee—another suitor, already inside her apartment—as a "tick ob wood," making it abundantly clear that both men are firm in their desire. Finally, Rose invites Sambo inside, Sambo spots Cuffee, the two men fight, and the song ends with Sambo chasing after his rival, who has "cut dirt and run."[68] This simple narrative, with its catchy melody and salacious lyrics, lent itself to dramatic adaptation, and before long, Dixon was performing a lost playlet called *Love in a Cloud* based on "Coal Black Rose." A playbill for *Love in a Cloud* from the Chatham Theater, dated October 19, 1829, lists an all-male cast: "Sambo, Mr. Dixon; Rose, Mr. Madden; Cuffee, Mr. Orson."[69] Lhamon remarks that this performance "apparently established the convention of the blackface wench," a staple of the antebellum minstrel show, which featured white male actors in burlesque impersonations of black women.[70] By the end of October Dixon had added seven white characters to *Love in a Cloud* and cast white actresses in the new, female roles—a choice that must have made Rose's racial and gendered drag appear all the more ludicrous and degrading.[71]

Rice also adapted "Coal Black Rose" into a short play, entitled *Oh! Hush! Or the Virginny Cupids!*, which premiered at Philadelphia's Walnut Street Theater on July 20, 1833.[72] *Oh! Hush!* refashions Sambo from "Coal Black Rose" into a character named Sam Johnson, a bootblack who "quit

Fig. 14. White Snyder, composer, "The Coal Black Rose," ca. 1827–29. Courtesy Brown University Library.

his old perfersion" after winning the lottery (note the pun on *perversion* and *profession* in this line). Johnson puts on airs, proclaiming himself "Bacchus, God of Love," and taunting his former friends—especially Cuffee, a fellow bootblack, whom Rice renames Gumbo Cuff. At the climax of the play, Johnson tries to kiss Rose, and Cuff falls off a shelf in Rose's kitchen, where he was hiding while Rose entertained Johnson. As Cuff tumbles, he spills a jar of flour on his head, coating his blackface makeup with a powdery layer of white. Rose takes Johnson's side in the ensuing melee, striking Cuff with a frying pan and dismissing him as "noffin' else but trash." But Cuff prevails over Rose and Johnson after he miraculously recovers from Rose's attack. In the final tableau, "[Cuff] breaks his fiddle over Johnson's head. Rose faints. . . . Johnson falls at her feet, [and] Cuff stands with uplifted hands."[73]

Unlike Dixon, who played Sambo in *Love in a Cloud*, Rice chose to play Cuff in his adaptation of "Coal Black Rose," hitching his emergent star power to an underclass bootblack rather than to a dandified lottery winner. To accommodate this choice, *Oh! Hush!* tweaks the finale of "Coal Black Rose" to make Cuff come out on top, lifting his hands in victory rather than fleeing from his rival in defeat. The final stage picture in *Oh! Hush!* arguably reimagines Cuff as a whiteface-on-blackface representative of the working class, standing in triumph over the nouveau riche pretensions of Johnson and Rose. But this class-based reading of the play cannot fully overcome the racist and sexist depiction of Rose as a blackface wench, given that the text of *Oh! Hush!* echoes both the form and content of Clay's *Life in Philadelphia*. In the ninth plate of Clay's series, a garishly dressed black man asks a black woman for her opinion about his attire: "How you like de new fashion shirt, Miss Florinda?" "I tink dey mighty elegum," she replies; "you look jist like Pluto de God of War."[74] This cheap joke is formally identical to Johnson's proclamation in *Oh! Hush!* that he is Bacchus, the god of love. In both cases, presumptuous black characters unwittingly reveal their ignorance of Western classical mythology, stoking the audience's laughter. Whether or not Rice lifted this bit of fun from Clay (and it is entirely possible that he did), both *Life in Philadelphia* and *Oh! Hush!* invent and ridicule failed social performances by upwardly mobile African Americans—the same fictive "Ethiopian Mobility" that Rice lampooned in his stage version of *Life in Philadelphia*, which premiered within months of *Oh! Hush!*. In sum, Rice's adaptation of "Coal Black Rose" may champion the proletariat, but this radical critique is structurally dependent upon the derogation of the black middle class.

TURKISH DANCING GIRLS

Looking back on Clay's Miss Minta from the constellation of performances surrounding "Coal Black Rose," Minta herself starts to resemble a wench—a failed, burlesque impersonation of a "real" woman. After all, Minta is "as big, if not bigger, than Cato."[75] Does her ball gown conceal a white man in blackface and drag rather than the muscled flesh of a black female laborer? This is a hypothetical question, of course, since Clay's image—unlike an actor playing a part—does not possess a body beneath its costumed surface. But the contrast between Miss Minta and the dancing white women in *An Amalgamation Waltz* (figure 7) suggests that Clay confines the successful performance of femininity—understood according to nineteenth-century social conventions—to *white* women. To unpack the relationship between femininity and whiteness in Clay's oeuvre, this section focuses on Clay's orientalist paintings, since they are the only examples of his work that construct images of women outside the black/white racial dyad. Clay's painting *A Turkish Dancing Girl* shows a young female figure in a colorful costume holding a pair of castanets. She extends her arms laterally with her elbows unlocked and lifts her heels just a touch above the floor. She also appears phenotypically white, with a small mouth, a receding chin, rosy cheeks, and straight, brown hair.

Eleven years after he executed this painting, Clay drew a picture of the ballet prodigy Augusta Maywood that mimicked the composition of his *Turkish Dancing Girl*. Maywood wears a different costume than her predecessor (though with a similar blue and yellow color scheme), and she holds a long, pink scarf rather than a pair of castanets. She dances *en pointe* with her feet close together, and although her hair and face do not match those of the Turkish dancing girl, the poses of the two figures strongly resemble one another. The drawing of Maywood ostensibly depicts her performance as Zoloé in *The Maid of Cashmere*, an adaptation of the ballet *Le dieu et la bayadère* (1830), composed by Daniel Auber and choreographed by Filippo Taglioni. According to dance historian Maureen Needham Costonis, "the high point of the ballet occurs when two dancing *bayadères*"—the French term for *devadasis*, or Hindu temple dancers—"[compete] to win the love of the Unknown. In the end, the Unknown shows himself to be the god Brahma when he rescues Zoloé from death and carries her up to paradise."[76] Maywood debuted as Zoloé at Philadelphia's Chestnut Street Theater in December 1837, when she was twelve years old. Clay, who had moved to New York City in 1835, probably saw her perform at the Park Theater, where she appeared as Zoloé in February 1838.[77]

Fig. 15. Edward Williams Clay, *A Turkish Dancing Girl*, 1827. Courtesy Cowan's Auctions, Inc.

Fig. 16. Edward Williams Clay, *La Petite August, Aged 12 Years, in the Character of Zoloé, in the Bayadere*, 1838. Courtesy Jerome Robbins Dance Division, New York Public Library for the Performing Arts.

According to the nineteenth-century ballet librettist and dance critic Théophile Gautier, a November 1837 production of *La bayadère* at the Paris Opera included a noxious corps de ballet of French *devadasis* in blackface. "Their faces are carelessly daubed with ochre or licorice juice," he complained, "which makes them look more like chimney-sweeps than those voluptuous charmers, gilded by the sun, who tinkle the silver bells on their bracelets on the steps in front of the temple doors."[78] Gautier, enamored of a troupe of South Asian dancers that toured to Paris in 1838, lamented that he never saw *La bayadère* performed by an Indian company. "Having admired and accepted [Marie] Taglioni," choreographer Filippo Taglioni's daughter, "as the typical bayadère, the French public did not appreciate the genuine article." Given that Marie Taglioni performed *La bayadère* in "white gauze tutus" and "delicate pink tights," it seems that French stagings of this ballet in the second quarter of the nineteenth century vacillated between crude racial impersonation and the ethereal costumes of the romantic *ballet blanc*.[79] Because *The Maid of Cashmere* borrowed heavily from *La bayadère*—and because none of the available evidence suggests that Maywood played Zoloé in blackface, brownface, or oriental dress—I suspect that Maywood's performance was just as "white" as Taglioni's. But the orientalism of Clay's *Turkish Dancing Girl* nonetheless haunts his drawing of Maywood in *The Maid of Cashmere*.

Edward W. Said famously argues that nineteenth-century orientalism privileged "a style of thought based on an ontological and epistemological distinction" between East and West.[80] Although European political and economic hegemony had taken root in parts of North Africa, the Middle East, and South Asia by the late eighteenth century, neither the colonial enterprise nor the academic study of oriental cultures displaced the *idea* of the Orient from the Western imagination. This idea fascinated Clay and countless other European and Euro-American artists, but visions of *devadasis* and seraglios tended to encourage the production of superficial and sexualized images of the East rather than intercultural engagement with actual oriental people. Gautier, for example, describes the Indian dances he saw in Paris as "unimpeachably authentic" because "they coincided exactly with the idea he had formed of them."[81] In light of this remark, symptomatic as it is of the epistemology of orientalism, I view Clay's images of exotic dancing girls as autochthonous fantasies, born of an imaginative and inward-looking conception of the Orient that Said casts in theatrical terms:

The Orient is the stage on which the whole East is confined. On this stage will appear figures whose role it is to represent the larger whole from which they emanate. The Orient then seems to be, not an unlimited extension beyond the familiar European world, but rather a closed field, a theatrical stage affixed to Europe.[82]

Given Clay's negrophobia, a closed field in which he could safely construct and contain the Other must have been an attractive proposition. But can such a field offer a refuge from racialist fears, especially given Fabio Ciaramelli's astute, Levinasian claim that "the heart of subjectivity [contains] a radical and anarchical reference to the Other which in fact constitutes the very inwardness of the Subject"?[83] This question pinpoints the stakes of Clay's orientalism, which at first appears incidental to processes of racialization in antebellum popular culture. Clay's harsh portrayal of African Americans could not fulfill his desire for what Homi K. Bhabha calls "a reformed, recognizable Other, *as a subject of difference that is almost the same, but not quite.*"[84] In other words, Clay's fantasy of a resolution to his divided feelings about black people—who simultaneously attracted and repelled him—could not be realized through racial caricature, which produced more and more outlandish and insulting fictions of black difference as the nineteenth century wore on. Minstrelized images possess a peculiar power of accretion, gathering steam as they circulate from graphic art to popular theater to street performance. But the fictive status of racial caricature marks its insufficiency as a technique for containing the ostensible threat of black freedom in the increasingly racist imagination of the antebellum North.

As Daniel R. Biddle and Murray Dubin argue, an "emboldened" generation of young black activists emerged in Philadelphia in the 1850s, demanding streetcar desegregation and aiding fugitives from slavery.[85] The growing strength of black political life and social institutions in the antebellum period called forth not only more and more vicious racial caricatures but also the direct expropriation of black rights, including the loss of the franchise for most black men in Pennsylvania in 1838.[86] In other words, the practice of racial caricature had real social effects, drawing and reinforcing a color line that hardened almost to the point of impermeability. Almost, but not quite—for the graphic art and performances that shored up the color line often depended for their efficacy on tactical maneuvers of symbolic inversion. Because these maneuvers threatened to introduce ambivalence into the rhetoric of racial difference, they also raised the possibility that a counterappeal *against* racism could be staged from within a deeply racialized popular culture. This counterappeal, glimpsed faintly in T. D. Rice's performances as Jim Crow, privileged class rather than race as the most important site of social struggle. But the fleeting cohesion of a proletarian audience through shared identification with blackface stage characters too often came at the expense of women and upwardly mobile blacks, undermining the insurgent potential of blackface performance.

By singling out middle-class blacks—and especially middle-class black women—as objects of derision, Clay's *Life in Philadelphia* prints served up a nasty mixture of racism and misogyny, which coalesced in the figure of the blackface wench. But Clay's *Turkish Dancing Girl* and his drawing of Maywood as Zoloé in *The Maid of Cashmere* operate according to a different logic, reflecting a subtle but important shift in the parsing of racial difference in early nineteenth-century Philadelphia. Whereas earlier orientalist performances like the Meschianza and *Slaves in Algiers* tended to align the Orient with blackness, Clay's orientalist paintings treat their subjects as "almost the same but not white."[87] Indeed, *A Turkish Dancing Girl* and *The Maid of Cashmere* draw such a fine distinction between oriental women and white women that both racial categories dissolve upon contact. The disappearance of whiteness into the Orient—and vice versa—exposes the fiction of racial difference in a manner that must have frightened Clay if he had the perspicacity to grasp it, which may explain why he eschewed oriental subjects for more than a decade after returning from Europe to the United States. But beyond such autobiographical conjecture, Clay's repressed fascination with the Orient marks a notable shift in the co-construction of orientalism, blackness, and femininity in antebellum Philadelphia, distinguishing the racial formation of this period from its revolutionary and early national antecedents.

FOUR | Parade Time

Colonel Pluck, Bobalition, and Minstrel Remains

Think of anything, of cowboys, or movies, or detective
stories, of anybody who goes anywhere or stays at home
and is an American and you will realize that it is something
strictly American to conceive a space that is filled with
moving, a space of time that is filled always filled with
moving.
  —Gertrude Stein

Susan G. Davis, Mary P. Ryan, David Glassberg, and Brooks McNamara
(among others) have documented the American infatuation with parades,
pageants, and other sorts of public celebrations in the nineteenth and early
twentieth centuries, but the spatiotemporal form of the American parade
has received little scholarly attention.[1] I begin this chapter by drawing cre-
atively on Gertrude Stein's paean to the Americanness of cowboys, movies,
and detective stories in order to theorize what I call *parade time*, a concept
that can be fruitfully applied to the historiography of parade performances—
and their attendant representation in visual and print media—in the
nineteenth-century United States. Parade time, as I conceive of it, takes
three forms: the time of the performer, the time of the spectator, and the
time of the voyeur.

  To perform in a parade is to occupy "a space of time that is filled always
filled with moving," to borrow Stein's phrase. Parade participants tend to
organize themselves into groups—bands, clubs, brigades, and so on—
processing along a route and performing for street-side audiences as they
go. These groups of parade performers are doubly on the move as they
dance, play music, engage spectators, and enact short scenes or tableaux,
all while processing along the street. In my experiences performing in the
Mummers Parade, time feels spatialized, shot through with this double
motion, as though a stage—or a parade float—is rolling along beneath my
feet as I strive to keep up with the group choreography and improvised

hijinks of my fellow performers. Parade participants experience the parade not as a series of events unfolding sequentially but rather as a continuous and reiterative "space of time," a mobile stage filled by the movement of the group of which one is a part.

The vantage points available to spectators—whether on the street, in a grandstand, or in front of a television screen—offer up a different temporal experience of the parade. For spectators, the parade unfolds as a nearly continuous flow of performances, punctuated by occasional pauses and gaps. As Robin Bernstein argues in her analysis of an 1892 parade based on *Uncle Tom's Cabin*, "The parade's scenes played out simultaneously, each on its own wagon, but they revealed themselves sequentially to a viewer who remained . . . in one place on the street."[2] Stand still and watch a parade from beginning to end, and it is easy to succumb to the illusion that one has seen it all. But each group of paraders, each "space of time," passes through the spectator's field of vision for only a few moments. It is impossible to see the entirety of any one group's performance without moving alongside the parade, thus surrendering the spectator's privilege of enjoying a series of discrete performances in procession.

Neither the time of the performer (a "space of time," a mobile stage) nor the time of the spectator (a sequential flow, one stage after another) allows for the parade to be grasped as a totality. Only a view from above would make the whole of the parade intelligible as a unitary event, forming at one end, dispersing at the other, and undulating in between according to the double motion of groups of performers on the street. Writing in 1980, Michel de Certeau marveled at the "voluptuous pleasure" of looking down on New York, "lifted out of the city's grasp" to the top of the World Trade Center, where "elevation [transfigured] him into a voyeur." With his body no longer "clasped by the streets" nor possessed "by the rumble of so many differences," the city became a form stripped of particularities, a "fiction of knowledge" in which he could not see the parts for the whole. Writing in 1938, Stein marveled that traveling across the United States by airplane could reveal "the lines of cubism" in the landscape below—a reduction of both city and countryside into a formalist image, purged of geographic specificity.[3] Thinking with de Certeau and Stein about parade time, the voyeurism of elevation and distance collapses the spatialized temporality of the performer and the sequential temporality of the spectator into an abstraction, a cubist line evacuated of content and thus open to ideological and formal appropriation.

Parades in the United States generally proceed along the broad, straight thoroughfares that have characterized American cities since William Penn laid out Philadelphia on a rectilinear grid in 1683. Wary of the fire that de-stroyed much of London in 1666, Penn envisioned Philadelphia as "a greene country towne, which will never be burnt, and allways be whol-some [sic]." As a result, his plan for the city eschewed the narrow, tortuous streets of medieval Europe, where, as Lewis Mumford argues, parades took on a distinctly recursive form:

> Those who walked about the [medieval] city on their daily business, who marched in a guild pageant or in a martial parade . . . in the very twisting and turning of the procession could, as it were, see themselves in advance, as in a mirror, by observing the other parts of the procession: thus, participant and spectator were one, as they can never be in a formal procession on a straight street.[4]

The interanimation of the time of the performer and the time of the specta-tor in Mumford's account suggests that medieval parades resisted the voy-eurism of a bird's-eye view, situated above and outside of the winding streets of the city. By contrast, I argue that the linearity of American pa-rades lends itself to voyeuristic appropriation. The impulse to capture and interpret the multiple moving stages of a parade in a single image or a concise text suffused the visual and print cultures of the northern United States throughout the 1800s. The experience of parade time at street level, for both performers and spectators, makes a totalizing apprehension of the parade all but impossible. But the desire to contain the parade in a unitary visual or textual representation is just as American as the skyscraper or the airplane—both of which produced new ways of voyeuristically looking down on city streets at the turn of twentieth century.

This chapter begins by following a single, nineteenth-century subject, John Pluck, whose transformation from a street performer into a visual icon offers a case study in the multiple forms of parade time. In the time of the performer and the time of the spectator, Pluck's parade performance bril-liantly satirized the antebellum militia system. But in the time of the voy-eur, Pluck was transformed through visual and print culture into an object of scorn rather than an agent of social critique. This ideological and formal appropriation of Pluck's parade performance relied upon the gradual blackening of Pluck in the popular imagination, a process that offers an unorthodox view of the racial, class, and ethnic implications of the antebel-lum blackface mask. Unpacking Pluck's oscillation from performance to print requires digressions on the carnivalesque iconography of pigs and brooms; on satires of black abolition celebrations in Boston's bobalition broadsides; on race riots, labor politics, and black parades in antebellum Philadelphia; and on orientalism in the postbellum minstrel show. Following Nick Salvato, I adopt digressiveness as "both a working style and a working strategy" in this chapter, stepping back from Pluck in order to grasp the representational economy of blackface that ultimately subsumes him, depositing his spectral remains in both the minstrel show and the Philadelphia Mummers Parade.[5] The result is a case study in parade time articulated through the figure of Pluck and, I hope, enriched by digressions that weave haunting and racial impersonation—this book's central themes—through Pluck's transformation from an agent of parody into an object of contempt.

COLONEL PLUCK'S PARADE TIME

In the early nineteenth-century United States, parading was not always a voluntary activity. The federal Militia Act of 1792 required all able-bodied white men between the ages of eighteen and forty-five to serve in locally organized, self-governing militia units—a requirement deeply resented by working-class Philadelphians. The Militia Act also compelled local regiments "to be exercised and trained"—an obligation satisfied on Muster Day, an annual springtime event when all militia companies *had* to parade.[6]

In 1825 the working-class white men of Philadelphia's Eighty-Fourth Militia Regiment elected John Pluck as their colonel. Pluck, a hostler at a tavern in the poor Northern Liberties neighborhood, was one of their own. But according to contemporary press accounts, he was also was five feet tall, bowlegged, hunchbacked, and mentally deficient—an inversion of the usual qualities expected of a militia officer. To the consternation of the respectable press and Philadelphia's elite militia regiments, Pluck's stint as a colonel made him an overnight celebrity. Within weeks of his first appearance at a militia muster, Susan G. Davis claims, "theater crowds were shouting for Pluck, and he was in demand at the circus."[7] In the summer of 1826 Pluck embarked on a national tour, "exhibiting himself at the rate of 12½ cents to the curious" in New York, Providence, Boston, Albany, and Richmond.[8] By the 1830s Pluck was famous enough to earn a mention on the floor of Congress, when James Nelson Barker—the comptroller of the treasury, a minor playwright, and a Philadelphian—made an unfavorable comparison between the treasury secretary and "Col. Pluck's spurs."[9]

The chronic racial, class, and ethnic strife in Philadelphia and other northern cities in the antebellum period found expression in performances like the burlesque parade of the Eighty-Fourth Militia Regiment with Pluck at the helm, as well as in press accounts, graphic art, and printed ephemera mocking Pluck. A description of the Eighty-Fourth Regiment in the *Saturday Evening Post*, a Philadelphia weekly magazine with a national circulation, belittled Pluck and his comrades with the tone of a supercilious theater review:

> On Wednesday last, was enacted the grand Military farce, in which the redoubtable John Pluck made his debut with considerable *éclat*, in the character of Colonel of the merry 84th. The sport was not, however, as great as was anticipated by the lovers of frolic and fun, from the complete impotence with which the Colonel went through his part.

The *Post* skewered Pluck for "scarce possessing spirit . . . to carry on the joke," even though he was "clamorously encored by the great crowd." Pluck seems to have understood the role in which his fellow militiamen had cast him, notwithstanding the *Post*'s claims of his "impotence" and lack of spirit. On taking command of his regiment, Pluck shouted, "Well, at least I ain't afraid to fight." He then dallied on the parade route, extending the Eighty-Fourth's performance to an "unwarrantable length" and violating "the rules of propriety and good order, to which some little respect, even on this occasion, should have been paid."[10] Clearly, Pluck and the other members of the Eighty-Fourth used the "space of time" allotted them on Muster Day to irritate middlebrow spectators (including the reporter for the *Post*) with a drawn-out parody of the militia system. This parody, enacted in the time of the performer, is partially contained by the *Post*'s caustic voyeurism, which appropriates Pluck's performance as a violation of propriety. But Pluck eluded capture in the time of the voyeur by taking advantage of the publicity conferred by negative press coverage, charging admission for his appearances in theaters and hotels throughout the country.

By October 1826 Pluck had returned to Philadelphia, where he was court-martialed, cashiered, and "pronounced incapable of holding a commission in the militia for seven years."[11] Nonetheless, Pluck's name and likeness circulated widely for more than a decade after his national tour and the inglorious end to his colonelcy. A series of mordant images denigrated Pluck's burlesque performances, culminating in a blackface graphic of Pluck that appeared on a song sheet printed in Boston in the late 1830s.[12] Like the racial caricatures in Edward Williams Clay's *Life in Philadelphia*, Pluck's rapid movement across media helped transform him from a local figure into a national phenomenon. But Pluck's appropriation into visual and print culture reduced him from an agent of his own politically piquant performances into a symbol of racialized disorder, immobilizing the insurgent parade time of the Eighty-Fourth Militia Regiment into a fixed image of social abjection.

Fifty years before Pluck's election as a colonel, militia service among artisans and wage earners in Philadelphia contributed to the emergent class-consciousness of the city's laboring poor. As Steven Rosswurm argues, "the militia experience" during the Revolutionary War politicized Philadelphia's working-class recruits by uniting them into "one body" and drawing their attention "toward established authority in the colony."[13] Organized pressure from Philadelphia's proletarian militiamen helped to secure Pennsylvania's support for the revolution and to usher in the radically democratic Pennsylvania Constitution of 1776.

Despite the Pennsylvania militia's populist leanings, a loyalist observer named Samuel Curwen noticed hints of class-based segregation at a Philadelphia militia muster in the spring of 1775. In his journal, Curwen described several regiments in which "Gentlemen, Merchants, tradesmen, old, young, English, Irish, German, and Dutch" all drilled together, but he also remarked on one militia group composed of "young gentlemen only," which he derided as a "Silk-Stocking Company." Curwen's observations anticipated the institutionalized, two-tier militia system that emerged in Pennsylvania in the early national period. As Davis explains it, elite volunteer companies "formed the upper tier" of Pennsylvania's militia from the 1790s until the Civil War, serving as the state's "federally sponsored peacekeeping force. Below the volunteers in prestige and legal status ranked the public militia [companies], in which all eligible white men unable to afford private company membership were required to enroll." The Northern Liberties' Eighty-Fourth Regiment was one such public company, made up of men who lacked the money and leisure to outfit themselves in fancy uniforms or to rehearse elaborate drills like those staged by their counterparts in the private militias. By electing Pluck as colonel, the Eighty-Fourth Regiment parodied Pennsylvania's unjust militia system, inverting and caricaturing the pretentious militia performances of their social betters—a common tactic among disgruntled public militia companies in a number of U.S. cities in the 1820s and 1830s.[14]

In Philadelphia, Center Square—the site of nineteenth-century Fourth of July festivities and the focal point of the contemporary Mummers Parade—served as the terminus of Muster Day processions, where white men too young to enlist in the militia and free blacks (who were barred from militia service) assembled to watch the parade.[15] The march of Pluck's regiment and other burlesque militia companies to Center Square introduces yet more ghosts to the haunted space now occupied by Philadelphia's City Hall, where an interracial crowd once gathered to take in both the elite pomp and the working-class parody of Pennsylvania's militia system. Before Pluck left Philadelphia for his national tour, he performed on Muster Day in 1825 for this street-side audience, puncturing the "glare and pageantry" and "martial scenes . . . of patriotism and glory" staged by the city's private militias.[16] In contrast to these disciplined and spectacular processions, Pluck paraded through Center Square in burlap pants and an oversized *chapeau de bras*, equipped with "a giant sword and spurs half a yard long."[17] According to Davis, the lengthy performance of the Eighty-Fourth Regiment riled not only the reporter for the *Saturday Evening Post* but also the members of the private militias, who "resented their forced public appearance with ill-trained, ragged companies" at city-wide militia musters.[18]

As a touring stage act the following summer, Pluck's parody of the militia system drew large audiences and the voyeuristic scorn of the respectable press. The crowds that thronged to see Pluck probably laughed *at* him because of the contrast between his marginal social status and his putative rank, but they also probably laughed *with* him at the "Silk-Stocking" militia companies travestied by his performance. *Niles' Weekly Register*, a Whiggish national newspaper, reported that Pluck appeared before the public "armed and equipped in the most ludicrous manner. . . . He was making money rapidly—but it seems, was sometimes too drunk to see company."[19] Pluck disquieted the upper classes in New York City, where the *New York Mirror and Ladies' Literary Gazette* expressed relief at the colonel's departure: "We are not sorry that his hour is past and his exit made."[20] In Boston Pluck's appearance outraged the local elite, and he "very precipitately retreated" from the city to avoid arrest.[21] Pluck's popular success ratifies Barbara A. Babcock's theory that "the socially peripheral is often symbolically central" to cultural performances of reversal and inversion, which have the potential to upset the established social order.[22] Of course, such carnivalesque performances, when licensed by authority, can function to reinforce existing structures of power, as Terry Eagleton and others have observed.[23]

The disquiet of local elites over Pluck's touring act suggests that his parody of the militia system could not be easily brushed off or co-opted by his social superiors. But even as newspapers like the *Saturday Evening Post*, *Niles' Weekly Register*, and the *New York Mirror* evinced anxiety about Pluck, graphic artists like David Claypoole Johnston subtly transposed Pluck's parade performance from the time of the participant and the time of the spectator to the time of the voyeur.

PICTURING PLUCK

In 1825 or 1826, at the height of Pluck's celebrity, the caricaturist and actor David Claypoole Johnston produced a satirical lithograph of Pluck on parade.[24] Johnston, a native Philadelphian, was one of the most successful graphic artists in the antebellum North, but his early caricatures of "dandies," "exquisites," and "the pompous, would-be-martial officers of the local militia" provoked accusations of libel.[25] When controversy made it difficult for him to sell prints, Johnston turned to acting for his livelihood, playing a variety of roles at the Walnut Street Theater from 1821 to 1824. Theater was a family business for Johnston. His father served as the treasurer of the Walnut Street Theater, and his maternal aunt, Susanna Rowson, had a remarkable career as a playwright and actress in Philadelphia.[26] In 1825 Johnston quit the stage and relocated from Philadelphia to Boston, where he opened an engraving business and began to publish the annual comic magazine *Scraps*, which made him nationally famous.

Johnston's caricature of Pluck reproduces two aspects of the colonel's costume often noted in contemporary press accounts: his ludicrous *chapeau de bras* and his giant, phallic sword, both of which make him appear dwarfish. Johnston accentuates his satire of Pluck by framing the colonel's image with a punning caption adapted from Shakespeare's *Henry IV, Part 1*, in which Bullingbrook boasts that he is "seldom seen"—a sharp contrast to Pluck's habit of exhibiting himself to all comers for 12½ cents per head.[27] In the background of the engraving, the men of the Eighty-Fourth Regiment carry tree branches and brooms in place of muskets, ride barnyard animals in place of horses, and fly banners emblazoned with images of quotidian labor (a man milking a cow, two men sawing a log). These details reflect "the popular-festive system of images" that Mikhail Bakhtin famously associates with carnival, in which "the kitchen and the battle meet and cross each other" in grotesque depictions of the human body.[28] Johnston's print is voyeuristic. It captures the spatialized temporality of the parade performer and the sequential temporality of the parade spectator in a single image, compressing the entirety of the Eighty-Fourth Militia Regiment's parade into a parody of Pluck. The background of the image, with its carnivalesque symbolism, sets the stage for this parody.

The figure of a black man mounted on a pig emerging into the fore-

Fig. 17. David Clay-
poole Johnston, *Col.
Pluck*, ca. 1825–26.
Courtesy Library of
Congress.

ground at the left of the engraving also plays an important role in Johnston's
composition. The black man is almost certainly a fictive addition to the
scene. Although hired black musicians sometimes accompanied private militias on parade in Philadelphia (much as hired black musicians accompany
some mummers brigades today), African Americans rarely if ever served in
the antebellum militia.[29] Thus the image of a black man riding on a pig at the
head of the Eighty-Fourth Militia Regiment strikes me not as an ahistorical
slip but as a deliberate reimagining of Pluck's parade performance, which
invokes blackness to malign the disorderly conduct of the white working
class. Gary B. Nash and Phillip Lapsansky both have noted examples of
virulent antiblack imagery elsewhere in Johnston's oeuvre, and in a detailed
study of Johnston's anti-Irish painting *Sound Asleep or Wide Awake* (ca. 1850),
Jennifer A. Greenhill argues that Johnston's work "depended heavily upon
vulnerable targets . . . already despised in the popular imagination and thus
primed for further derision through caricature."[30] In the carnivalesque context of the Pluck lithograph, the prominent conjunction of a black man and
a pig implicitly blackens Johnston's image of Pluck.

In an influential critique of Bakhtin's theory of carnival, Peter Stally-brass and Allon White argue that "there is no *a priori* revolutionary vector" to the inversive and grotesque tendencies of popular-festive images. On the contrary, the symbolic vocabulary of carnival "often violently abuses and demonizes *weaker*, not stronger, social groups—women, ethnic and religious minorities, those who 'don't belong'—in a process of *displaced abjection*." In early modern Europe the pig often served as the focus of this process, "the symbolic analogy of scapegoated groups and demonized 'Others.'" Proscribed by Jewish and Islamic dietary law, the pig has long been reviled in many parts of the world for "its ability to digest its own and human feces" and "its need to protect its tender skin from sunburn by wallowing in the mud." But as Stallybrass and White remark, the pig was *"celebrated* as well as reviled" in early modern Europe through both visual representations and public performances of carnival.[31] In Pieter Bruegel the Elder's famous painting *The Battle between Carnival and Lent* (1559), the allegorical figure of carnival, an obese man riding a wine barrel, also carries a pig's head on a spit. And at the Königsberg carnival in 1583, ninety butchers hauled a sausage weighing 440 pounds in a solemn procession through the streets of the city.[32]

The pig retained, or perhaps regained, its symbolic ambivalence in the nineteenth-century United States, with porcine imagery functioning both to demonize the low/Other and to license various forms of transgression and excess. The symbolic function of the pig in Johnston's caricature of Pluck can be seen more clearly through a comparison of this image with an account of a carnivalesque performance staged at a militia muster in Dedham, Massachusetts, in 1838. During militia exercises at the Dedham parade ground, "some mercenary and lawless wag" evaded the state's ban on retail liquor sales "by giving a drink to all who should patronize a certain wonderful exhibition . . . [of] a pig striped like a zebra from snout to tail." As temperance reformer Charles Jewett recalls it,

A picture of the wonderful animal adorned the tent under which it was exhibited. . . . Six cents was charged for admission. Of course the pig had been striped for the occasion with a paint brush, and the trick was rendered perfectly transparent by the first glance. The patrons of the show, however, after learning of the cheat, were solaced by a glass of grog, for which they were not required to pay . . . until the sheriff, with his posse, gobbled up the whole concern, tent, pig, and exhibitor, and took them from the field.

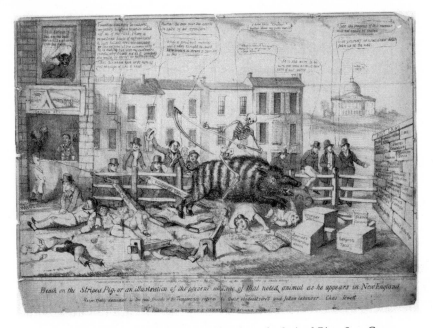

Fig. 18. David Claypoole Johnston, *Death on the Striped Pig*, 1839. Courtesy American Antiquarian Society.

Jewett put a pro-temperance spin on this incident by commissioning a print entitled *Death on the Striped Pig*, tentatively attributed to Johnston. In a style reminiscent of Johnston's political cartoons, this print portrays death as a skeleton with a scythe, riding a colossal striped pig and trampling over drunkards, a copy of the Bible, and a mother and child. As Jewett explains, "The press of the country, especially that portion of it controlled by whiskey-drinking editors, told the story of the Striped Pig with great *éclat*," and he responded by attempting to "turn the popularity of the pig . . . to the advancement of the temperance cause."[33]

Even in Jewett's teetotaling account it is clear that the grog seller at the Dedham militia muster leveraged both sides of the pig's symbolic ambivalence, simultaneously celebrating and duping the customers who paid to see the striped pig. Indeed, the collective laughter of carnival—"gay, triumphant, and at the same time mocking, deriding"—suffuses Jewett's description of the striped pig affair.[34] But Johnston's print precludes both the celebratory and the derisive aspects of carnival laughter by setting the striped pig on a rampage of indiscriminate destruction. Both the pig and his rider become agents of the devil, who appears in the print as a black, horned figure, standing at an upstairs window and surveying the violence below. "Go it, Stripes," he says. "You are the best servant I ever sent into the field." Through a dense series of visual associations, the print condemns drunkenness through the reviled figure of the striped pig, which thereby takes on the devilish power to crush everything in its path.

I am less interested in the temperance rhetoric of *Death on the Striped Pig* than in Johnston's intervention in the social semiotics of swine, which transforms the pig from an ambivalent figure into a demon. A similar, though more subtle, intervention in the carnivalesque symbolism of the pig appears in Johnston's caricature of Pluck in figure 17. In this engraving, the pig's fast trot, open mouth, and visible teeth render it slightly threatening, while the slurred speech of the pig's black rider—"Hurra for de Pennsylwamy light infamy"—lends an air of drunken revelry to the composition. But behind the festive surface of this image, Johnston compresses and elides racial dialect, black skin, and all the negative associations conjured by the pig—a filthy, demonic stand-in for the socially excluded and the culturally Other. As such, Johnston's print appears to draw a distinction between Pluck and the black, pig-riding interloper in the Eighty-Fourth Regiment's procession, who is being chased out of the scene by a white militiaman on a steer (and by Pluck's right foot, poised to kick both pig and rider in the behind).

The effect of this composition is to displace the burden of abjection from Pluck to the pig and rider on the left side of the engraving. Pluck remains the primary target of Johnston's satire, lampooned for his short stature and his preposterous mimicry of high militia style. But although Pluck may be *low* on the social scale, Johnston's print suggests that the black man riding a pig is *even lower*. Recall, however, that this is a voyeuristic image of the Eighty-Fourth Militia Regiment, the motion of the parade arrested and the actors rearranged to parody Pluck. If Johnston's print were animated, the "next frame" in the sequential, spectatorial time of the parade would show Pluck in the space previously occupied by the black man and the pig, stepping into the position of these low/Others while simultaneously displacing them from the scene. In this view, Pluck proleptically takes the place of the black man and the pig, an act of substitution that anticipates the blackening of Pluck in antebellum visual culture as the colonel's image continued to circulate in printed ephemera and graphic art.

PLUCK'S BROOM

Circa 1832 the woodcut graphics on a broadside entitled *Bobalition of Slavery* juxtaposed a white, burlesque militia officer—clearly inspired by

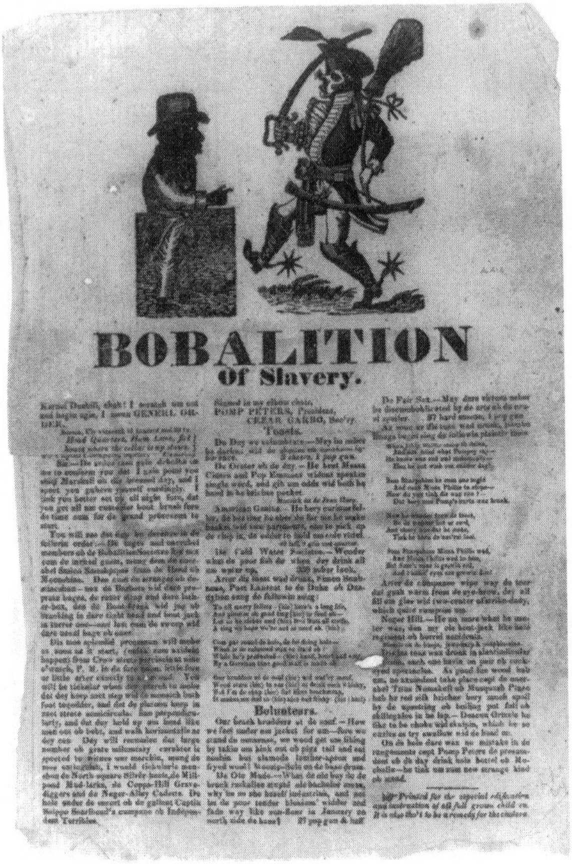

Fig. 19. *Bobalition of Slavery*, 1832. Courtesy Library of Congress.

Pluck—and a crudely carved figure of a black man. *Bobalition of Slavery* is one of about thirty so-called bobalition broadsides, published anonymously in Boston between 1816 and 1837, that satirize African American celebrations of the British abolition of the slave trade.[35] Beginning in 1808 Boston's black community staged an annual procession on July 14 to commemorate abolition, and in the 1810s and 1820s large and "increasingly hostile" crowds of white spectators turned out "to watch and to harass the marchers verbally and physically."[36] By 1816 broadsides featuring graphic racial caricatures and mock epistles in racialized dialect "began to appear all over Boston in advance of July 14."[37]

The next section discusses the form of parade time posited by *Bobalition of Slavery*, but first I would like to pause and digress over an important prop added to the Pluckish white militiaman's costume in this print. Unlike Johnston's rendition of Pluck (or the historical Pluck as described in press accounts), the figure of the white militiaman in *Bobalition of Slavery* carries a broom. Brooms were common props in Anglo-Atlantic popular performance in the eighteenth and nineteenth centuries, closely associated not only with domestic labor but also with blackface masking in mummers' plays, street performance, and early minstrelsy. Theater historian E. K. Chambers dates the first appearance of the word *mummers* in English to 1377, and mummers' plays were staged throughout northern Europe from the late Middle Ages until the early twentieth century.[38] Dale Cockrell argues that mummers' plays traveled to the Americas with immigrants from England, Ireland, and Germany, contributing to a diverse range of performance traditions, including Jamaican Jonkonnu, New Orleans Mardi Gras, and the mumming practices of Newfoundland, New England, and Pennsylvania.[39] Mummers' plays should not be confused historically with the Philadelphia Mummers Parade, though both form part of a what Herbert Halpert calls a "mumming complex" in the performance cultures of the North Atlantic world.[40]

English mummers' plays could be menacing to the audience. One script collected by Chambers ends with these lines, delivered by Devil Dout (elsewhere known as Devil Doubt or Little Devil):

In come I, little Devil Dout;
If you don't give me money, I'll sweep you out.
Money I want and money I crave;
If you don't give me money, I'll sweep you to the grave.[41]

Frequent references to brooms and sweeping appear in other English mummers' plays, attributed not only to Devil Dout—a role likely performed in blackface—but also to the male-to-female transvestite characters who often appear in the mummers' repertory.[42] Chambers argues that the broom "serves a practical purpose in clearing a space" for the mummers to perform "but it also, especially as used by Little Devil Dout, carries a suggestion of good or ill luck about it."[43]

Brooms also appeared with some regularity in nineteenth-century English street performances. For example, the May Day procession at Hertfordshire in 1823 was headed by "two men with blackened faces, one dressed as a woman in rags and tatters, and the other, with a large, artificial lump on his back, carrying a birch broom," who "[swept] road dust into the face of the crowd and [chased] them about with his broomstick."[44] This parade figure calls to mind not only the hunchbacked Colonel Pluck but also the grotesque antics of the Punch and Judy show, popular in both England and the United States in the early nineteenth century, in which the eponymous puppets beat each other with ladles, laundry paddles, mops, and broomsticks.[45]

Cockrell links the sweeping trope in English popular theater and street performance to the U.S. blackface song "Clare de Kitchen," which appeared in numerous editions throughout the 1830s:

> In old Kentuck in de arter noon,
> We sweep de floor wid a bran new broom,
> And arter dat we form a ring,
> And dis de song dat we do sing,
> Oh! Clare de kitchen old folks, young folks,
> Clare de kitchen old folks young folks,
> Old Virginny never tire.[46]

The images of brooms and sweeping in these lyrics function much as they do in mummers' plays, proclaiming the kitchen to be "a temporary extension of the mummers' domain . . . thus converting a private space into a public one."[47] However, a comparison of "Clare de Kitchen" with another popular song of the period demonstrates the ambivalent symbolism of brooms in the antebellum United States. In the late 1820s Baltimore music publisher John Cole—who printed one of the earliest extant copies of "Clare de Kitchen"—issued a song entitled "Buy a Broom," in which a Bavarian immigrant girl hawks her wares on the street:

> Oh buy of the wand'ring Bavarian a Broom
> Buy a Broom, Buy a Broom, Buy a Broom,
> Oh buy of the wand'ring Bavarian a Broom.
>
> To brush away insects that sometimes annoy you,
> You'll find it quite handy to use night and day
> And what better exercise pray can employ you,
> Than to sweep all vexatious intruders away.
> Buy a Broom
> And sweep all vexatious intruders away.[48]

Considered together, "Clare de Kitchen" and "Buy a Broom" suggest a dialectic associated with brooms in the popular imagination: brooms could sweep seamy, lower-class maskers *into* the home, but they could also sweep *out* "vexatious intruders." Either way, the broom functioned not only as a whisk but also as a weapon. Thus the white militiaman's broom in *Bobalition of Slavery* endows this figure with a threatening edge by portending his incursion into the kitchens and parlors of prosperous homes, where female maids rather than unruly male street performers usually did the sweeping.

IMPOSSIBLE PARADES

Read back into *Bobalition of Slavery*, the subtle blackface associations of the broom—derived from both English popular performance and "Clare de Kitchen"—further the gradual blackening of Pluck in nineteenth-century visual culture. The broadside's juxtaposition of the Pluckish white militiaman and the black figure contribute to a "double-voiced critique of blacks . . . and of unruly whites," which Corey Capers identifies as a "consistent rhetorical feature" of the bobalition broadside genre.[49] The carnivalesque language of *Bobalition of Slavery* amplifies this double-voiced critique, casting black abolition celebrations and burlesque militia parades beyond the abstract and appropriative gaze of the voyeur into a realm of temporal impossibility, where there is simply *no time* that such parade performances can occur.

Historians David Waldstreicher and Joanne Pope Melish both remark on the "inverted world" of "disorder and misrule" constructed by the language of the bobalition broadsides.[50] Waldstreicher reads this language as a form of "literary blackface," in which the white authors of the broadsides employ "exaggerated dialect and malapropism . . . in order to ridicule black pretensions to speak (and write) as whites did."[51] This literary interpretation of the broadsides overlooks the *performative* tendency of racial impersonation across media, whether in print, in graphic art, onstage, or in the streets. As Phillip Lapsansky argues, "The bobalition broadsides are performance pieces of a sort, as the intended humor"—nasty though it may be—"is evident only when they are read aloud."[52] In a similar vein, Douglas A. Jones Jr. reads the bobalition broadsides as scripts, "not simply something northerners laughed at, but, more important, something they acted from."[53] In *Bobalition of Slavery* the performative ventriloquism of ostensibly "black" language takes on a carnivalesque quality. The text begins with a letter from the president and secretary of the July 14 festivities to a parade marshal, which relates the following instructions:

Dis mos splendid processun will mobe as soon as it start . . . percisele at nine o'watch, P.M. in de fore noon, little fore or little after exactly to a second. You will be tickular when dey march to mobe dat dey keep zact step wid de moosick both foot togedder, and dat de pla-toon keep in zact strate semicircula line perpendicularly . . . and walk horizontalle as dey can. Dey will recumlec dat large number ob grate milumtary carakter is spected to witness our marchin, mung de mos extinguish, I would tickularle menshun de North-square Silver-heels, de Millpond Mud-larks, de Copps-Hill Gravediggers and de Neger-Alley Cadetts. De hole under de escort ob de gallant Captin Snippo Snarlhead's cumpane ob Independent Terribles.[54]

Bobalition of Slavery describes an African American abolition celebration as though it were a burlesque militia parade. The marchers form a "pla-toon," witnessed by an audience "ob grate milumtary carakter," with spec-tators drawn from several groups with ridiculous, martial-sounding names. Although these names have a racializing (and racist) tinge, they nonetheless bear a formal resemblance to the monikers adopted by white militia companies in Philadelphia and other northern cities in the 1820s and 1830s. For example, the *Pennsylvania Gazette* reported that Philadel-phia's Eighty-Fourth Regiment, Pluck's old company, carried a banner pro-claiming themselves "Hollow Guards, the Terror of the World" at a militia muster in May 1833.[55] Like the names of the fictive black militia groups in *Bobalition of Slavery*, the name "Hollow Guards" betokens an empty and laughable threat. But unlike black abolition celebrants in Boston, the men of the Eighty-Fourth Regiment chose a name for themselves—which was then reported in the newspaper—whereas "poor and nonexistent press coverage" of black abolition parades limited and distorted the impact of these events.[56]

It would be historically irresponsible to dissect an odious artifact like *Bobalition of Slavery* without trying to recover the celebrations of abolition placed under erasure by the self-canceling language of the broadside. A procession cannot begin "at nine o'watch P.M. in de fore noon." It cannot start "little fore or little after" this unattainable hour if it is also timed "ex-actly to a second." The marchers cannot move in "zact step wid de moosick" while keeping "both foot together." They cannot march "strate" while ar-ranged in a "semicircula line." And they cannot march "perpendicularly" while also marching "horizontalle." This linguistic assault on the very pos-sibility of an African American parade suggests that public performance played a crucial role in black politics in the early nineteenth century—not only as a tactic for asserting "a right to the streets," as Shane White argues, but also as a vehicle for ideas and forms of expression threatening enough to drive two decades of bobalition broadside production.[57]

Drawing on records from New York City and Salem, Massachusetts, Jones outlines "the standard structure of black parades" in the beginning of the nineteenth century: "processional ranks to and from the primary meeting place, orations, communal meals, sartorial accouterment, and musical accompaniment.... With this reproduction of form, the parades functioned as rituals of continuity and rejuvenation."[58] This standard structure persisted among some black fraternal organizations through the eve of the Civil War. In Philadelphia, the Grand United Order of Odd Fellows Carthagenian Lodge Number 901 regularly processed in full regalia throughout the 1850s, prompting white abolitionist Thomas P. Cope to worry "how far it is prudent in them" to march "while so much prejudice exists against them."[59] As Daniel R. Biddle and Murray Dubin argue, "White Philadelphia—for that matter, the white North—was not enamored of the sight of Negroes in uniform," which implied black power and authority.[60] Nonetheless, the Odd Fellows Carthagenian Lodge sometimes enjoyed police escorts for their parades, a protection rarely (if ever) afforded to black abolition celebrations earlier in the century.[61]

If most black parades in the antebellum North aimed for respectability and "reproduction of form," then who read and who listened to the accounts of carnivalesque disorder in the bobalition broadsides when they were posted on the streets of Boston each year in advance of July 14? Capers interprets the mode of address in the bobalition broadsides as "a rapprochement between the Federalist desire for proper order and the Jeffersonian Republican desire for a horizontal white national manhood, paving the way for herrenvolk democracy."[62] In other words, the bobalition broadsides appealed to both elite and populist political sensibilities among white northerners, contributing to the formation of whiteness by excluding both blacks and the most unruly elements of the white working class from the national imaginary. Hence the rhetorical importance of the graphic of a burlesque militiaman in *Bobalition of Slavery*, which would otherwise be a visual non sequitur in a work preoccupied with staging the alleged impossibility of black abolition parades.

Pace Waldstreicher, I view black abolition parades not only as an appropriation of white nationalist celebrations but also as an affective performance of black collectivity.[63] In his landmark book *The Black Atlantic*, Paul Gilroy distinguishes between "the politics of fulfillment" and "the politics of transfiguration." Through the politics of fulfillment, which operate according to the discursive norms of the Habermasian public sphere (print, literacy, debate), disenfranchised racial groups demand that "bourgeois civil society live up to the promise of its own rhetoric" — that is, the rhetoric of freedom. The politics of transfiguration, on the other hand, "exists at a lower frequency, where it is played, danced, and acted, as well as sung . . . in a partially hidden public sphere of its own." For Gilroy, a utopian impulse drives the politics of transfiguration, a desire for "qualitatively new . . . social relations and modes of association within the racial community."[64] By marching to commemorate abolition, black Bostonians did more than advocate freedom; they *practiced* it, transfiguring their community into a politicized public.

In a Freudian vein, the inversive language of *Bobalition of Slavery* can be read as a skeptical joke with a hostile purpose.[65] Skeptical humor pushes radical doubt to the point of absurdity, undermining any sense of epistemological order. *Bobalition of Slavery* fits this pattern, evoking an impossible parade by describing a series of mutually exclusive actions. The carnivalesque pleasure of this playful skepticism seduces the reader or listener into discounting the abolition celebrations and burlesque militia parades ridiculed by the joke, situating these performances outside of time, as though they had never occurred. "Every joke," writes Freud, "calls forth a public of its own," and the broad, herrenvolk public called forth by the bobalition broadsides participates through laughter in the "psychical conformity" of racism and classism.[66] This laughter suppresses both the black public sphere and working-class protest, dismissing (and equating) abolition celebrations and burlesque militia parades like those of Pluck's Eighty-Fourth Regiment as below the threshold of political intelligibility.

PLUCK IN BLACKFACE

Another image of Pluck carrying a broom appears on a song sheet published in Boston between 1837 and 1840 — and this time, he is in blackface. The air for the colonel's eponymous song is a "parody on 'St. Patrick was a Gentleman,'" an Irish Catholic nationalist ballad. By juxtaposing an image of Pluck in blackface and a recognizably Irish Catholic tune, this song sheet elides any meaningful distinction between African Americans and Irish Catholic immigrants — a reflection of the anxieties of native-born whites in cities like Boston and Philadelphia, who felt increasingly threatened by black upward mobility, abolition, amalgamation, and immigration.

Until 1815 most immigrants from Ireland to North America were

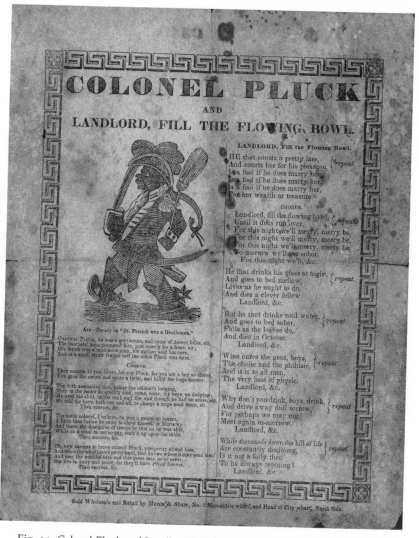

Fig. 20. *Colonel Pluck and Landlord Fill the Flowing Bowl*, ca. 1837–40.
Courtesy Library Company of Philadelphia.

Scotch-Irish Protestants, but this pattern shifted radically when poor, un-skilled Irish Catholics crossed the Atlantic en masse after the end of the Napoleonic Wars and the War of 1812.[67] Even before the Irish Potato Fam-ine of 1845–52, the scale of Irish emigration in the nineteenth century was enormous. According to Timothy Meagher, "as many as 800,000 to one mil-lion men and women left Ireland for North America from 1815 to 1845," during which time the Irish made up nearly half of all immigrants to the United States.[68] As David R. Roediger points out, Irish Catholics and African Americans "often lived side by side in the teeming slums of American cities," which invited racial comparisons between the two groups.[69] In antebellum Philadelphia, according to one account, "to be called an 'Irishman' [was] . . . nearly as great an insult as to be called a 'nigger.'"[70] Roediger argues that Irish Catholics and African Americans in Philadelphia "often celebrated and socialized together, swapping musical traditions and dance steps" through the early 1830s.[71] These informal exchanges likely served as an incubator for early blackface songs like "Clare de Kitchen," as well as for Philadelphia-born blackface performers like Eph Horn, who allegedly organized a "band of mummers" in his native city before becoming a national and international minstrel-show star.[72]

By the mid-1830s, Irish-black relations in Philadelphia began to sour as the ongoing influx of Irish immigrants and the recession of 1833–34 exacerbated job competition among the city's large and growing pool of unskilled laborers. Labor historian Bruce Laurie contends that newly arrived Irishmen were "thirsting for work" at construction sites and on Philadelphia's waterfront, where large numbers of black men labored as hod carriers and stevedores.[73] On August 12, 1834, the heavily Irish Catholic Moyamensing district—situated along the Delaware River just south of the city limits— erupted into Philadelphia's first full-blown race riot. In a neighborhood encompassing both Walnut Grove (the site of the Meschianza) and the row of mummers' clubhouses that now stands along Second Street, a violent mob attacked black homes, businesses, and public buildings for three consecutive nights. According to a detailed study by John Runcie, "The rioters were mostly young and from the bottom rungs of the occupational ladder. Some of them were of Irish origin, some of them had criminal records, a few of them were skilled craftsmen," and most of them lived in or near Moyamensing.[74] Contemporary newspaper accounts demeaned the rioters as "brutal and cowardly miscreants" from the "lowest cast of society."[75]

Job competition doubtless contributed to the Moyamensing riot, but Runcie concludes that "an aggressive, emotional negrophobia was just as important as economic rivalries" in spurring the mob that assaulted black people and their property in August 1834.[76] Although few in number, the native-born white artisans who participated in the riot faced little or no job competition from Philadelphia's mass of unskilled black laborers or from the city's small black elite.[77] Because economic tensions cannot fully account for racial violence in antebellum Philadelphia, Emma Jones Lapsansky historicizes the race riots of the 1830s and the 1840s by focusing on the targets singled out for attack. In the riots of 1834 and 1835, black churches, black Masonic halls, and the homes and businesses of "outstanding black leaders" bore the brunt of the rioters' aggression.[78] On May 17, 1838, a mob set fire to Pennsylvania Hall—the largest public building in the city—which had opened just three days earlier as a meeting place for abolitionists, temperance reformers, and advocates of women's rights.[79] On August 1, 1842, rioters attacked a black temperance parade.[80] And on October 9, 1849, an angry mob descended on a tavern owned and operated by an interracial couple near Sixth and Lombard Streets—the heart of black Philadelphia—after hearing a rumor that a white man had been shot on the premises.[81] These five major race riots suggest three root causes of antiblack violence just as potent as interracial job competition: a fear of black social institutions, like churches and Masonic halls, that signaled black upward mobility; a loathing of social reform movements, like temperance and abolitionism, which drew much of their support from blacks and upper-class whites; and anxiety over "amalgamation," or race mixing.

African Americans were not the only victims of collective violence in the cities of the antebellum North, where mobs also persecuted Catholics, Mormons, German immigrants, and abolitionists of any hue.[82] In Philadelphia, a series of bloody clashes between white Protestants and Irish Catholics rocked the outlying Kensington district in the spring and summer of 1844. This protracted melee stood out to contemporary observers not only because of the scale of the violence but also because religion rather than race motivated the attacks.[83] In the words of a popular song about the Kensington riots, "I guess it wan't de niggas dis time."[84] This lyric evokes both the equation of and the distinction between African Americans and Irish Catholics in the antebellum imagination, with Irish Catholic identity oscillating between "quasi blackness" and "ethnic whiteness."[85] Blackface masking by Irish immigrants to the United States in the 1830s and 1840s leveraged the ambivalence of Irishness, helping Irish Catholics become white (or at least "ethnically" white) in the eyes of their native-born neighbors. In a firsthand account of the Moyamensing riots, abolitionist E. S. Abdy claims that "men in black masks, and disguised with shabby coats and aprons" participated in the destruction of African American homes in August 1834.[86] Although Abdy does not specify the ethnicity of the maskers, it is likely that Irish Catholic immigrants and native-born whites blacked up together in racialist solidarity.

The lyrics to the first verse of the blackface Pluck's song reveal a heightened preoccupation with issues of labor:

> Colonel Pluck, he was a gentleman, and came of decent folks, sir,
> The butchers' boys promoted him, just merely for a hoax, sir;
> His father was a mud-scow man, his mother sold hot corn,
> And in a small straw feather bed the noble Pluck was born.[87]

The remaining verses give satirical descriptions of Pluck on parade, but the opening lines of the song lampoon Pluck by linking him to three trades—butchering, dredging, and food vending—all of which had specific racial and class associations in the antebellum period.

The phrase *butchers' boys*, much like imagery of pigs and brooms, functioned as a rich but unstable signifier in the early nineteenth century. In March 1821 a butcher named William White organized Philadelphia's annual Procession of the Victuallers on a scale never seen before. After a weeklong exhibition of "Cattle, Sheep, and other animals, which for numbers and excellence . . . have never been surpassed in any country," a parade featuring two hundred butchers and 86,731 pounds of meat wound its way from the slaughterhouses of the Northern Liberties along the waterfront and through the city's central business district.[88] Approximately three hundred thousand spectators turned out to watch the two-mile-long procession, which painter John Lewis Krimmel captured in *Parade of the Victuallers* (1821), the last of his many watercolors of Philadelphia's vibrant street life. According to *Poulson's American Daily Advertiser*, "two hundred Butchers Carts, each carrying a portion of the meats," made up the bulk of the parade, driven by "boys with white frocks ornamented with artificial flowers and gay ribbons."[89] Alexander Nemerov argues that "the recasting of the butchers as boys . . . emphasized their innocence in the business of slaughter."[90] This symbolic separation of butcher and butchered militated against the vernacular epithet *butchers' boys*, which Philadelphians used to describe dog fighters, brawlers, and other "blackguards" from the early nineteenth century through the Civil War.[91]

The "butchers' boys" who "promoted" Pluck in the blackface song sheet were no doubt the reluctant militiamen of the Eighty-Fourth Regiment, some of whom probably worked in the slaughterhouses of the Northern Liberties, a neighborhood of "native and foreign-born wage earners" for most of the nineteenth century.[92] For the residents of this neighborhood and other poor, outlying districts like Moyamensing and Kensington, laboring on the Delaware River as a "mud-scow man" was at least as dirty and dangerous an occupation as working in a slaughterhouse. In 1804 the Philadelphia Board of Health commissioned inventor Oliver Evans to create "a machine for cleansing docks," which consisted of a large scow (or flat-bottomed boat) "with a steam engine of the power of five horses on board" to dredge mud from the river.[93] In a meticulous study of dredging in early Baltimore, Seth Rockman describes the grueling conditions aboard a nineteenth-century mud-scow. "Many of the workers stood knee-deep in the water while shoveling debris," which consisted of "excrement, kitchen scraps, and spoiled produce and meat cast off from the market." One Baltimore mud-scow man died on the job in 1816, and another lost a hand a few years later. Unlike many unskilled occupations in the early United States, dredging offered a subsistence wage, but "the vast majority of men" who labored on Baltimore's mud-scows "did not last a month." The perils of the job ensured that mud-scow work fell primarily to "the segments of society most vulnerable to economic and physical coercion: slaves, free blacks, recent immigrants, and transients."[94]

Mud-scow men left work soiled, their clothes and skin blackened by harbor sludge. In 1854 journalist Solon Robinson published a saccharine, patronizing, and probably fictional account of the lives of outdoor corn vendors, who had one of the dirtiest urban occupations in the nineteenth-century United States. Over the course of *Hot Corn: Life Scenes in New York*, Robinson introduces several characters from a variety of backgrounds— black and white, young and old, women and men—all of them filthy and impoverished.[95] Robinson's text implies that both the labor market and popular print culture relegated butchers' boys, mud-scow men, and hot-corn vendors to the substratum of the poor disdained as the "scum, offal, refuse of all classes" by Karl Marx in *The Eighteenth Brumaire of Louis Bonaparte*. For Marx, this class—which he calls the "lumpenproletariat"— consists not only of "vagabonds, discharged soldiers, discharged jailbirds, escaped galley slaves, swindlers, mountebanks, *lazzaroni* (beggars), pickpockets, tricksters, gamblers, *maquereaus* (pimps), brothel keepers," and so on, but also of "decayed *roués* with dubious means of subsistence" and "ruined and adventurous offshoots of the bourgeoisie . . . in short, the whole indefinite, disintegrated mass, thrown hither and thither, which the French term *la bohème*."[96]

Reading Marx against the grain, W. T. Lhamon Jr. argues that *The Eighteenth Brumaire* provides the best summary of the "cross-class, cross-ethnic, cross-gender, and transatlantic cohort" brought together through shared identification with T. D. Rice's performances of blackface characters like Jim Crow and Long Tail Blue. But Lhamon's accent on the inner dynamics of Rice's lumpen audience—its hybridity, its critique of authority, its celebration of emancipation and escape—leads him to exaggerate the potential of blackface performance to galvanize "cross-racial charisma and union" between "working whites and disdained blacks."[97] The blackface image of Pluck signifies a lumpen identity imposed from above on African Americans and Irish Catholics by native-born whites, themselves mostly laborers or artisans. Blackening Pluck and associating him with degraded forms of labor served to draw a bright line between the native-born working class and the dirty occupations dominated by blacks and recent immigrants in the first half of the nineteenth century. This interpretation of Pluck in blackface offers a noteworthy challenge to the prevailing analysis of blackface makeup as the mask through which the Irish became white. For example, Eric Lott argues that the rise of the blackface minstrel show in the 1840s offered Irish immigrants "a means of cultural representation from behind the mask," since "those who 'blacked up' and those who witnessed minstrel show were often working-class *Irish* men."[98] By impersonating blacks in the streets and onstage (and by driving the market for blackface minstrelsy), Lott believes, first- and second-generation Irish Americans claimed the conceit of universal performability, negotiating a place for themselves as white in the fluid racial formation of the antebellum North.

A staple of mid-nineteenth-century popular culture, the antebellum minstrel show usually featured a group of musicians arranged in a semicircle, with an interlocutor in the middle and blackface comedians known as Tambo and Bones (named for their respective musical instruments) on each end. The banter between the pompous interlocutor, who did not wear blackface, and the two "endmen" loosely structured a full evening of performances, which included song-and-dance numbers, parodic stump speeches, novelty acts, and short skits, usually set on southern plantations. Following Carl Wittke, Lhamon argues that minstrelsy's audiences "were on the side of the spontaneous Tambo and Bones rather than that of the interlocutor, whose correct speech and elaborate attire" represented the "mercantile" perpetrators of class oppression.[99] Fair enough; but as I argue throughout this book, the contents of blackface stage performance—rarely more than a hairsbreadth away from unmitigated racism—attracted working-class audiences by mocking not only those at the top of the social hierarchy but also those at the bottom, whose rise posed a threat to the power of laboring white men. As such, the minstrel show rarely overcame its penchant for denigrating upwardly mobile blacks and women of all classes and colors, compromising the form's revolutionary potential.

The song sheet with a blackened Pluck shows that blackface could function to ridicule the dirtiest and least desirable forms of working-class labor, racializing butchers' boys, mud-scow men, and hot-corn vendors as black and Irish. This hardly suggests that class, race, and ethnicity were coterminous in the antebellum United States, especially given that native-born whites and Irish Catholics probably blacked up together in violent street clashes like the Moyamensing riot of 1834. But the symbolic overlap of dirty work, blackening, and Irishness encoded in the blackface image of Pluck marks this figure's class, racial, and ethnic attributes as interchangeably contemptible. The blackface song sheet is the culmination of a voyeuristic process of blackening that haunts Pluck from 1825 through the late 1830s, dogging the colonel as he and his image circulate from street parades and theater into print and visual culture.

MINSTREL REMAINS

After stinging defeats to the Union Army in the first year of the Civil War, Congress overhauled the militia system in July 1862, allowing "persons of African descent" to enlist in "any military or naval service for which they may be found competent."[100] For the first time since the passage of the Militia Act of 1792, African Americans could serve in local militias—a cherished goal of young black activists in Philadelphia like Octavius V. Catto and Jake White, who assembled "a colored company of ninety volunteers" in June 1862, the month before Congress opened military service to blacks. Catto and White's martial ambitions unnerved both local and federal authorities. Mayor Alexander Henry declined to issue the men rifles when they mustered at Independence Hall, and Major General Darius Couch refused to accept their service in the Union cause.[101]

Surprisingly, an armed black group called the Frank Johnson Guards had paraded through the streets of Philadelphia in August 1859—two years before the start of the Civil War and three years before the summary rejection Catto and White's company of black volunteers. Named for the African American composer Francis Johnson, the Johnson Guards marched in the style typical of black parades in the antebellum North, with uniforms, ornaments, and musical accompaniment. However, each of the roughly eighteen members of the group "carried a U.S. musket," which alarmed the editors of the *Philadelphia Public Ledger*:

> The law of the State requires that none but "able bodied white male citizens" shall be liable to do military duty. . . . Under what law do our colored military friends organize themselves into a military company? Whence do they procure their arms, and who commissions the officers?

With a whiff of bobalitionist derision, the *Public Ledger* remarked that "the men appeared to have but little knowledge of company movements or manual of arms."[102] Black diarist Amos Webber complained about this newspaper report in his private journal, lambasting the prohibition on black military service as "a Law aginst the colered mans progress [sic]."[103]

With the Civil War looming and a tradition of black parades well established in Philadelphia, the *Public Ledger* could question and criticize the Johnson Guards, but it could not discursively restage a public performance by armed black men as though such a performance were impossible. However, the remains of bobalition secreted in the *Public Ledger* article did not entirely fade away in the latter half of the nineteenth century. Even though 1,903 black Philadelphians died in the Civil War—more than one in six of the city's casualties—minstrel shows mocked the alleged cowardice and ineptitude of black soldiers throughout the 1860s and 1870s.[104] In the song "Black Brigade" (sometimes called "Greeley's Brigade" in a jab at abolitionist Horace Greeley), black soldiers join the Union Army only to flee from the battlefield:

> We're gwine to fight de South, O,
> All by de word ob mouth, O
> To fight for death an' glory,
> Am quite anudder story . . .
> I'll take my boat an' paddle
> For freedom will skydaddle.[105]

"Black Brigade" was performed regularly in Philadelphia by Carncross and Dixey's Minstrels, as well as by minstrel troupes and glee clubs throughout the country.[106] According to Robert C. Toll, one popular "Ethiopian Military Sketch" from the 1870s featured a group of blackface soldiers, formed into "ragtag ranks," that "marched right into its own officers, pushing them off the stage."[107]

Both the bobalition broadsides and the burlesque militia parades of the early nineteenth century haunt these postbellum caricatures of black military service—one aspect of a general coarsening of the practice of racial impersonation in late blackface minstrelsy. An overview of the repertoire at Philadelphia's Eleventh Street Opera House from the 1850s to the early twentieth century demonstrates that the minstrel show skewered black soldiers, romanticized slavery, and broadened its objects of ridicule to include oriental peoples and cultures. John L. Carncross and E. F. Dixey operated a resident minstrel company at the Eleventh Street Opera House from 1862 to 1871, assuming the management of the theater from Samuel S. Sanford, who had leased the venue beginning in 1855.[108] Under Sanford, the theater's productions evinced the increasingly proslavery bent of the minstrel show in the years leading up to the Civil War. According to an advertisement printed for "city passenger railway reading," Sanford's performance as "Happy Uncle Tom" won praise for "showing the slaves in their proper light, and not the abuse as written by Mrs. Beecher Stowe."[109] Carncross and Dixey not only satirized black soldiers with songs like "The Black Brigade" but also participated in a national trend toward East Asian impersonations on the minstrel stage. Their 1865 repertoire included an act called "The Flying Black Japs," which parodied a troupe of Japanese acrobats on tour in the United States. Carncross and Dixey made much of the putatively strange sound of the Japanese language, advertising that "hamsandwich-cellar-kitchen and his beautiful son all wrong . . . will appear assisted by eleven or eight other 'japs.'"[110]

Although never a minstrel staple like the wench act or the plantation sketch, Japanese impersonation gained currency on the minstrel stage through Thomas Dilverd, or "Japanese Tommy," a "Celebrated Minstrel and great female impersonator, height 37 in."[111] Along with the dancer William Henry Lane, or "Master Juba," Dilverd was one of the only African Americans to perform alongside white minstrels in blackface, touring widely with such companies as Christy's Minstrels, Bryant's Minstrels, and Kelly and Leon's Minstrels from 1853 through his death in 1887.[112] Frank Dumont, who succeeded Carncross and Dixey as the manager of the Eleventh Street Opera House, lists Japanese Tommy among the "grand procession of minstrel stars" who performed at his theater.[113] Dilverd likely earned his stage name through his aural parody of East Asian speech. According to John Russell Bartlett's *Dictionary of Americanisms*, Japanese Tommy coined the phrase *hunky-dory*, which he allegedly derived from "the name of a street, or a bazaar, in Yeddo"—an Anglicized corruption of Edo, or Tokyo.[114] Dilverd's stage name suggests that *hunky-dory* and the other Japanese-sounding locutions he used in performance eclipsed his blackness, his dwarfism, and his female impersonations in the popular imagination, underscoring the prominence of oriental impersonation in late minstrel shows.

Minstrel orientalism at the Eleventh Street Opera House persisted through the early twentieth century, when most minstrel-show venues in the United States had either switched to vaudeville or shut their doors. A playbill from 1911, for the "Last Night of the 11th Street Opera House," includes the song "'Funny Little Chinaman,' followed by a program of clas-

Last Performance of Dumont's Minstrels, at the Eleventh Street Opera House, in Philadelphia, May 13, 1911.

Fig. 21. *Last Performance of Dumont's Minstrels*, 1911. Courtesy Harry Ransom Center, University of Texas at Austin.

sics like 'My Old Kentucky Home.'"[115] Here an orientalist tune, almost certainly laden with malapropisms and invented phrases, precedes a nostalgic restaging of landmark minstrel songs. A souvenir photograph of this closing show displays a company of some thirty performers, more than half of them in blackface, against a backdrop painted with Chinese lanterns and a large pagoda. This oriental mise-en-scène may have been used for only part of the program, but the fact that it appears in a commemorative photo of the last show at a legendary minstrel theater suggests the deep imbrication of blackface and oriental impersonation in the performance culture of late minstrelsy.

After closing the Eleventh Street Opera House, Dumont "transferred his minstrel activities to the old Dime Museum building, at Ninth and Arch Streets," where he died of a sudden heart attack in the box office in 1919. By this time, Philadelphia was the last city in the United States with a resident minstrel theater.[116] Even before Dumont's move to Ninth Street, his company included former minstrel-show stars like the African American composer and singer James Bland, who could no longer find work in London, New York City, or Washington, DC.[117] Bland composed "Oh! Dem Golden Slippers" (1879), the anthem of the Philadelphia Mummers Parade, and local lore holds that Charles Dumont—Frank Dumont's nephew—introduced

Bland's tune to the mummers in 1905.[118] Corey Elizabeth Leighton speculates that Charles Dumont probably first heard "Oh! Dem Golden Slippers"
while "working backstage at his uncle's theater."[119] However, neither
Leighton nor I have found evidence that Charles Dumont performed in the
Mummers Parade before 1912 or that the mummers played Bland's tune
much before 1920.[120] Even if the popular history of the Mummers Parade is
more than a decade off in dating the debut of "Oh! Dem Golden Slippers"
in Philadelphia's iconic New Year's Day procession, it seems almost certain
that Charles Dumont served as a vector for transmitting the remains of
blackface minstrelsy into the mummers' repertoire.

Theater is a time-based art form, and scenes on a proscenium stage usually
unfold in succession, even when their temporal arrangement is nonlinear.
A stationary spectator experiences a parade as something akin to street
theater—a sequential flow of performances traversing a specific vantage
point. The time of the performer and the time of the voyeur fragment this
sequential, theatrical structure. For the performer, a parade is repetition in
motion, a continuous reenactment of the same songs, dances, and scenes
played while processing down the street. This temporal experience is performative rather than theatrical, insofar as it overturns the sequential unfolding of one scene after another. As Tracy C. Davis argues, "Performative
time participates promiscuously in the past yet is ongoing"—much like the
reiterative burlesques, recycled minstrel material, and recondite orientalism of the Philadelphia Mummers Parade. For Davis, performative time is
"crucially dependent upon citationality," and mummers frequently cite
both the past and the present as they negotiate the parodic, nostalgic, and
competitive impulses that animate their parade.[121] Nonetheless, it would
strain belief to claim that twenty-first-century mummers consciously cite
Colonel Pluck, bobalition, the Johnson Guards, "The Flying Black Japs," or
any of the historical moments of street and stage performance discussed in
this chapter. These moments haunt the Mummers Parade, and the historiography of parade performance requires attention not only to citationality
and lines of descent but also to ghosts—to the half-forgotten and site-
specific performances that seep through the time of the parade performer
and into an ongoing present.

The time of the voyeur attempts to repress the past by apprehending
the parade as a totality, stilled in a single image or a pithy description. Voy-
eurism is most obvious when it formalizes and abstracts the street into a
fiction of knowledge (de Certeau) or a cubist line (Stein) rather than a route
for the movement of bodies. But the voyeuristic blackening of Pluck's pa-

rade performance unfolds not only through a bird's-eye view of the street but also through a series of canny juxtapositions and displacements across media and across the racial formation of the antebellum North. Through this media hopping and racializing process, Pluck is stripped of his agency as a political parodist and rendered abject by the voyeur's gaze. The historical Pluck—the performing, embodied Pluck—becomes a specter, overlaid by his variegated representations in graphic art and print, but remaining, however faintly, to haunt the minstrel show and the Mummers Parade.

| The Minstrel Wench and the Mummers Wench

A Performance Genealogy

In December 1963, under pressure from civil rights activists, the city of Philadelphia banned blackface makeup from the Mummers Parade. To protest the ban, a group of white mummers staged a sit-in that briefly halted the 1964 procession up Broad Street. As mummers historian Charles E. Welch Jr. recalls it,

> Members of the H. Philip Hammond Comic Club sat down in the middle of the street, some shouting, "Negroes sat down in City Hall, we'll sit down here." A new chant started: "One, two, three, four, we hate Cecil Moore" (local leader of the NAACP [National Association for the Advancement of Colored People]). The police quickly moved in and forced the mummers to rise. The entire incident lasted about twenty minutes, after which the paraders again started up the Street.[1]

The appropriation of the sit-in, a tactic of the civil rights movement, to defend the practice of racial impersonation is among the more ironic examples of the interracial history of the Mummers Parade.

To stop in the middle of a parade route is to seize control over the audience's experience, disrupting the sequential procession of performances moving along the street. By intervening in the temporal flow of the 1964 Mummers Parade, the members of the Hammond Club attempted to intervene in the parade's history to preserve the mummers' longstanding practice of blackface masking. This chapter measures the impact of Hammond's intervention by tracing a performance genealogy of the mummers wench, one of the most enduringly popular figures in the parade. This genealogy begins with early nineteenth-century black and blackface performance and extends through the present, highlighting new, progressive possibilities for disrupting the Mummers Parade's unfinished history.

Frank Dougherty and Ron Goldwyn, who spent decades reporting on the Mummers Parade for the *Philadelphia Daily News*, describe the mummers wench as "the most traditional, outrageous, and politically incorrect of all mummers. Basically, it's a guy in a dress. The hairier the legs, the longer the braids, the colder the beer, the better."[2] The persistence of racial and gender impersonation among the wenches of the Philadelphia Mummers Parade suggests a genealogical connection between the mummers wench and the "wench act" of the early 1840s: a burlesque form of gender impersonation performed by white men in blackface, often in the context of the antebellum minstrel show. Although many midcentury minstrel troupes incorporated blackface gender impersonation into their routines, the wench act first became popular in 1842, before the conventional format of the antebellum minstrel show—with two endmen, an interlocutor, and a semicircle of musicians—had come into its own. Thus the wench act stands at a threshold between the short blackface scenes and sketches of early nineteenth-century popular theater and the emergence of the minstrel show as a full-fledged theatrical genre.

The genealogy of the mummers wench encompasses not only the wench act but also two other, equally complex performance traditions: the cakewalk, an antebellum slave dance absorbed into blackface minstrelsy, African American theater, and the "strut" of the mummers wench; and Philadelphia's African American brass bands, which have played music for white men on parade since the early nineteenth century. These three genealogical strands came together in the performances of the early twentieth-century mummers wench and then frayed when confronted with the 1960s civil rights campaign to rid the Mummers Parade of blackface makeup—a campaign that brought important changes, though hardly an ending, to wench performances of racial and gendered impersonation.

Until 1964 mummers wenches usually marched in blackface, recalling the frequent concurrence of blackface makeup and male-to-female transvestism in rowdy Christmas celebrations in nineteenth-century Philadelphia. As Susan G. Davis has shown, disorderly bands of young, working-class white men roamed the streets of the city on Christmas Eve from the 1830s through the 1880s, intimidating "respectable Philadelphians" and mocking women, blacks, and ethnic minorities.[3] After 1854 Philadelphia's new central police force cracked down on unruly Christmas celebrations, and holiday revelers responded by forming organized clubs and competing for prizes in neighborhood parades. In 1901 these neighborhood competitions converged on Broad Street for a New Year's Day procession, with prizes funded by the city. According to Goldwyn, wenches participated in the Mummers Parade for much of the twentieth century thanks to a tense but mutually beneficial arrangement with the comic clubs:

> For decades and decades, people [who performed as wenches] would do it on their own. They bought badges from comic clubs, who would put them up for sale. A lot of the comic club officials didn't like wenches; they felt the wenches gave them a bad name. But [some officials] would sell or hand out badges . . . so that the wenches could march.[4]

By the 1990s the wenches had organized a few large brigades of their own, which now compete in the Mummers Parade as an independent division, unaffiliated with the comic clubs.

Since the 1964 sit-in on Broad Street, both the comic clubs and the wench brigades have occasionally challenged the city's authority over the Mummers Parade—most notably in 1995, when the seven hundred wenches of the James "Froggy" Carr brigade sat down in the middle of the parade route to protest the arrest of their captain and the confiscation of their beer. More often, the comics and wenches wait until their after-hours party on Second Street (or "Two Street") to flout city-imposed rules. In 1964 some mummers donned blackface makeup on Two Street after the official parade had ended, an act of defiance foreshadowed by a large poster of a blackface minstrel displayed on Broad Street earlier in the day. The caption: "Gone Yes, Forgotten Never"—a testament to the indelible memory of blackface performance that continues to haunt the Philadelphia Mummers Parade.[5]

"LUCY LONG"

> Given that North American blackface musical performance goes back at least to 1815, probably in Albany first, why is the minstrel show said to begin in 1843 in New York City? Given that the minstrel show has seeped well beyond its masked variants into vaudeville, thence into sitcoms; into jazz and rhythm 'n' blues quartets, thence into rock 'n' roll and hip hop dance; into the musical and the novel, thence into radio and film; into the Grand Old Opry, thence into every roadhouse and the cab of every longhaul truck beyond the Appalachians—why, then, is the minstrel show said to be over?[6]

On June 15, 1842, six months before the "first" minstrel show at the Chatham Theater in New York City, five blackface performers appeared in an entr'acte entertainment at Philadelphia's Walnut Street Theater. Billed as a performance of "Negro Oddities, by Five of the Best Niggers in the World," the program featured "Jim Sanford, Master Diamond, Ole Bull Myers, Pickanniny Coleman, and Master Chestnut, in a grand trial dance: 'Lucy Long' by Jim Sanford; 'Piney Woods Jig,' by Master Diamond."[7] This performance lacked the full-evening format that probably originated with the Virginia Minstrels at the Chatham Theater in January or February 1843, but already in the summer of 1842 it signaled a trend toward larger blackface troupes performing multipart programs—a structural transformation in North American blackface performance that facilitated the emergence of the minstrel show.[8]

This structural transformation coincided with the rise of wench songs like "Lucy Long," which Robert B. Winans has called "unquestionably *the* most popular song of the first minstrel decade."[9] According to S. Foster Damon, "Lucy Long" circulated in numerous versions copyrighted 1842 or 1843, "all popular and many of them claiming to be the original."[10] Jim Sanford and Ole Bull Myers—who later became principals in the Virginia Serenaders, Philadelphia's most popular early minstrel troupe—both appeared at the Walnut Street Theater on June 15, 1842, which suggests that the "Negro Oddities" act probably featured the Virginia Serenaders' version of "Lucy Long":

> Oh, I jist come out afore you,
> To sing a little song,
> I plays it on de banjo,
> And dey calls it Lucy Long.
>> Oh, take your time Miss Lucy,
>> Take your time Miss Lucy Long.
>
> Miss Lucy she is handsome,
> Miss Lucy she is tall,
> And de way she spreads her ancles,
> Is death to de niggers all.
>> Oh, take your, &c.
>
> Oh, Miss Lucy's teeth is grinning,
> Just like an ear ob corn,
> And her eyes dey look so winning,

The Dancing Lucy Long.

Fig. 22. "The Dancing Lucy Long," *White's New Illustrated Melodeon Song Book*, 1848. Courtesy Brown University Library.

I wish I ne'er was born.
    Oh, take your, &c . . .

If I had a scolding wife,
I'd lick her sure as I'm born;
I'd take her down to New Orleans,
And trade her off for corn.
Oh, take your time, &c.[11]

The popular song "Coal Black Rose" and the plays derived from it put white men in blackface and drag onstage as early as 1829, as discussed in chapter 4. But the performance structure of the 1840s wench act differed significantly from that of "Coal Black Rose." According to Eric Lott, the 1840s wench "usually did not sing the songs she starred in"; rather, she became the "theatrical object of the song, exhibiting [her]self in time with the grotesque descriptions" in the lyrics, sung by an onstage accompanist while the wench performer danced.[12] Lott reads the "popular misogyny" of antebellum wench songs like "Lucy Long" against a background of changing gender roles among the urban working class in the northern United States. As Christine Stansell argues, "Hard times and the irregularity of employment made many husbands poor providers and weakened their control of their families, [while] at the same time, female wage work, however lowly, provided many women some means of support apart from men."[13] Lott relates this theater of gender relations outside the playhouse to what he calls the "social unconscious" of the wench act, which converted the gender anxiety of its white, working-class, male audience into a source of "comic pleasure." This psychoanalytic interpretation ultimately locates the blatant sexism of the wench act within the larger symbolic economy of "white male desire for black men," which Lott believes is "everywhere to be found" in the minstrel show. For the spectator, this volatile combination of gender anxiety and interracial desire led to an "unsteady oscillation in 'wench' acts between a recoil from women into cross-dressing misogyny and a doubling-back from the homoeroticism that this inevitably also suggested, with the misogyny serving as a convenient cover story for or defense against the homoerotic desires."[14]

    Bruce McConachie disputes this conclusion, arguing that it is "very difficult to believe that actor-dancers playing minstrel wenches would try to induce erotic desire in their spectators." McConachie's "cognitive simulation" of wench act spectatorship—putting himself "in the shoes of an antebellum spectator at a minstrel show in order to imagine what would interest me if I were seeking to enjoy a wench act"—allows him to recover the humor of these performances with remarkable specificity. In the wench act, McConachie argues, "the fun occurred in the contrast between the pose of frail femininity adopted by the wench and the reality of male muscle underneath"—a contrast suggested in the Virginia Serenaders' version of "Lucy Long."[15] In verse 2, for example, the words *handsome* and *tall* hint at Miss Lucy's masculinity, a subtlety punctured when she "spreads her ancles" and brings "death to niggers all"—presumably by revealing masculine undergarments beneath her frilly dress. The analogy of Miss Lucy's teeth to an ear of corn in verse 3 lends her a grotesque aspect, and the last verse recycles this corn imagery when a "scolding wife"—perhaps Miss Lucy, perhaps another woman—is traded off for corn. The final lines of the song laminate a misogynistic fantasy of conjugal control—connected, no doubt, to the anxieties of working-class male audiences about changing gender roles in society at large—to the sale of flesh. And given that the antebellum wench dancer usually impersonated a black woman, trading "her" off for corn cruelly exploits the flesh trades of slavery and prostitution as fodder for the audience's fun.

Later minstrel show female impersonators like Frances Leon departed from the burlesque style of the wench act, abandoning blackface makeup and achieving verisimilitude in their performances of gendered drag. "Some of the men who undertake this business are marvelously well-fitted by nature for it," wrote Olive Logan in 1879, "having well-defined soprano voices, plump shoulders, beardless faces, and tiny hands and feet. Many dress most elegantly as women." However, Logan also noted that the wench, or "funny old gal," remained a part of the postbellum minstrel show, appearing in the "walk-around" finale: "Clad in some tawdry old gown of loud, crude colors, whose shortness and scantness display long frilled 'panties' and No. 13 valise shoes . . . the funny old gal is very often a gymnast of no mean amount of muscle, as her saltatory exercises in the break-down prove."[16] These "saltatory exercises" included the cakewalk, appropriated into the minstrel show walk-around in the late nineteenth century. Dance historian Lynne Fauley Emery describes the cakewalk as "originally a kind of shuffling movement, which evolved into a smooth, walking step with the body help erect. . . . [As] the dance became more of a satire on the dances of the white plantation owners, the movement became a prancing strut."[17]

I view the cakewalk as the template for the signature "strut" of the mummers wench: a high, walking step, danced by the contemporary wench with his knees bent, one hand on his waist or the hem of his dress, and the other hand gleefully swinging a parasol through the air. As Dougherty and Goldwyn note, "the high-stepping gyrations of the [wench's] strut are ideal for revealing the matching satin bloomers that each wench wears beneath his skirts."[18] According to dress historian Gayle V. Fischer, the term *bloomers* first appeared in newspaper satires of the thin, loose-fitting trousers popular among advocates of women's dress reform in the early 1850s.[19] Named for women's rights activist Amelia Jenks Bloomer, the "bloomer costume" featured pantaloons elasticized at the ankles and worn under a knee-length skirt. Although "dress reformers . . . stressed that there was nothing inherently male about trousers," critics, including some feminists, condemned bloomers as "a travesty of male attire."[20]

Marjorie Garber argues that the bloomer costume carried Turkish connotations in the late nineteenth century, leading to charges of heathenism directed at dress reformers and provoking chauvinistic commentaries on "the lack of freedom of Middle Eastern women" compared to their counterparts in the United States (who, of course, could not vote in most state and federal elections until 1920).[21] Unlike Lady Mary Wortley Montagu, an Englishwoman who savored the "perpetual masquerade" of the Turkish veil while living in Constantinople in the eighteenth century, women's dress reformers in the nineteenth-century United States espoused the utilitarian aims of comfort and hygiene. "In Turkey," wrote dress reformer Mary Walker in 1871, "the fact is recognized, that the women's limbs are flesh and blood, as well as the men's."[22] The tinge of orientalism that haunts the bloomer costume adheres to the blackface wenches of the minstrel show and the Mummers Parade, suggesting another node in the intertwined histories of oriental and blackface impersonation traced throughout this study.

The mummers wench strutting in feminine dress while simultaneously displaying hairy legs and bloomers recalls the blackface wench act of the prebloomer era, which contrasted women's costumes with masculine undergarments and "saltatory" choreography. Although Dale Cockrell argues that the lyrics to early versions of "Lucy Long" contained "no hint of anything fraught with political or social concerns," later iterations of the blackface wench act often used the satire of women's dress reform to explicitly political ends.[23] As Garber remarks, the minstrel show frequently lampooned "bloomers in particular, and women's desire to wear pants in general."[24] One New Orleans minstrel show program, for example, advertises Lucy Long appearing "à la bloomer," suggesting the appropriation of the bloomer costume and its oriental connotations into minstrelsy's persistent assault on women's rights.[25]

Fig. 23. A wench
strutting in the 1987
Mummers Parade.
Photo by Vicki Vale-
rio. Courtesy the
Philadelphia Inquirer.

When I first began to study the historical relationship between the minstrel show and the Mummers Parade, the retention of bloomers as a costume piece by the mummers wench struck me as an obvious remnant of
minstrel-show sexism, amplified by the ongoing exclusion of women from
the wench brigades.[26] But on New Year's Day 2010 I saw a street-side performance that challenged my inclination to connect the minstrel wench and
the mummers wench. About a mile south of City Hall, an older woman
stood watching the parade and enthusiastically waving a large, hand-
lettered sign. "Real Men Wear Bloomers," it said. I vividly recalled this sign
two years later at a retrospective of photographer Zoe Strauss's work at the

Philadelphia Museum of Art, which included a portrait of two mummers wenches pulling back their skirts and bloomers to reveal tattooed penises underneath.[27] Strauss began her career as a street photographer in Philadelphia and Camden, New Jersey, in 1995, snapping candid images of urban life and exhibiting them under Interstate 95—along the same haunted stretch of Delaware River shoreline where contemporary mummers clubs rehearse and where the British Army celebrated the Meschianza in 1778. All of Strauss's photographs of mummers wenches exude masculinity, but none more so than *Tattooed Penises*, which updates the 1840s stage gag of Lucy Long "spreading her ancles" for the full-frontal sensibilities of the twenty-first century.[28]

Both the "Real Men Wear Bloomers" sign and *Tattooed Penises* raise fundamental questions about the performance genealogy of the mummers wench. In the nineteenth-century women's movement, white women wore bloomers to assert their right to dress in practical, "masculine" garb, thereby transgressing both gendered and racial norms. In the nineteenth-century minstrel show, male wenches wore bloomers to mock women's political aspirations, crossing barriers of gender and race in order to consolidate them. In the twenty-first century, could it be that bloomers in the Mummers Parade had come to embody masculinity *tout court* rather than a series of gendered and racial inversions in which white men in blackface imitate white women imitating an imagined, Turkish fashion? Could this be so, even though the mummers wench wears a dress over his bloomers? Are the minstrel-show wench act and the women's dress-reform movement even valid historical referents for understanding the contemporary mummers wench?

These questions, from field notes composed after a long day at the Mummers Parade, assume that the past vanishes from a performance as soon as the actors and the audience forget that performance's history. But as Mikhail Bakhtin points out, carnivalesque celebrations like the Mummers Parade have often served as "a reservoir into which obsolete genres [are] emptied."[29] Viewed genealogically, the dance steps and costume pieces of the mummers wench are haunted by the obsolete genre of the wench act, despite what contemporary wenches and their fans may say. The slogan "Real Men Wear Bloomers" implies an historical disconnect between the mummers wench and the minstrel wench, and indeed, most of the mummers I have interviewed offer ahistorical explanations of the appeal of performing as a wench in today's parade. In the words of Rich Porco, president of the Murray Comic Club, "Going in the parade in a wench suit is cheap and easy, and it's a fun thing to do."[30] Ed Smith, captain of the O'Malley Wench Brigade, explains that he left a fancy brigade in 1988 to help start O'Malley because "marching with the fancies takes a lot of time and a lot of money. I decided to go with the [wenches] because it was easier." He adds, "You don't have to have talent to be a part of the wenches. All you have to be able to do is swing an umbrella in the air, and everybody's got enough talent for that."[31]

Porco and Smith are correct that the wench brigades offer the least demanding avenue for participation in the contemporary Mummers Parade. Most clubs in the four other competitive mummers divisions spend significant time and money designing and building their costumes and rehearsing their music and choreography. Although wench brigades choose a different theme for each year's parade, most wenches wear identical costumes; for the casual spectator, only the color of the dress, bloomers, and parasol distinguishes one wench brigade from another. In addition, many wench brigades hire African American brass bands to march with them rather than playing or recording their own music, and the wenches spend little or no time rehearsing their choreography before New Year's Day. The minimal commitment and preparation required to parade as a wench help explain why the wench brigades are among the only mummers groups adding rather than losing members. In 2010 roughly two thousand wenches in seven brigades marched up Broad Street; "for comparison, the string bands [had] about eleven hundred costumed marchers."[32] Just before the 2011 Mummers Parade, the Oregon New Year's Association, a venerable fancy club, changed its affiliation to become a wench brigade, and a new wench brigade called the Americans launched in 2015. But accepting low-hassle fun as a sufficient explanation of the wench brigades' explosive growth skirts the question of *why* so many white men enjoy strutting in the Mummers Parade in costumes borrowed from the antebellum wench act.

Although the vast majority of mummers now obey the 1964 ban on blackface, the anachronistic style of the mummers wench registers an affective affiliation with the cross-dressed, blackface performers who walked the streets and stages of nineteenth-century Philadelphia. As such, the performance practices of the contemporary mummers wench tap into what W. T. Lhamon Jr. calls "the blackface lore cycle," a reservoir of expressive gestures that crystallized in minstrel and protominstrel performances in the early nineteenth century.[33] Through the lore cycle, blackface shifts and recurs across historical contexts, accreting new meanings without necessarily shedding old ones. Lhamon's suggestive list of examples quoted at the beginning of this section shows blackface on the move, seeping "well beyond its masked variants" into U.S., Atlantic, and global popular culture—both past and present. The minstrel show is not over, and the mummers wench continues to evoke both "Lucy Long" and the emergence of blackface minstrelsy in 1842–43.

TOM AND JERRY

The performance of "Lucy Long" in the "Negro Oddities" act in June 1842 not only pre-enacts aspects of the minstrel show and the Mummers Parade, it also reenacts the blackface dance scene in W. T. Moncrieff's play *Tom and Jerry; or, Life in London*, a staple of U.S. playhouses in the 1820s and 1830s. *Tom and Jerry*, a plotless romp by three young men of leisure through the slums of London, immediately followed the "Negro Oddities" act on the June 15, 1842, program at the Walnut Street Theater. Moncrieff based his play on Pierce Egan's popular novel *Life in London*, with illustrations by the celebrated caricaturists I. R. and George Cruikshank, whose work Edward Williams Clay absorbed when he traveled to London in 1823–24. A program for the Philadelphia premiere of *Tom and Jerry* in April 1823 advertised "scenery and dresses . . . copied from the plates" of Egan's novel, one of which shows Tom, Jerry, and Logic (Egan's three principal characters) visiting an East London club called All Max.[34] In Egan's novel, Tom, Jerry, and Logic immerse themselves in the revelry at the club, where "Lascars, blacks, jack tars, coal-heavers, dustmen, women of colour, old and young, and a sprinkling of the remnants of once fine girls, &c. [are] all *jigging* together."[35] But in Moncrieff's dramatic adaptation, the three gentlemen visitors to All Max remain aloof from the action, choosing to watch a "comic *pas de deux*" by "Dusty Bob and African Sal" rather than joining in the dance themselves.[36]

Peter P. Reed argues that white men in blackface usually played the roles of Dusty Bob and African Sal in early U.S. productions of *Tom and Jerry*, presaging the wench acts of the 1840s.[37] As such, the juxtaposition of *Tom and Jerry* and "Lucy Long" on a June 1842 playbill at the Walnut Street Theater suggests a threshold in cross-dressed blackface performance between Moncrieff's play, a waning theatrical fad of the previous two decades, and the wench act, a popular form of blackface gender impersonation that would soon emerge as a staple of the antebellum minstrel show. Unlike the wenches of the 1840s, who most often danced solo, *Tom and Jerry*'s Dusty Bob and African Sal performed as a couple—a detail underscored by Moncrieff's stage directions, which call for Bob and Sal's "black Child" to "[squall] violently . . . thinking there is

Fig. 24. I. R. and George Cruikshank, *Lowest Life in London*, 1821. Courtesy Printed Book and Periodical Collection, Winterthur Library.

something the matter with its mother" as Sal, "in the fullness of her spirits, keeps twirling about."[38] This primal scene unfolds as a command performance for the three white gentlemen onstage, witnessed on June 15, 1842, by the predominantly working-class, male audience at the Walnut Street Theater.[39]

Reed contends that Bob and Sal's pas de deux "imagines blackface dance as constructed and patronized, conjured into being by upper-class observers."[40] Although this analysis illuminates the racial and class dynamics of the scene, it overlooks the importance of gender and sexuality in a performance where two white men in blackface makeup—one of them dressed as a woman—dance hysterically before the gaze of a squalling child. If white male desire for black men permeates the minstrel show, as Lott argues, then U.S. productions of *Tom and Jerry* should be read as a genealogical tributary of this cross-racial homoeroticism. Just before Bob and Sal begin dancing, Logic—a member of the onstage upper-class audience for their performance—"gives [the] Fiddler gin and snuff, and begrimes his face," staging rituals of intoxication and blackening to license the gender-bending and homoerotic scene ahead.[41]

Flash forward to the Mummers Parade, which refracts the racial, gendered, sexual, and class dynamics enmeshed in the performance and attendant spectatorship of Bob and Sal's comic dance scene in *Tom and Jerry*. "Decades ago," write Dougherty and Goldwyn, mummers wenches "marched with dudes, tuxedoed figures who carried a cane. Both wore blackface, until it was banned following civil rights protests in 1964. At that point, dudes went extinct" — a change that transformed the strutting of the mummers wench from a couples dance à la *Tom and Jerry* to a solo dance à la "Lucy Long."[42] This transformation shifted mummers wench performances away from the explicit homoeroticism of wench-dude partnering and toward the homosocial dynamic of the contemporary wench brigades, in which large groups of cross-dressed men dance together — a transformation that resulted at least in part from the city-imposed ban on blackface. Indeed, the fierce attachment of some wenches and comics to blackface makeup prior to 1964 may have had as much to do with the homoerotic license it provided as with its racializing and racist implications.

The 1964 blackface ban and the extinction of dudes had little immediate impact on the practices of spectatorship surrounding the Mummers Parade. With the exception of brief stints on Market Street (the city's central business corridor) in 1995 and 2000–2003, the mummers have always paraded up Broad Street through South Philadelphia, where a predominantly white, working-class crowd gathers to watch the mummers strut to City Hall. Even when city officials reversed the direction of parade in 2015, the wench brigades insisted on starting their march in South Philadelphia, where their fans are concentrated, and moving upstream against the rest of the procession. This refusal to comply with authority resulted in a bidirectional procession, disrupting the spectator's temporal experience of the parade as a linear, sequential flow of events. But through these changes to the route and direction of the Mummers Parade, the judging stand has remained at City Hall, where an elite panel made up of "deans of musical colleges, people with doctorates in their fields, artists, writers [and] TV producers" awards prizes for the best performances.[43] Although the judges enforce the 1964 blackface ban by disqualifying any group that appears in black makeup, other forms of racial and ethnic impersonation in the parade continue to flourish unchecked. And thus a small, privileged group of spectators authorizes performances of racial and gender impersonation to be enjoyed by a largely working-class crowd, a pattern of spectatorship homologous to that found in early nineteenth-century stagings of *Tom and Jerry* on this side of the Atlantic.

WHITE STRUTTING AND BLACK BRASS BANDS

There are but two couples, and as the cake is now in evidence, the walkers promptly get down to business. One pair holds the floor at a time, and the men's manners are in strong contrast. One chap is clownish, though his grotesque paces are elaborate, practiced, and exactly timed, while the other is all airiness. . . . Away upstage he and his partner meet and curtsy, she with utmost grace, he with exaggerated courtliness. Then down they trip, his elbows squared, his hat held upright by the brim, and with a mincing gait that would be ridiculous were it not absolute in its harmony with the general scheme of airiness. . . . The other chap's rig is rusty, and his joints work jerkily, but he has his own ideas about high stepping, and carries them out in a walk that begins like his companion's but that ends at the other side of the stage. Then the first fellow takes both women, one on each arm, and leaving the other man grimacing vengefully, starts on a second tour of grace.[44]

This passage from the *Indianapolis Freeman*, the first illustrated black newspaper in the United States, reviews Bert Williams and George Walker's cakewalk act, which they performed with their female dance partners to great acclaim. After meeting in San Francisco in the early 1890s, Williams (the "clownish" chap) and Walker (described as "all airiness") found success with their cakewalk act in New York City in 1895, billing themselves as "Two Real Coons"—a sly dig at white minstrels in blackface, whose performances still drew large though dwindling crowds in the late nineteenth century. In March 1897, the same month that the *Indianapolis Freeman* review appeared, a Philadelphia correspondent for the *New York Dramatic Mirror* called Williams and Walker "the greatest negro comedy act ever witnessed in this city, their cakewalk act creating a genuine sensation."[45]

The cakewalk was hardly new to Philadelphia, which had hosted one of the earliest cakewalking exhibitions in the North at the 1876 Centennial Exposition.[46] In his 1899 study *The Philadelphia Negro*, W. E. B. Du Bois identified "gambling, excursions, balls and cake-walks" as the "chief amusements" of poor black Philadelphians.[47] As the cakewalking craze of the 1890s unfolded, working-class whites in the emerging mummers' stronghold of South Philadelphia got in on the act. White women began offering cakes as prizes at street performance competitions among predominantly white, male mummers clubs, many of which hosted "cake-cutting balls" to raise money for their New Year's Day processions.[48] By 1920 several mummers clubs had begun dancing their cakewalk-inspired strut to black minstrel composer James Bland's 1879 tune "Oh! Dem Golden Slippers," a song that remains integral to the contemporary Mummers Parade.[49]

In his biography of Bert Williams, Louis Chude-Sokei recovers the subversion of racial stereotypes in Williams and Walker's stage performances. Like many black entertainers at the turn of the century, Williams frequently performed in blackface, and Chude-Sokei contends that Williams's blackface makeup "signified" on the conventions of the white minstrel show "by ironizing and reclaiming the previously white artifice . . . of the 'darky' or the 'coon.'"[50] In his landmark book *The Signifying Monkey*, Henry Louis Gates Jr. argues that "signifyin(g) in jazz performances and in the play of black language games is a mode of formal revision . . . [that] most crucially, turns on repetition of formal structures and their differences."[51]

Unlike Williams and Walker's cakewalk act, which signifies on the minstrel show, Bland's "Oh! Dem Golden Slippers" signifies on black music while remaining firmly confined by minstrel-show stereotypes. In a detailed study of Bland's oeuvre, William R. Hullfish shows that "Oh! Dem Golden Slippers" uses both "the typical spiritual rhythm . . . and the cakewalk rhythm."[52] In light of the song's minstrelized lyrics, this rhythmic blend of sacred and secular signifies on the black spiritual tradition, as the words to the second verse amply demonstrate:

Oh, my ole banjo hangs on de wall,
Kase it aint been tuned since way last fall,
But de darks all say we will hab a good time,
When we ride up in de chariot in de morn;
Dar's ole Brudder Ben and Sister Luce,
Dey will telegraph de news to Uncle Bacco Juice,
What a great camp-meetin' der will be dat day,
When we ride up in de chariot in de morn.[53]

Because Bland played and composed on the banjo (an unusual trait for a minstrel-show songwriter), the music of "Oh! Dem Golden Slippers" lends itself well to the banjo and brass instrumentation of mummers string bands. And the mummers' adoption of "Oh! Dem Golden Slippers" in about 1920, well after the heyday of stage minstrelsy, suggests not only a musical affinity for the tune but also a misplaced nostalgia for the racial caricatures of the minstrel show.

"Oh! Dem Golden Slippers" still reigns as the anthem of the Mummers

Parade, played on New Year's Day not only by the predominantly white string bands but also by the African American brass ensembles that march as paid accompanists for some of the wench brigades. These musicians both play and playfully revise "Oh! Dem Golden Slippers," and it is likely that black brass bands hired to accompany white mummers have long signified on Bland's tune. Black brass bands have deep roots in Philadelphia, first emerging in significant numbers in the early nineteenth century. In 1780 Pennsylvania became the first state to enact legislation gradually abolishing slavery, and within a generation Philadelphia had grown into "the largest and most important center of free black life in the United States."[54] The hostility of white Philadelphians toward their black neighbors mounted from the late 1820s through the Civil War, as evinced by the prolific production of racial caricatures and the scourge of race riots that rocked the city in this period. But despite its history of racial strife, Philadelphia has remained a major cultural and population center for African Americans from the revolutionary era through the present day.

At the beginning of the nineteenth century, Philadelphia boasted a vibrant community of black artists and musicians, including Francis Johnson—a bandleader, a master performer on the bugle and French horn, and a pioneer in staging "concerts à la Musard" (or promenade concerts) in Philadelphia.[55] The most important African American composer of his era, Johnson catapulted to fame soon after the War of 1812, composing and playing music for elite white militia regiments and society soirees. In 1819 the Philadelphia businessman and politician Robert Waln identified Johnson as "leader of the band at all balls, public and private; sole director of all serenades, acceptable and not acceptable; inventor-general of cotillions; to which add, a remarkable taste in distorting a sentimental, simple, and beautiful song, into a reel, jig, or country-dance."[56] Johnson wrote and played music in a variety of styles, including military marches and minstrel songs; but as Waln suggests, it was his dance music that made him a celebrity.

John F. Szwed and Morton Marks argue that European dance forms like the cotillion and the quadrille were "flexible and open to transformation and improvisation" in nineteenth-century African American musical performance, and they speculate that Johnson's dance band played music akin to what later listeners would recognize as ragtime or jazz.[57] Eileen Southern makes a similar claim, suggesting that Johnson infused his performances "with rhythmic complexities such as are found in black folk music or twentieth-century jazz" to make his cotillions and quadrilles infectiously danceable. Southern also argues that black musicians in Philadelphia continued to cultivate Johnson's legacy after his death in 1844—a claim evinced by the Johnson Guards, a black musical and militia organization, which paraded at least twice in 1859.[58]

This musical heritage, along with the dizzying performance genealogy of the cakewalk, complicates the relationship between white strutting and black brass band music in both historical and contemporary wench performances of "Oh! Dem Golden Slippers." As the cakewalk migrated from southern plantations to the urban streets and stages of the Atlantic rim, its racial, gendered, sexual, and class implications were constantly in flux. Will Marion Cook's 1898 musical *Clorindy, the Origin of the Cakewalk*—which he wrote for Williams and Walker, though they were unable to perform in the show's Broadway run—created "a story of how the cakewalk came about in Louisiana in the early 1880s."[59] An 1897 article in the *New Orleans Times-Democrat* also traces the origin of the cakewalk to Louisiana, where blacks in the antebellum period used the dance to circumvent the prohibition on slave marriage "by allowing a man . . . to show his preference for a woman and thus to publicly claim her as wife."[60] Jurretta Jordan Heckscher argues that heterosexual partnering in African American dance "represented a fundamental break with African traditions," and even among enslaved blacks in the United States, Roger D. Abrahams notes, the organization of dancers into male-female couples was "far from the norm."[61] Thus it is striking that many black performers, unlike their white minstrel counterparts, retained the heterosexual partnering of the plantation cakewalk when they put the dance onstage later in the nineteenth century. African American showman Tom Fletcher recalls that *The Creole Show*, with an all-black cast and a white producer, included women in the cakewalk finale as early as 1890; "from then on," he writes, "nearly every colored show, minstrels and all, put women in the cast."[62] Some "colored shows," like the 1892 hit *South Before the War*, even capitalized on the vogue for amateur cakewalking contests, directly involving their interracial audiences in cakewalk competitions.[63]

In their exhaustive history of jazz dance, Marshall Stearns and Jean Stearns quote the recollections of a former slave and cakewalking champion regarding the plantation cakewalk:

> Us slaves watched white folks' parties . . . where the guests danced a minuet and then paraded in a grand march, with the ladies and gentlemen going different ways and then meeting again, arm in arm, and marching down the center together. Then we'd do it, too, *but we used to mock 'em*, every step. Sometimes the white folks noticed it, but they seemed to like it; I guess they thought we couldn't dance any better.

Clearly, some plantation cakewalkers reveled in signifying on the dances of their masters, and as Stearns and Stearns point out, there was little the "white folks" could do about it: "any reprimand would be an admission that they saw themselves in the dance, and they would be the only ones— apparently—to whom such a notion had occurred."[64] A courtship dance in which slaves parodied their masters, parodied in turn by white minstrels in blackface, copied and adapted from plantation life and the white minstrel show by African American theater, and staged in a variety of interracial contexts as a public competition, the cakewalk is, in David Krasner's view, a "hall of mirrors."[65]

Mimetic vertigo overwhelms me as I look down cakewalking's mirrored hallway to try to see whom contemporary mummers wenches are imitating.[66] But the reflections dancing in the mirror—white planters, enslaved blacks, minstrel-show wenches, African American theater artists— disclose no original at the end of the hall. Viewed genealogically, there *is* no original, since "genealogists resist histories that attribute purity of origin to any performance." Instead, argues Joseph Roach, "they have to take into account the give and take of joint transmissions, posted in the past, arriving in the present, delivered by living messengers, speaking in tongues"—or dancing in movements—"not entirely their own."[67] Today's mummers wenches are the living messengers of both the antebellum wench act and the turn-of-the-century cakewalk, strutting to the music of black brass bands, produced by and producing an interracial performance genealogy with no single origin and no single end.

THE BLACKFACE CONTROVERSY

Of all the stereotypes that have dogged the mummers over the years, "white guys only" is the most persistent. Mummers have always argued vehemently, but unsuccessfully, against this label, and their arguments are valid. . . . News clippings document that "all-Negro" units competed throughout the first quarter-century of the Broad Street parade, and it is likely that they were part of the free-for-all neighborhood parades prior to that time.[68]

On New Year's Day 1901, three African American groups—the Ivy Leaf Club, the Blue Ribbon Club, and the Homebreakers String Band— competed for prizes in Philadelphia's first city-sponsored Mummers Parade.[69] Regular African American participation in the parade continued

through 1929, when the Octavius V. Catto String Band, named for a mar-
tyred nineteenth-century civil rights leader, made its final appearance.
Patricia Anne Masters attributes the withdrawal of independent African
American clubs from the 1930 Mummers Parade to the Depression, which
hit Philadelphia's black community especially hard.[70] As Charles Pete T.
Banner-Haley argues, lower-class blacks in Philadelphia "experienced
the Depression long before the Crash of 1929, while the Black middle
class was pushed perilously close to lower class levels."[71] Deteriorating
economic conditions, along with the Catto String Band's last-place finish
in 1928 and 1929, clearly discouraged African American groups from
competing for city prize money.[72] In addition, mummers documentarian
E. A. Kennedy III suggests that the prolific use of blackface by white
mummers contributed to black disillusion with the parade: "Since the
1930s, the African American community [in Philadelphia] has taken justified offense over the mummers' historic use of the blackface minstrel as a
theme for disguise."[73] Nonetheless, black brass bands continued to march
as paid accompanists for white mummers groups through the 1930s, a
practice that remains common today.

The black community's "justified offense" over blackface erupted into
full-blown conflict in December 1963, when Cecil B. Moore, head of the
Philadelphia chapter of the NAACP, and Louis Smith of the Congress of
Racial Equality (CORE) successfully pressured parade director Elias Myers, a city official, to ban blackface from the Mummers Parade. This deci-
sion prompted two hundred outraged mummers—in blackface—to
picket Myers's home, leading to a compromise that pleased neither side:
blackface makeup would be allowed in the parade "if it was used to create a character, but not if it was to be used to ridicule any ethnic group."[74]
Civil rights activists were dissatisfied with Myers's equivocation, and
NAACP attorney Charles Bowser petitioned the Philadelphia Court of
Common Pleas to uphold the blackface ban: "We feel that the city should
not take part in a parade where Negroes are depicted in an unfavorable
light, provoking, taunting, humiliating, and embarrassing to them. We
are taxpayers and we do not think our money should be used to support
it."[75] Under Moore's leadership, the Philadelphia chapter of the NAACP
combined its traditional tactics of legal action and economic pressure
with public protests and threats to demonstrate, and the controversy over
blackface in the Mummers Parade was no exception. Matthew J. Countryman argues that "Moore's charisma . . . convinced large number of
working-class black Philadelphians to join explicit and collective racial
protest," many of them for the first time.[76] As such, the NAACP's collabo-

ration with CORE to fight blackface in the Mummers Parade marked a high point of organizational cooperation and community involvement in the civil rights movement in Philadelphia.

A snowstorm on New Year's Day 1964 forced a delay in the Mummers Parade until January 4, and on January 3 the Philadelphia Court of Common Pleas issued a preliminary injunction banning blackface on Broad Street—though not on Second Street—and prohibiting civil rights protestors from picketing the parade. Despite the ruling, one white mummer recalls that a group of Moore's supporters tried to stop the comic clubs from marching:

There was a lot of bad feelings on both sides. And this Cecil [B.] Moore brought down all these people from North Philadelphia from the black community, and they tried to stop the mummers; it was a mistake on their part because when [the mummers are] all together, they're not easily dissuaded. There was a big fight and a lot of black people got hurt very bad.[77]

If the antiblackface campaign led to this tragic but predictable incident of interracial violence, it also functioned less predictably to aggravate political fissures within Philadelphia's African American community. On December 31, 1963, the *Philadelphia Tribune* (the city's principal African American newspaper) reported that "four hundred Negro ministers went into their pulpits . . . and urged members not to watch the [mummers] parade either on television or in person."[78] But as the *Tribune* revealed four days later, "At least five and possibly more Negro marching bands will participate in the Mummers Parade . . . despite the controversy which has arisen over blackface."[79] According to Masters, an African American bandleader was thrown down a subway stairwell by civil rights activists for refusing to boycott the mummers, prompting one comic club president to ask his club's black accompanists if they wanted to be released from their obligation to parade—to which they replied, "Definitely not."[80] In an interview in the *Tribune*, George E. Hawkins, a prominent African American brass player who marched with the Catto String Band in the 1920s, defended black musicians like himself who chose to participate in the 1964 Mummers Parade.[81] The danger faced by Hawkins and his compatriots suggests that support for white mummers, as well as economic considerations, may have spurred some black musicians to defy the boycott, inspiring a show of interracial solidarity that coalesced in *opposition* to a just and powerful civil rights campaign.

In 1965 Philadelphia's civil rights movement succeeded in greatly reducing the visibility of blackface makeup in the Mummers Parade. At the behest of Mayor James Tate, the police enforced the 1963 ban on blackface, ejecting twenty-five mummers from the parade route for wearing burnt-cork makeup. Even the Hammond Comic Club largely acquiesced to the blackface ban, with only four of its members marching in blackface.[82] But to some extent, this show of compliance has deflected attention from the persistence and development of other forms of racial and ethnic impersonation in the Mummers Parade. In a controversial performance in 2009, the B. Love Strutters Comic Brigade paraded up Broad Street with a skit entitled "Aliens of an Illegal Kind," in which a group of white mummers impersonated immigrants clashing with the border patrol. An editorial in the *Philadelphia Daily News* chastised the performance for its "blatant racism," correctly pointing out that "Arabs had long beards and turbans, Mexicans wore sombreros, and Asian women were depicted as geishas."[83] The B. Love Strutters finished in eleventh place out of seventeen in the judges' scoring of the comic brigades, and none of the other 2009 Mummers Parade performances involving racial and ethnic impersonation garnered negative media coverage or sparked public debate.

Considered alongside demographic changes in contemporary Philadelphia, the impersonation of Hispanics and Asians by white mummers functions as a symbolic attempt to retake possession of space occupied by recent immigrants from Mexico, China, Vietnam, and Cambodia, who have settled in large numbers in the southern part of the city. Pennsport, home to the row of mummers' clubhouses on Two Street, saw its Hispanic population jump 47 percent and its Asian population grow 29 percent between 2000 and 2010, while the number of white residents in the neighborhood hardly budged. In South Philadelphia East, a census tract adjacent to Pennsport, the Hispanic population grew by 222 percent and the Asian population by 94 percent. Census figures also show a 16 percent decline in the number of white residents in the neighborhood—a surprising statistic, given that gentrification has followed close on the heels of large-scale immigration in this part of the city.[84] In March 2010 the *New York Times* travel section reported on the "fresh, hipster-ready cafes and boutiques" popping up along East Passyunk Avenue in South Philadelphia, a once-moribund commercial corridor best known for Pat's and Geno's, its dueling cheesesteak emporia.[85]

"Aliens of an Illegal Kind" is a troubling response to the increasing racial and ethnic diversity of South Philadelphia. At the beginning of the performance, the late Joey Vento—owner of Geno's Steaks on East Passyunk—

popped out of a small float emblazoned with the words "When Ordering, Speak English," a copy of the infamous sign over the counter at his sandwich shop. As the crowd cheered Vento's surprise appearance, an announcer hollered, "Uh-oh, here comes the border patrol," which sent a dozen men with American-flag jackets, cowboy hats, and wooden rifles rushing into the street. Parade marshals quickly set up a fence dividing the "border patrol" from a crowd of "immigrants," who stormed the "border" waving an assortment of foreign flags—including the Italian and Irish tricolors, a nod to the immigrant roots of Philadelphia's two largest white ethnic communities. A mummer dressed as President Barack Obama handed out green cards to all and sundry, and as the "immigrants" crossed the "border," they traded their national flags for the Stars and Stripes. This three-minute performance ended with the "immigrants" and "border patrol" strutting up Broad Street together as Vento threw fake cheesesteaks into the crowd, prompting one television commentator to remark, "This looks like a celebration of diversity."[86]

It is tempting to view the denouement of "Aliens of an Illegal Kind" as a carnivalesque suspension of hierarchy that mitigates the racism, sexism, and xenophobia evident earlier in the performance. But because most comic routines in the Mummers Parade end with all the performers dancing together, this interpretation would be misleading. Adherence to the conventions of genre does not excuse the malicious series of racial and gendered impersonations enacted by the B. Love Strutters in 2009, and other, similarly nasty comic sketches have appeared in more recent Mummers Parades. The Venetian New Year's Association's 2013 performance "Indi-Insourcing," for example, featured a group of white mummers in Native American dress overrunning a "New Delhi Call Center" as they performed the tomahawk chop.[87] Although not anti-immigrant per se, this performance springs from the same xenophobic anxieties over globalization that animate "Aliens of an Illegal Kind," transmuted into retrograde racism under the guise of satire.

UTOPIA/DYSTOPIA

The Murray Comic Club, one of the largest and most successful competing organizations in the contemporary Mummers Parade, sponsors both the B. Love Strutters, the brigade that staged "Aliens of an Illegal Kind," and the Vaudevillains, the self-consciously progressive comic brigade that I joined in 2009. As I describe in chapter 1, the Vaudevillains confront issues like global warming and nuclear proliferation by sewing costumes, dousing them with glitter, and dancing in the streets on New Year's Day. Vaudevillains cocaptain Danielle Redden describes the brigade's 2016 parade performance, entitled "Love Buzz: The Matriarchal World of Bees," as a "vision for a feminist utopian world of abundance, cooperation, harmony, and, of course, partying!"[88] In theoretical terms, the group aspires to stage what Jill Dolan calls *utopian performatives*, "small but profound moments in which performance . . . [makes] palpable an affective vision of how the world might be better."[89] Of course, any one affective vision of a better world might appear dystopic from elsewhere on the political spectrum, and multiple, conflicting visions of utopia compete for the audience's allegiance in the contemporary Mummers Parade. When I asked Rich Porco, president of the Murray Club, how he felt about sponsoring both the B. Love Strutters and the Vaudevillains, he replied that "we're not a politically motivated organization."[90] Porco plays to win, and the broad range of groups that perform under the Murray Club banner have earned eighteen consecutive victories for Murray as the best overall club in the comic division.

While documenting the 2006 Mummers Parade, Kennedy snapped a photograph of a mummer named Tom Spiroploulos wearing a rainbow-colored wig, blackface makeup, a wench dress, and a Murray Club badge. Spiroploulos, who was carried up Broad Street as an infant in the Mummers Parade on January 4, 1964, told Kennedy that he "don't mean nothing" by blacking up: "I'm not trying to put nobody down. It's just tradition. It's the way my father paraded."[91] Spiroploulos's remarks may strain belief, but they also point to the changing implications of blackface makeup for the mummers in the years since the 1964 blackface controversy. Blackface performance on both stages and streets helped to define the emergent category of whiteness for working-class immigrant men in the nineteenth-century United States while also producing occasional flashes of cross-racial identification. But for Spiroploulos and the few other recalcitrant mummers who still black up today, blackface serves an additional purpose. Masters argues that, by the 1960s, blackface as a mummers "tradition" had come to imply "a symbolic link to grandfathers and fathers," a point Spiroploulos echoes in defense of his blackface makeup.[92] By claiming blackface as a patriarchal inheritance, Spiroploulos identifies with an earlier generation of mummers as a tactic to mitigate the racist sting of his blackface mask. Such a tactic is insensitive at best, but it also discloses an ambivalent fantasy, at once nostalgic for a time of white male dominance and loaded with interracial desire.

Fig. 25. E. A. Kennedy III, photograph of Tom Spiroploulos, 2006.
Courtesy The Image Works.

From an antiracist perspective, a lone wench in blackface in the contemporary Mummers Parade embodies a dystopic politics of white male
privilege, naturalized as a mummers "tradition." But among the wench
brigades, most of which eschew blackface, the communal spirit in evidence on New Year's Day suggests a utopian performative. The genealogy of the wench brigades carries generations of displacements and com-
promises in its train: the grudging acceptance of the blackface ban, the
disappearance of dudes, and the vertiginous history of parodic mimesis
embodied in the mummers' strut. This performance genealogy does not
absolve the wench brigades of their racist and sexist tendencies, past or
present, but it reveals an ongoing, cross-racial engagement that keeps
white wenches and black brass bands parading together. This may not be
utopia, but the rush of a wench brigade strutting in front of City Hall
sends both the performers and the audience into a joyful abandon where
boundaries between people blur and anything feels possible. This is the
promise of carnival in the classic, Bakhtinian sense, where dance, music,
laughter, crowds, intoxication, and disguise coalesce into a fleeting illusion of harmony. To spurn cross-racial engagement by wearing blackface
in the midst of this revelry is to reinstate the unequal power relations that
carnival, at its best, always gestures beyond.

My distaste for blackface wenches and "Aliens of an Illegal Kind" made me hesitant to join the Vaudevillains, given the brigade's association with the Murray Comic Club. But as one member of the Vaudevillains explained to me,

> What we [are] doing, if I may dare say, is making history, . . . tackling weird and interesting issues [in the Mummers Parade] while integrating . . . the festive debauchery that is Philadelphia's New Year's Day. There are a lot of things deeply rooted and historically unjust about the Mummers Parade, but I am proud of this brigade's contradictions and its approach to infiltrating, invigorating, and intervening into [the parade's] cultural conventions.[93]

Indeed, the best way to intervene in the Mummers Parade, to enact a utopian performative, is to join the festivity: to broaden the diversity of participation, to claim the parade as a site of political protest, and to counter dystopic performances of racial and gendered impersonation, which attempt to justify their presence by denying their past.

Conclusion

Carnival, the Public Sphere, and Performance in Place

On New Year's Day 1995 the Philadelphia Department of Recreation moved thousands of reluctant mummers from Broad Street to a new, downtown parade route wending past many of the city's most famous tourist attractions. In Max Raab's film *Strut*, a 2001 documentary on the Mummers Parade, mummer Ed Kirlin describes how he and the other members of the Froggy Carr Wench Brigade responded to this change. On the way to their starting position, Kirlin and his seven hundred white, male, cross-dressed confederates

> had to go through a really ritzy neighborhood, and apparently lots of guys were stopping to pee, and the people who lived in the neighborhood were appalled. If the city had any sense they woulda put some port-o-johns along the way because you can't march three miles, drink beer the whole way, and not have to pee. It's not our fault! So by the time we got to the parade route, the police captain was furious . . . and when we got to Fifth and Market [Streets], he ordered that our beer be confiscated, and when our captain protested, he was arrested. . . . He got arrested at Independence Hall, right in front of the Liberty Bell, and by the time we got to Eighth Street, word spread through the group that Tooth [Renzi], our captain, had been arrested, so we all sat down in the middle of the street—all seven hundred of us—and the Pirates [another wench brigade] heard what was happening. They brought their beer truck up, so we all started drinkin' right away. . . . Tooth was in jail, we sat down and said we would not get up until they released our captain. . . . One of our guys . . . knew the superintendent of the police, and he said to him, he said, "you got four hundred cops out here, we got twelve hundred guys. It's gonna take every cop you have in the city to arrest everybody and, you know, it's gettin' that way, it's get-

tin' ugly." Now it's still only 9:00 in the morning! So they let Tooth go, and it was like Gandhi had arrived on the scene.[1]

This showdown between the Froggy Carr wenches and the Philadelphia police echoed the mummers' 1964 sit-in to protest the city-imposed ban on blackface—although unlike their counterparts thirty-one years earlier, the Froggy Carr wenches were not blacked up. In the spirit of Philadelphia's burlesque parade tradition, Froggy Carr and other mummers wench brigades use gender inversion to assert social and political power from below. In so doing, they constitute a public—not through the rational discourse of the Habermasian public sphere but rather through the carnivalesque symbolic vocabulary of popular street performance. This mode of publicity bears a formal resemblance to Paul Gilroy's politics of transfiguration, through which disenfranchised racial and ethnic groups enact new forms of collectivity and resistance in a "partially hidden public sphere" of their own.[2] And this formal resemblance poses a theoretical problem, insofar as the Froggy Carr wenches harness the politics of transfiguration to reinforce white male privilege, successfully placing themselves above the law.

The Froggy Carr wenches make a queer sort of public, situated somewhere between Habermas's normative conception of the public sphere and the minoritarian alternatives to bourgeois publicity celebrated by scholars like Gilroy. In a passage redolent of Gilroy's comments on the politics of transfiguration, Michael Warner argues that "counterpublics . . . structured by alternative dispositions and protocols" can and do emerge "against the background of the public sphere," enabling "new forms of intimate association, vocabularies of affect, styles of embodiment."[3] Without discounting Gilroy or Warner's generative theories of (counter)publicity, the sit-in by the Froggy Carr wenches suggests that performances of social and symbolic inversion can also forge conservative and exclusionary publics, even when these publics take a direct stand against official authority.

In *New World Drama*, Elizabeth Maddock Dillon posits the "performative commons" as a more robust model than the public sphere for performance historiography in the Atlantic world. In her view, "the 'sphere' model implies that a boundary delimits the space of the sphere, but the precise nature of that limit is often not addressed by those who envision the public as a sphere: what, for instance, lies beyond the edges of the sphere?"[4] *Pace* Dillon, I contend that any public must imagine its own limit, its own outer boundary, in order to constitute itself as a public. And as this book argues throughout, the impersonation of racial, ethnic, or gendered social groups that lie outside the boundary of a particular public's self-conception can be a potent tactic to define and defend that boundary.

In the 2013 Mummers Parade, the Joseph A. Ferko String Band performed a routine entitled "Bringin' Back Those Minstrel Days."[5] This unabashed homage to minstrelsy, performed in brownface rather than blackface to avoid censure by the judges, incorporated visual and musical references to both Stephen Foster and Al Jolson. At one point in the performance, band captain Anthony Celenza mouthed the lyrics to "My Mammy" into a three-way mirror, eerily evoking Jolson's signature blackface song from the 1927 film *The Jazz Singer*. This efflorescence of minstrel-show nostalgia, performed in front of City Hall, summons the ghosts of blackface to wishfully reconstruct a racially exclusive public sphere. The implicit omission of women and African Americans from the Froggy Carr sit-in is here made explicit through the reenactment of the maudlin sexism and racism of late blackface minstrelsy.

The performance of blackface or its most noxious variants (brownface, etc.) undermines the equalizing, carnivalesque potential of the Mummers Parade. But politically ambivalent mummers' performances like the sit-in of the Froggy Carr wenches can be productively understood through a rapprochement of public sphere theory and carnival theory. Thirty years after the publication of his landmark book *The Structural Transformation of the Public Sphere*, Jürgen Habermas suggested precisely such a rapprochement when he acknowledged Bakhtin's theory of carnival as an indispensible complement to his own work:

> Only after reading Mikhail Bakhtin's great book *Rabelais and His World* have my eyes become really opened to the *inner* dynamics of a plebeian culture. This culture of the common people apparently was by no means only a backdrop, that is, a passive echo of the dominant culture; it was also the periodically recurring violent revolt of a counterproject to the hierarchical world of domination, with its official celebrations and everyday disciplines. Only a stereoscopic view of this sort reveals how a mechanism of exclusion that locks out and represses at the same time calls forth countereffects that cannot be neutralized.[6]

In their 1995 sit-in, the Froggy Carr wenches refused to accept the transformation of the Mummers Parade—already a disciplined form of festivity—into an "official celebration," staged for tourists against the picturesque backdrop of Independence Hall. But through carnivalesque gender inversion, haunted by the long history of blackface associated with the mummers wench, the public constituted by Froggy Carr's performance not only posed a successful challenge to hierarchical domination but also locked out racial and gendered others from partaking in the power and revelry of licensed disorder. Viewing events like the Froggy Carr sit-in as *carnival in the public sphere* brings both the resistant and the exclusionary aspects of the performance into focus, suggesting a new model for the historiography of politically ambivalent parade performances and the (counter)publics they delimit.

DIVERSITY IN DIGITAL TIMES

To date, "Bringin' Back Those Minstrel Days" (2013) marks the nadir of racial impersonation in the twenty-first-century Mummers Parade, but the past several years have witnessed their share of insensitive parade performances. In 2015 "a member of one of the nine wench brigades held a sign reading 'Wench Lives Matter,'" an apparent satire of the Black Lives Matter movement, and "another marcher, dressed as President Obama, bore a sign that read 'Illegal Aliens Allowed.'"[7] The unabashed racism of these displays sparked both official and grassroots agitation to reform the Mummers Parade. Rue Landau, the executive director of Philadelphia's Human Relations Commission, and Leo Dignam, the city's coordinator of parade logistics, worked together to launch a new unit of the parade called the Philadelphia division, organized with the explicit goal of increasing the diversity of the Mummers Parade.[8] Meanwhile, the Taller Puertorriqueño gallery curated an exhibit called *Filadelfia: New Perspectives*, which brought together Jesse Engaard of the Rabble Rousers New Year's Brigade and Edgar Ramirez of San Mateo Carnavalero, a local carnival organization founded by immigrants from Puebla, Mexico. While delivering a gallery talk entitled "Mumming Forward: A Tradition of Inclusion," Engaard formally invited the *carnavaleros* to participate in the Mummers Parade.[9]

Both the Rabble Rousers and the Vaudevillains (the mummers group to which I belong) have been labeled "hipster mummers" and "artsier, younger brigades," a step outside the mainstream of Philadelphia mummery.[10] Engaard and Danielle Redden, the cocaptain of the Vaudevillains, have been the mummers' most vocal and visible activists for diversity, but a broad consensus to promote inclusion has recently emerged as the result of an egregious act of homophobia in the 2016 Mummers Parade. In the midst of a performance satirizing Caitlyn Jenner's gender transition—a theme that the city's director of LGBT affairs deemed "unacceptable"—a member of the Finnegan Comic Brigade shouted "fuck the gays." Nick Kurczewski of the *New York Daily News* captured the slur with his smartphone video camera and posted it to his Twitter feed, unleashing a deluge of social media commentary.[11] A few days later, the offending mummer was permanently banned from the parade, and the presidents of the five "traditional" mummers divisions issued a press release promising to "condemn any expression of hate" and to foster "awareness, sensitivity, community standards, and inclusion."[12]

Notably, the leaders of the new Philadelphia division—which includes not only the San Mateo Carnivalero but also a Puerto Rican *bomba* group, an African American drill team, and a brigade of drag queens—did not sign the press release. This lapse bespeaks the segregation of minority and LGBT mummers groups into a separate division of the parade, excluded from the collective voice of "traditional" mummery. Furthermore, the Finnegan Brigade refused to apologize for staging a transphobic parade performance, which featured a placard juxtaposing an image of Olympic decathlete Bruce Jenner from a Wheaties cereal box with a mockup of Caitlyn Jenner adorning a box of Froot Loops.[13] Finnegan's captain, Michael J. Inemer Sr., expressed regret for the "gross and disturbing" slur shouted by one of his members but defended the rest of the performance as harmless parody. "Folks need to lighten up," he said.[14] For Finnegan and many other mummers brigades, sensitivity is an unfinished project. But a large contingent of mummers from the Murray Comic Club (the Vaudevillains' parent organization) marched in the Philadelphia Pride Parade in June 2016—a sign of growing awareness among mummers of the need to embrace diversity.

Whether this embrace is tactical or sincere, pressure will continue to mount on the mummers to police offensive material as digital recordings of the parade by street-side spectators immediately expose the mummers' most bigoted performances on social media. This *sousveillance*, or "citizen undersight," of the Mummers Parade could pose as much of a risk to the mummers' tradition of licensed parody as state and corporate *surveillance*, or oversight, of the content of the mummers' performances.[15] When the Rabble Rousers staged an irreverent critique of Comcast, the largest corporation in Philadelphia, in the 2015 Mummers Parade, the live coverage on local television station PHL17 "cut away, and stayed away."[16] Both the online shaming of offensive parade performances and the television censorship of anticorporate satire have the potential to erode what Kirlin, of Froggy Carr, calls the mummers' "right to mock."[17] In practice, the Froggy

Carr wenches, the Ferko String Band, the Finnegan Comic Brigade, and many other mummers clubs, through racial, gendered, ethnic, and LGBT impersonation, exclude large groups of citizens from the public sphere constituted by the parade. The challenge for the future of the Mummers Parade is to protect the right to mock while also extending the right to participate, so that anyone who wishes may join in the equalizing laughter of Philadelphia's carnivalesque celebration of the New Year.

PERFORMANCE IN PLACE

To understand and intervene in the Mummers Parade requires attention to local haunts, in both senses of the term. Like Center Square and South Philadelphia, the neighborhood around Independence Hall—where Froggy Carr staged a sit-in—is a haunted place, a place that lights up the bodies that pass through it with flashes of the past. Today, Independence Hall is a monument, a revered symbol of liberty in the national imagination—but it was not always thus. Charlene Mires argues that the building's Georgian architecture "worked against its emergence as a national symbol" until well into the nineteenth century.[18] After hosting various iterations of the Continental Congress from 1775 through 1787, Independence Hall served as Pennsylvania's capitol building until the state government decamped to Lancaster in 1799. In the 1790s, the neighborhood south of the hall emerged as the center of Philadelphia's black community—a position it maintained until the 1950s, when the area was redeveloped and gentrified into the "ritzy neighborhood" that Kirlin complains about in *Strut*. In the early nineteenth century, artist and collector Charles Willson Peale lamented the decline of the square in front of Independence Hall into "vice and indecorum," and the state government allowed him to move his museum into the building in hopes that visitors drawn to Peale's exhibits would revitalize the neighborhood.[19] From 1802 to 1827, Peale displayed a Linnaean history of man in Independence Hall, with portraits and life-size wax figures arranged in a strict racial hierarchy.[20] As recounted in chapter 3, a series of prints based on Edward Williams Clay's *Life in Philadelphia* ended up on display at Independence Hall in 1911—another derogatory representation of racial "types" in the building now claimed as the birthplace of the nation.

On New Year's Day 1876, five months before the massive Centennial Exhibition opened in Philadelphia, a motley assortment of masqueraders staged a proto–Mummers Parade terminating at Independence Hall. As recounted in the *Philadelphia Public Ledger*,

The Fantasticals . . . were out in force during the whole day and caused much boisterous amusement. Indians and squaws, princes and princesses, clowns, columbines, and harlequins . . . Negroes of the minstrel hall type, Chinese and burlesque Dutchmen, bears, apes, and other animals promenaded the streets to the music of the calethumpian cowbell or the more dignified brass bands, and kept up the racket until late at night. Independence Hall was the grand objective for them all, and the old building received many a cheer and serenade, both burlesque and serious. In the middle of the day, several of these parties united in one grand parade and made quite a striking display.[21]

In this passage, street performances replete with racial impersonations borrowed from the nineteenth-century stage recall the visual practices of racialization on display inside Independence Hall over the course of the nineteenth and early twentieth centuries. Here again, print, performance, and visual culture animate each other in a discrete, haunted place, blurring the distinction between the archive and the repertoire and unsettling the progressive time of performance genealogy.

Throughout this book, I try to show that communing with local ghosts like those at Independence Hall need not preclude broader historical concerns. As Brian Connolly argues, "the desire for ever larger geographical scales as arbiters of historical truth" can lead to uncritical universalism unless local knowledge subtends and challenges the practice of transnational, oceanic, hemispheric, and global historiography.[22] By this logic, recovering the orientalism of eighteenth- and nineteenth-century blackface masking contributes not only to scholarship on the minstrel show but also to a critique of "the Atlantic" as an historical model—a critique that acknowledges cultural and economic relations beyond the shores of Europe, the Americas, and West Africa as immanent to *intra*-Atlantic constructions of race. Secreted in dance steps and costume pieces, caricatures and photographs, play texts and masks, the specters of racial impersonation that haunt Philadelphia produce effects radiating outward to geographies and genealogies far beyond the City of Brotherly Love. Passing through the wormhole of the local into a reconfigured understanding of the global, the historiography of performance *in place* affords a glimpse of unexpected affinities across media, across bodies, and across time—lost connections that haunt the present, flashing up at moments of danger from the threshold of invisibility.

Notes

CHAPTER ONE

Epigraph: Michel de Certeau, *The Practice of Everyday Life*, trans. Steven Rendall (Berkeley: University of California Press, 1984), 108.

1. Jill Lane and Marcial Godoy-Anativia, introduction to "Race and Its Others," special issue of *e-misférica* 5.2 (2008), http://www.emisferica.org

2. Howard Pyle, "Christmas-Time Two Hundred Years Ago: Fragments from the Diary of Richard Pennyworth, Esq.," *Harper's Weekly*, December 9, 1882, 780.

3. Christopher Marshall, qtd. in Charles E. Welch Jr., *Oh! Dem Golden Slippers: The Story of the Philadelphia Mummers*, rev. ed. (Philadelphia: Book Street Press, 1991), 22–23.

4. Natalie Zemon Davis, *Society and Culture in Early Modern France* (Stanford, CA: Stanford University Press, 1975), 124–51.

5. Bryan Palmer, "Discordant Music: *Charivaris* and Whitecapping in Nineteenth-Century North America," *Labour/LeTravailleur* 3 (1978): 5–62.

6. Dale Cockrell, *Demons of Disorder: Early Blackface Minstrels and Their World* (Cambridge: Cambridge University Press, 1997), 52.

7. Robert C. Toll, *Blacking Up: The Minstrel Show in Nineteenth-Century America* (New York: Oxford University Press, 1974); Eric Lott, *Love and Theft: Blackface Minstrelsy and the American Working Class* (New York: Oxford University Press, 1993); David R. Roediger, *The Wages of Whiteness: Race and the Making of the American Working Class*, rev. ed. (London: Verso, 2007).

8. *Pennsylvania Gazette*, December 29, 1827, qtd. in Alfred L. Shoemaker, *Christmas in Pennsylvania: A Folk-Cultural Study* (1959; repr., Mechanicsburg, PA: Stackpole Books, 1999), 77–78. On the etymology of the term *belsnickling*, see Stephen Nissenbaum, *The Battle for Christmas* (New York: Alfred A. Knopf, 1996), 99.

9. Nissenbaum, *Battle for Christmas*, 100, 102.

10. *Philadelphia Sunday Dispatch*, December 27, 1857, qtd. in Shoemaker, *Christmas in Pennsylvania*, 4.

11. Claire Sponsler, *Ritual Imports: Performing Medieval Drama in America* (Ithaca, NY: Cornell University Press, 2004), 85–86.

12. Samuel Breck, *Recollections of Samuel Breck, with Passages from His Note-Books, 1771–1862*, ed. H. E. Scudder (Philadelphia, 1877), 35–36.

13. Herbert Halpert, "A Typology of Mumming," in *Christmas Mumming in*

Newfoundland: Essays in Anthropology, Folklore, and History, ed. Herbert Halpert and G. M. Story (Toronto: University of Toronto Press, 1990), 57.

14. J. Thomas Scharf and Thompson Westcott, *History of Philadelphia, 1609–1884* (Philadelphia, 1884), 2:935.

15. Susan G. Davis, "'Making Night Hideous': Christmas Revelry and Public Order in Nineteenth-Century Philadelphia," *American Quarterly* 34.2 (1982): 185.

16. Susan G. Davis, *Parades and Power: Street Theatre in Nineteenth-Century Philadelphia* (Philadelphia: Temple University Press, 1986), 110.

17. S. Davis, "Making Night Hideous," 196. Until 1854 the borders of the city of Philadelphia extended from the Delaware River in the east to the Schuylkill River in the west and from Vine Street in the north to Cedar Street (later renamed South Street) in the south—an area of about three square miles. The Act of Consolidation, passed by the state legislature in 1854, made the city and county of Philadelphia coterminous, enlarging the size of the city to over 140 square miles.

18. "First Day of the New Century," *Philadelphia Public Ledger*, January 2, 1901, in T. Dinote, "Mummers Parade Scrapbook: 1901 to 1929," n.p., Philadelphia Mummers Museum.

19. I draw these statistics from a review of the coverage of the Mummers Parade in the *Philadelphia Daily News* from 1984 to 2015.

20. The fancy brigades' performances are judged indoors at the Pennsylvania Convention Center, although they also parade on Broad Street with the other mummers divisions.

21. Maria Panaritis, "With a New Division, Mummers Embrace Diversity," *Philadelphia Inquirer*, December 28, 2015, www.philly.com

22. Ron Goldwyn, "Top Drill Team Answers Call to Glory," *Philadelphia Daily News*, December 24, 1984, 6.

23. Deborah Wong, *Speak It Louder: Asian Americans Making Music* (New York: Routledge, 2004), 53–68.

24. Sonja Trauss, qtd. in Christian DuComb, "The Wenches of the Philadelphia Mummers Parade: A Performance Genealogy," in *Performing Utopia*, ed. Rachel Bowditch and Pegge Vissicaro (London: Seagull Books, 2017), 182.

25. Jared Brown, *The Theatre in America during the Revolution* (Cambridge: Cambridge University Press, 1995), 51.

26. Charles A. Poulson, collector, "Durang's History of the Philadelphia Stage Scrapbook, 1854–1863," 1:18, Library Company of Philadelphia.

27. "Champions by Year," Philadelphia Mummers Fancy Brigade Association, http://www.fancybrigade.com/fancy_brigades/champions.php. Although the first Philadelphia Mummers Parade took place in 1901, city-sponsored prizes were not awarded to the fancy brigade division until 1950.

28. "2013 Results," Mummers.com, http://Mummers.com/2013-results

29. Joseph Roach, *Cities of the Dead: Circum-Atlantic Performance* (New York: Columbia University Press, 1996); W. T. Lhamon Jr., *Raising Cain: Blackface Performance from Jim Crow to Hip Hop* (Cambridge, MA: Harvard University Press, 1998).

30. Shannon Steen, *Racial Geometries of the Black Atlantic, Asian Pacific, and*

American Theatre (Basingstoke, UK: Palgrave Macmillan, 2010), 33. Steen and a number of other scholars have fruitfully explored the coarticulation of blackness and Asianness in twentieth- and twenty-first-century performances of racial impersonation. For example, see the essays by Steen, Deborah Elizabeth Whaley, Mita Banerjee, and Cathy Covell Waegner in Heike Raphael-Hernandez and Shannon Steen, eds., *AfroAsian Encounters: Culture, History, Politics* (New York: New York University Press, 2006).

31. Roach, *Cities of the Dead*, 5.

32. Ibid., 122.

33. Ibid., 190.

34. John Kuo Wei Tchen, *New York before Chinatown: Orientalism and the Shaping of American Culture, 1776–1882* (Baltimore: Johns Hopkins University Press, 1999), xvi.

35. Marc Friedlaender and L. H. Butterfield, eds., *Diary of Charles Francis Adams: November 1834–June 1836* (Cambridge, MA: Belknap Press of Harvard University Press, 1974), 6:9.

36. Elizabeth Bisland, *The Life and Letters of Lafcadio Hearn* (Boston: Houghton Mifflin, 1906), 452.

37. Henry James, *The American Scene* (1907; repr., Bloomington: Indiana University Press, 1968), 280, 282, 286.

38. William Penn, Pennsylvania Charter of Privileges (1701), Constitution Society, http://www.constitution.org/bcp/penncharpriv.htm

39. Steven Conn, *Metropolitan Philadelphia: Living with the Presence of the Past* (Philadelphia: University of Pennsylvania Press, 2006), 37.

40. An Act for the Gradual Abolition of Slavery, 1780, in *The Avalon Project: Documents in Law, History, and Diplomacy*, http://avalon.law.yale.edu/18th_century/pennst01.asp

41. Gary B. Nash, *Forging Freedom: The Formation of Philadelphia's Black Community, 1720–1840* (Cambridge, MA: Harvard University Press, 1988), 2.

42. Joseph Sturge, *A Visit to the United States in 1841* (London, 1842), 40.

43. Phillip Lapsansky, "Graphic Discord: Abolitionist and Antiabolitionist Images," in *The Abolitionist Sisterhood: Women's Political Culture in Antebellum America*, ed. Jean Fagan Yellin and John C. Van Horne (Ithaca, NY: Cornell University Press, 1994), 220.

44. Scharf and Westcott, *History of Philadelphia*, 2:1090.

45. Ibid., 3:2199. This omnibus preceded by over three decades the introduction of segregated "Jim Crow cars" on some of Philadelphia's streetcar lines. On the Civil War–era struggle to make Philadelphia's streetcars accessible to black passengers, see Daniel R. Biddle and Murray Dubin, *Tasting Freedom: Octavius Catto and the Battle for Equality in Civil War America* (Philadelphia: Temple University Press, 2010), 323–54.

46. Edward William Clay, *Mr. T Rice as the Original Jim Crow* (New York, ca. 1830), Lester S. Levy Collection of Sheet Music, Johns Hopkins University Library, http://levysheetmusic.mse.jhu.edu

47. Walnut Street Theater Playbills, January 1, 1835, and September 2, 1835, Harvard Theatre Collection.

48. S. Davis, *Parades and Power*, 77. Cf. Raymond Williams, "The Press and

Popular Culture: An Historical Perspective," in *Newspaper History from the Seventeenth Century to the Present Day*, ed. George Boyce, James Curran, and Pauline Wingate (London: Constable, 1978), 41–50.

49. Diana Taylor, *The Archive and the Repertoire: Performing Cultural Memory in the Americas* (Durham, NC: Duke University Press, 2003), 19.

50. Ibid., 20.

51. Ibid., xvii.

52. Ibid., 20.

53. Ibid., 19, 36–37.

54. Michel Foucault, "Nietzsche, Genealogy, History," in *Language, Counter-Memory, Practice: Selected Essays and Interviews*, trans. Donald F. Bouchard and Sherry Simon (Ithaca, NY: Cornell University Press, 1977), 142.

55. Ibid., 148.

56. Roach, *Cities of the Dead*, 25.

57. Frank Dougherty and Ron Goldwyn, "Anatomy of a Mummer: Yo, Wench!," *Philadelphia Daily News*, December 30, 1994, M8.

58. Donald F. Bouchard, preface to Foucault, *Language, Counter-Memory, Practice*, 9.

59. Roach, *Cities of the Dead*, 26.

60. Welch, *Oh! Dem Golden Slippers*; Andrea Ignatoff Rothberg, "Philadelphia Mummery: Individual Rewards and Social Interaction" (PhD diss., University of Wisconsin–Madison, 1980); Patricia Anne Masters, *The Philadelphia Mummers: Building Community through Play* (Philadelphia: Temple University Press, 2007); E. A. Kennedy III, *Life, Liberty, and the Mummers* (Philadelphia: Temple University Press, 2007); Corey Elizabeth Leighton, "Strutting It up through Histories: A Performance Genealogy of the Philadelphia Mummers Parade" (PhD diss., Louisiana State University, 2009).

61. Ron Goldwyn, "Mummers Folk Art Struts into City Hall," *Philadelphia Daily News*, December 17, 1987, 6.

62. "Mummers Pictures Rejected," *New York Times*, December 31, 1987, http://www.nytimes.com

63. Qtd. in Tommie St. Hill, "Blackface Mummers Display in City Hall Angers Officials," *Philadelphia Tribune*, December 29, 1987, 1.

64. James Conroy, letter, *Philadelphia Tribune*, January 22, 1988, 10A.

65. Robin Wagner-Pacifici, *Discourse and Destruction: The City of Philadelphia versus MOVE* (Chicago: University of Chicago Press, 1994), 16–17.

66. Sonia Sanchez, "elegy (for MOVE and Philadelphia)," in *Under a Soprano Sky* (Trenton, NJ: Africa World Press, 1987), 14.

67. Norma T. Gwynn, Patrice LaJeunesse, and Marian Locks, et. al., letter, *Philadelphia Tribune*, January 5, 1988, 6.

68. Mark Bricklin, "Mummers Parade Minstrels Can Paint Faces Any Color but Black," *Philadelphia Tribune*, December 28, 1963, 3.

69. Welch, *Oh! Dem Golden Slippers*, 154.

70. Leighton, "Strutting It up through Histories," 52.

71. Richard Schechner, *Between Theater and Anthropology* (Philadelphia: University of Pennsylvania Press, 1985), 123. Schechner argues that "all effective performances" take place "in the field between a negative and a double nega-

tive, a field of limitless potential, free as it is from both the person (not) and the person impersonated (not not)." I agree, although I would add that the "limitless potential" at the threshold between "not" and "not not" can turn sinister when impersonation (i.e., "acting" in the broadest sense) verges into *racial* impersonation.

72. Leighton, "Strutting It up through Histories," 75.

73. Walter Benjamin, "Little History of Photography" (1931), in *Walter Benjamin: Selected Writings*, trans. Rodney Livingstone (Cambridge, MA: Belknap Press of Harvard University Press, 1999), 2:510–12.

74. Avery F. Gordon, *Ghostly Matters: Haunting and the Sociological Imagination* (Minneapolis: University of Minnesota Press, 1997), 6–7.

75. Herbert Blau, *Take Up the Bodies: Theater at the Vanishing Point* (Urbana: University of Illinois Press, 1982), 281, 204.

76. Marvin Carlson, *The Haunted Stage: The Theatre as Memory Machine* (Ann Arbor: University of Michigan Press, 2001).

77. Alice Rayner, *Ghosts: Death's Double and the Phenomena of Theatre* (Minneapolis: University of Minnesota Press, 2006), xvii.

78. Peggy Phelan, *Unmarked: The Politics of Performance* (London: Routledge, 1993), 146; Rebecca Schneider, *Performing Remains: Art and War in Times of Theatrical Reenactment* (London: Routledge, 2011), 101–2.

79. Rayner, *Ghosts*, 61.

80. Schneider, *Performing Remains*, 141.

81. William Penn, qtd. in Scharf and Westcott, *History of Philadelphia*, 3:1773.

82. Ibid., 3:1773.

83. Allen M. Hornblum and George J. Holmes, *Philadelphia's City Hall* (Mt. Pleasant, SC: Arcadia, 2003), 8.

84. S. Davis, *Parades and Power*, 27.

85. Scharf and Westcott, *History of Philadelphia*, 3:1842–44.

86. S. Davis, *Parades and Power*, 27–32.

87. Roland Barthes, "Semiology and the Urban" (1967), in *Rethinking Architecture: A Reader in Cultural Theory*, ed. Neil Leach (London: Routledge, 1997), 169, 171.

88. Robert Wharton, qtd. in Scharf and Westcott, *History of Philadelphia*, 3:1844.

89. Ibid., 3:1844.

90. William Rogers, qtd. in David Waldstreicher, *In the Midst of Perpetual Fetes: The Making of American Nationalism, 1776–1820* (Chapel Hill: University of North Carolina Press, 1997), 311.

91. Ibid., 314.

92. S. Davis, *Parades and Power*, 46.

93. *New York Evening Post*, July 12, 1804, qtd. in Nash, *Forging Freedom*, 176.

94. Nash, *Forging Freedom*, 176–77. On the history of the Pennsylvania Abolition Society in the context of the U.S. abolitionist movement, see Richard S. Newman, *The Transformation of American Abolitionism: Fighting Slavery in the Early Republic* (Chapel Hill: University of North Carolina Press, 2002).

95. Absalom Jones, "A Thanksgiving Sermon" (1808), in *Lift Every Voice: African American Oratory, 1787–1900*, ed. Philip S. Foner and Robert J. Branham

(Tuscaloosa: University of Alabama Press, 1998), 79; Nash, *Forging Freedom*, 189. A similar, black celebration of New Year's Day occurred in New York City, but African Americans in Boston tended to commemorate emancipation on July 14.

96. James Forten, *A Series of Letters by a Man of Color* (1813), in *A Documentary History of the Negro People in the United States*, ed. Herbert Aptheker (New York: Carol, 1990), 1:64.

97. John Lewis Krimmel, compositional sketches for *Return from Market*, in "Sketchbooks, 1809–1821," 6:3, 5, Winterthur Library.

98. Anneliese Harding, *John Lewis Krimmel: Genre Artist of the Early Republic* (Winterthur, DE: Winterthur Museum, 1994), 222–23.

99. Al Heller, qtd. in Masters, *Philadelphia Mummers*, 108.

100. Miriam Hill, Melissa Dribben, and Troy Graham, "Police Clear Occupy Encampment, 52 Arrested," *Philadelphia Inquirer*, November 30, 2011, http://www.philly.com

101. W. J. T. Mitchell, "Image, Space, Revolution: The Arts of Occupation," *Critical Inquiry* 39.1 (Autumn 2012): 9–10.

102. Hill, Dribben, and Graham, "Police Clear Occupy Encampment."

103. Ibid.

104. Barthes, "Semiology and the Urban," 171.

105. Jack Walsh, qtd. in Masters, *Philadelphia Mummers*, 107. Eddie Cantor made his Broadway debut in 1917 as a blackface comedian in the Ziegfeld Follies, playing opposite the Afro-Caribbean actor Bert Williams. Jimmy Durante also performed in blackface, most notably in the 1934 film *George White's Scandals*. See Camille F. Forbes, *Introducing Bert Williams: Burnt Cork, Broadway, and the Story of America's First Black Star* (New York: Basic Civitas, 2008), 272–73; and David Bakish, *Jimmy Durante: His Show Business Career* (Jefferson, NC: McFarland, 2007), 79.

106. Roach, *Cities of the Dead*, 224–25.

107. "2010 Orleans Parish Parade Rankings," *Carnival New Orleans News* (blog), http://blog.carnivalneworleans.com

108. Roach, *Cities of the Dead*, 231–32.

109. Rosemarie K. Bank, *Theatre Culture in America, 1825–1860* (Cambridge: Cambridge University Press, 1997), 2.

110. De Certeau, *Practice of Everyday Life*, 108.

111. Tere O'Connor, "500 Words," *Artforum*, September 23, 2008, http://artforum.com/words/id=21170

CHAPTER TWO

1. John André, "Particulars of the Mischianza Exhibited in America at the Departure of Gen. Howe," *Gentlemen's Magazine*, August 1778, 356. André wrote another, slightly different account of the Meschianza in a manuscript entitled "The Mischianza, Humbly Inscribed to Miss Peggy Chew" and published over one hundred years later in Sophie Howard Ward, "Major André's Story of the Mischianza: From the Unpublished Manuscript," *Century: A Popular Quarterly*, March 1894, 684–91. These and other contemporary descriptions

of the Meschianza use a variety of spellings (Meschianza, Mischianza, Misquianza, etc.), which I have standardized to *Meschianza* in this chapter. In addition to André, four other British officers—Sir John Wrottesley, Sir Henry Calder, Colonel Charles O'Hara, and Captain John Montresor—helped to organize the Meschianza, though André was the only one to leave written accounts of the event.

2. John Fanning Watson, *Annals of Philadelphia and Pennsylvania, in the Olden Time* (Philadelphia, 1850), 300, Library Company of Philadelphia.

3. André, "Particulars of the Mischianza," 354.

4. André, qtd. in Ward, "Major André's Story," 688.

5. Paul Engle, *Women in the American Revolution* (Chicago: Follett, 1976), 116.

6. J. Thomas Scharf and Thompson Westcott, *History of Philadelphia, 1609–1884* (Philadelphia, 1884), 2:898.

7. *Pennsylvania Gazette*, May 23, 1778, n.p. For a comprehensive history of the British occupation of Philadelphia, see John W. Jackson, *With the British Army in Philadelphia, 1777–1778* (San Rafael, CA: Presidio Press, 1979).

8. Israel Mauduit, *Strictures on the Philadelphia Mischianza, or, Triumph upon Leaving America Unconquered* (London, 1779); Joseph Galloway, *Letters to a Nobleman on the Conduct of the War in the Middle Colonies* (London, 1779), 37.

9. Elaine Forman Crane, ed., *The Diary of Elizabeth Drinker* (Boston: Northeastern University Press, 1991), 1:306; "Extracts from the Letter-Books of Captain Johann Heinrichs of the Hessian Jager Corps, 1778–1780," *Pennsylvania Magazine of History and Biography* 22.2 (1898): 139.

10. William Dunlap, *André*, in *Early American Drama*, ed. Jeffrey H. Richards (New York: Penguin, 1997), 61; the quotation is from Richards's introductory remarks on the play.

11. Charles A. Poulson, collector, "Durang's History of the Philadelphia Stage Scrapbook, 1854–1863," 1:17, Library Company of Philadelphia.

12. On the theater seasons in Boston (1775–76), New York (1777), and Philadelphia (1778) during General Howe's North American campaign, see Jared Brown, *The Theatre in America during the Revolution* (Cambridge: Cambridge University Press, 1995), 22–50.

13. Peter A. Davis, "Puritan Mercantilism and the Politics of Anti-theatrical Legislation in Colonial America," in *The American Stage: Social and Economic Issues from the Colonial Period to the Present*, ed. Ron Engle and Tice L. Miller (Cambridge: Cambridge University Press, 1993), 26.

14. *Journals of the Continental Congress*, October 20, 1774, in *A Century of Lawmaking for a New Nation: U.S. Congressional Documents and Debates, 1774–1875*, American Memory, Library of Congress, http://memory.loc.gov/cgi-bin/query/r?ammem/hlaw:@field(DOCID+@lit(jc00137)).

15. Constitution of Pennsylvania, September 28, 1776, in *The Avalon Project: Documents in Law, History, and Diplomacy*, http://avalon.law.yale.edu/18th_century/pa08.asp#1

16. David S. Shields and Fredrika J. Teute, "The Meschianza: Sum of All Fêtes," *Journal of the Early Republic* 35 (Summer 2015): 190, 199.

17. Ibid., 192.

18. My research has uncovered little specific information on the dancing at the Meschianza, although Kate Van Winkle Keller speculates that some of the dances collected by Hezekiah Cantelo in his *Twenty-Four American Country Dances* (London, 1785) may have been performed at the event. See Kate Van Winkle Keller, "Hezekiah Cantelo, an Eighteenth-Century Dance Collector in British-Occupied New York," in *Vistas of American Music*, ed. Susan L. Porter and John Graziano (Warren, MI: Harmonie Park Press, 1999), 19–38.

19. André, "Particulars of the Mischianza," 354.

20. André, qtd. in Ward, "Major André's Story," 689.

21. Ibid., 688–89.

22. Terry Castle, *Masquerade and Civilization: The Carnivalesque in Eighteenth-Century English Culture and Fiction* (Stanford, CA: Stanford University Press, 1986), 60.

23. Aileen Ribeiro, *Dress in Eighteenth-Century Europe, 1715–1789*, rev. ed. (New Haven, CT: Yale University Press, 2002), 259.

24. Daniel O'Quinn, "Diversionary Tactics and Coercive Acts: John Burgoyne's *Fête Champêtre*," *Studies in Eighteenth-Century Culture* 40 (2010): 133–55.

25. John Burgoyne, *The Maid of the Oaks: A New Dramatic Entertainment as It Is Performed at the Theater Royal, Drury Lane* (Dublin, 1775).

26. Edward W. Said, *Orientalism* (1978; repr., New York: Penguin, 2003), 3, 122.

27. On Burgoyne's legislative activities, see Gerald Howson, *Burgoyne of Saratoga: A Biography* (New York: Times Books, 1979), 59–61.

28. Daniel O'Quinn, "Theatre and Empire," in *The Cambridge Companion to British Theatre, 1730–1830*, ed. Jane Moody and Daniel O'Quinn (Cambridge: Cambridge University Press, 2007), 233.

29. Linda Colley, *Britons: Forging the Nation, 1707–1837* (New Haven, CT: Yale University Press, 1992), 147–48.

30. André, "Particulars of the Mischianza," 355.

31. Randall Fuller, "Theaters of the American Revolution: The Valley Forge *Cato* and the Meschianza in their Transcultural Contexts," *Early American Literature* 34.2 (1999): 141.

32. John W. Jordan, ed., *Colonial and Revolutionary Families of Pennsylvania* (Baltimore: Clearfield, 2004), 511–12.

33. Alexander Garden, *Anecdotes of the Revolutionary War in America, with Sketches of Character of Persons the Most Distinguished, in the Southern States, for Civil and Military Services* (Charleston, SC, 1822), 413.

34. Engle, *Women in the American Revolution*, 122–27.

35. "Some Account of the Meschianza, by One of the Company," in "Accounts of Theatrical Performances for the Entertainment of British Soldiers during the Revolution, 1775–1780," n.p., Historical Society of Pennsylvania.

36. Ernst Kipping, ed. and trans., *At General Howe's Side, 1776–1778: The Diary of General William Howe's Aide de Camp, Captain Friedrich von Muenchhausen* (Monmouth Beach, NJ: Philip Freneau, 1974), 52.

37. Hannah Griffitts, "Meschianza: Answer to the Question: 'What Is It?' by a Lady of Philada," in Watson, *Annals of Philadelphia*, n.p., Library Company of Philadelphia.

38. Robert B. Winans, "Bibliography and the Cultural Historian: Notes on the Eighteenth-Century Novel," in *Printing and Society in Early America*, ed. William L. Joyce et. al. (Worcester, MA: American Antiquarian Society, 1983), 178.

39. Ronald Paulson, *Don Quixote in England: The Aesthetics of Laughter* (Baltimore: Johns Hopkins University Press, 1998), 41.

40. Sarah F. Wood, *Quixotic Fictions of the USA, 1792–1815* (Oxford: Oxford University Press, 2005), 43.

41. Miguel de Cervantes Saavedra, *The History and Adventures of the Renowned Don Quixote*, trans. Tobias Smollett, ed. Martin C. Battestin and O. M. Brack Jr. (1755; repr., Athens: University of Georgia Press, 2003), 27, 30. Citations are to Smollett's translation of *Don Quixote*, except where otherwise noted, because it was the most popular version of Cervantes's novel among English-language readers in the early United States. Further references to this edition are cited parenthetically.

42. William Childers, *Transnational Cervantes* (Toronto: University of Toronto Press, 2006), 33.

43. Miguel de Cervantes Saavedra, *El ingenioso hidalgo Don Quijote de la Mancha*, ed. Florencio Sevilla Arroyo (1605; repr., Barcelona: Lunwerg Editores, 2004), 133, 49. The translations from this edition are my own. Smollett incorrectly translates "morisco aljamiado" as "Potugeze Moor" (66).

44. Cervantes, *Don Quijote*, ed. Arroyo, 258. For a detailed analysis of racial hybridity as an aspect of the narrative structure of *Don Quixote*, see María Rosa Menocal, *The Ornament of the World: How Muslims, Jews, and Christians Created a Culture of Tolerance in Medieval Spain* (Boston: Little, Brown, 2002), 253–65.

45. Shields and Teute, "The Meschianza," 190.

46. Homi K. Bhabha, *The Location of Culture* (1991; repr., London: Routledge, 2004), 122.

47. André, "Particulars of the Mischianza," 356.

48. Jackson, *With the British Army*, 248.

49. Bernhard A. Uhlendorf and Edna Vosper, eds. and trans., "Letters of Major Baurmeister during the Philadelphia Campaign, 1777–1778, III," *Pennsylvania Magazine of History and Biography* 60.2 (1936): 180.

50. André, "Particulars of the Mischianza," 356.

51. André, qtd. in Ward, "Major André's Story," 691.

52. *Royal Pennsylvania Gazette*, May 26, 1778, 3.

53. André, qtd. in Ward, "Major André's Story," 691; *Royal Pennsylvania Gazette*, May 26, 1778, 3.

54. André, "Particulars of the Mischianza," 356.

55. Thomas Postlewait and Tracy C. Davis, "Theatricality: An Introduction," in *Theatricality* (Cambridge: Cambridge University Press, 2003), 30.

56. Greg Dening, *Performances* (Chicago: University of Chicago Press, 1996), 105.

57. Odai Johnson, "What Never Happened," plenary paper, annual conference of the American Society for Theatre Research, Nashville, TN, November 2, 2012.

58. Gary B. Nash, *First City: Philadelphia and the Forging of Historical Memory* (Philadelphia: University of Pennsylvania Press, 2002), 99.

59. Monica L. Miller, *Slaves to Fashion: Black Dandyism and the Styling of Black Diasporic Identity* (Durham, NC: Duke University Press, 2009), 6, 49.

60. *Tatler*, November 2, 1710, qtd. in ibid., 52. As Miller notes, this letter was probably "a satirical, ghostwritten gesture" by Richard Steele, the editor of the *Tatler*.

61. Ibid., 50.

62. Gary B. Nash, *Forging Freedom: The Formation of Philadelphia's Black Community, 1720–1840* (Cambridge, MA: Harvard University Press, 1988), 11.

63. Ibid., 44.

64. John Murray, Earl of Dunmore, "A Proclamation," 1775, Black Loyalist Heritage Society, http://www.blackloyalist.com.

65. Nash, *Forging Freedom*, 55.

66. Lady Mary Wortley Montagu to Lady Mar, Constantinople, April 1, 1717, in *Embassy to Constantinople: The Travels of Lady Mary Wortley Montagu*, ed. Christopher Pick (New York: New Amsterdam, 1988), 108, 111.

67. Shields and Teute, "The Meschianza," 198.

68. Francis B. Lee, ed., *Documents Relating to the Revolutionary History of the State of New Jersey* (Trenton, NJ: John L. Murphy, 1903), 2:157.

69. Anthony Wayne to Richard Peters, Paramus, NJ, July 12, 1778, in Charles J. Stillé, *Major-General Anthony Wayne and the Pennsylvania Line in the Continental Army* (Philadelphia, 1893), 153–54.

70. Ruth H. Bloch, "The Gendered Meanings of Virtue in Revolutionary America," *Signs: Journal of Women in Culture and Society* 13.1 (1987): 37–38, 41, 44–45.

71. André, qtd. in Ward, "Major André's Story," 690.

72. Kate Haulman, *The Politics of Fashion in Eighteenth-Century America* (Chapel Hill: University of North Carolina Press, 2011), 174.

73. Bloch, "Gendered Meanings of Virtue," 45.

74. Joseph Reed to Nathanael Greene, Philadelphia, November 5, 1778, in Charles Lee, *The Lee Papers*, vol. 3, *1778–1782* (New York: New York Historical Society, 1873), 252.

75. Drinker, in Crane, *Diary of Elizabeth Drinker*, 1:314.

76. Richard Henry Lee to Francis Lightfoot Lee, Philadelphia, July 5, 1778, in *Letters of Delegates to Congress, 1774–1789*, ed. Paul H. Smith (Washington, DC: Library of Congress, 1976), 10:224; Garden, *Anecdotes of the Revolutionary War*, 413.

77. Josiah Bartlett to Mary Bartlett, Philadelphia, August 24, 1778, in Smith, *Letters of Delegates*, 10:496.

78. Susan E. Klepp, "Rough Music on Independence Day: Philadelphia, 1778," in *Riot and Revelry in Early America*, ed. William Pencak, Matthew Dennis, and Simon P. Newman (University Park: Pennsylvania State University Press, 2002), 169.

79. Ibid., 165.

80. E. P. Thompson, *Customs in Common* (New York: New Press, 1991), 467.

81. Dale Cockrell, *Demons of Disorder: Early Blackface Minstrels and Their World* (Cambridge: Cambridge University Press, 1997), 52; John Emigh, email to author, June 7, 2010.

82. *Pennsylvania Packet*, August 22, 1778, qtd. in Frank Moore, *Diary of the*

American Revolution from Newspapers and Original Documents (New York, 1863), 2:87.

83. Lemuel Clift, qtd. in ibid.

84. Julie Ellison, *Cato's Tears and the Making of Anglo-American Emotion* (Chicago: University of Chicago Press, 1999), 49, 162.

85. Leman Thomas Rede, *The Road to the Stage* (London, 1827), 38. On the publication history of Rede's book, see David Worrall, *Harlequin Empire: Race, Ethnicity, and the Drama of the Popular Enlightenment* (London: Pickering and Chatto, 2007), 36.

86. Heather S. Nathans, *Slavery and Sentiment on the American Stage, 1787–1861: Lifting the Veil of Black* (Cambridge: Cambridge University Press, 2009), 12.

87. W. T. Lhamon Jr., *Raising Cain: Blackface Performance from Jim Crow to Hip Hop* (Cambridge, MA: Harvard University Press, 1998), 59.

88. Nathans, *Slavery and Sentiment*, 122.

89. Miller, *Slaves to Fashion*, 28–29.

90. Nathans, *Slavery and Sentiment*, 20; Isaac Bickerstaffe, *The Padlock: A Comic Opera in Two Acts* (New York, 1825), 15.

91. Miller, *Slaves to Fashion*, 38.

92. Rede, *Road to the Stage*, 36.

93. Hans Nathan, *Dan Emmett and the Rise of Early Negro Minstrelsy* (Norman: University of Oklahoma Press, 1962), 24.

94. Charles Dibdin, *A Collection of Songs, Selected from the Works of Mr. Dibdin* (London, 1790), 4:191.

95. Nathan, *Dan Emmett*, 27.

96. Miller, *Slaves to Fashion*, 73.

97. Jenna M. Gibbs, *Performing the Temple of Liberty: Slavery, Theater, and Popular Culture in London and Philadelphia, 1760–1850* (Baltimore: Johns Hopkins University Press, 2014), 44.

98. William Dunlap, *A History of the American Theatre from Its Origins to 1832*, ed. Tice L. Miller (Urbana: University of Illinois Press, 2005), 35; Poulson, "Durang's History," 1:29. Neither Dunlap nor Durang saw Hallam's earliest performances as Mungo, though both saw him reprise the role several times before his death in 1808.

99. Felicity A. Nussbaum, "The Theatre of Empire: Racial Counterfeit, Racial Realism," in *A New Imperial History: Culture, Identity, and Modernity in Britain and the Empire, 1660–1840*, ed. Kathleen Wilson (Cambridge: Cambridge University Press, 2004), 78.

100. Nathans, *Slavery and Sentiment*, 19; Miller, *Slaves to Fashion*, 71.

101. Laurence Hutton, "The Negro on the Stage," *Harper's New Monthly Magazine*, June 1889, 132. *Louisville Public Advertiser*, October 4, 1830, qtd. in Cockrell, *Demons of Disorder*, 76.

102. Peter P. Reed, *Rogue Performances: Staging the Underclass in Early American Theatre Culture* (New York: Palgrave Macmillan, 2009), 67.

103. Susanna Rowson, *Slaves in Algiers; or, A Struggle for Freedom: A Play, Interspersed with Songs, in Three Acts*, in *Plays by Early American Women, 1775–1850*, ed. Amelia Howe Kritzer (Ann Arbor: University of Michigan Press, 1995), 56–57. Further references cited parenthetically.

104. Winans, "Bibliography and the Cultural Historian," 174–85.

105. Wood, *Quixotic Fictions,* 69. Cervantes spent five years as a slave in Algiers in the late sixteenth century, before he wrote *Don Quixote.* In an example of the complex narrative layering at work in *Don Quixote,* Cervantes slips a reference to himself—"a Spanish soldier, called such-a-one de Saavedra"—into the text of "The Captive's Tale" (287).

106. Elizabeth Maddock Dillon, "*Slaves in Algiers*: Race, Republican Genealogies, and the Global Stage," *American Literary History* 16.3 (2004): 407.

107. Childers, *Transnational Cervantes,* 40.

108. Dillon, "*Slaves in Algiers,*" 419.

109. Heather S. Nathans, "A Much Maligned People: Jews on and off the Stage in the Early American Republic," *Early American Studies* 2.2 (2004): 328.

110. Gay Gibson Cima, *Early American Woman Critics: Performance, Religion, Race* (Cambridge: Cambridge University Press, 2006), 152–53.

111. Poulson, "Durang's History," 1:60. Durang fils doesn't date Rowson's sailor act, but it most likely featured in the repertoire of Ricketts's Circus for the 1795–96 season, after which Rowson and her family moved from Philadelphia to Boston. For a history of Ricketts's Circus, see James S. Moy, "Entertainments at John B. Ricketts's Circus, 1793–1800," *Educational Theatre Journal* 30.2 (1978): 187–202.

112. Peter Linebaugh and Marcus Rediker, *The Many-Headed Hydra: Sailors, Slaves, Commoners, and the Hidden History of the Revolutionary Atlantic* (Boston: Beacon Press, 2000), 151–52.

113. Poulson, "Durang's History," 1:60.

114. Dillon, "*Slaves in Algiers,*" 408.

115. Michael Ragussis, *Theatrical Nation: Jews and Other Outlandish Englishmen in Georgian Britain* (Philadelphia: University of Pennsylvania Press, 2010), 86.

116. Rosemarie K. Bank, *Theatre Culture in America, 1825–1860* (Cambridge: Cambridge University Press, 1997), 2.

117. Jacques Derrida, *Specters of Marx: The State of the Debt, the Work of Mourning, and the New International,* trans. Peggy Kamuf (New York: Routledge, 1994), 4.

CHAPTER THREE

1. Elaine Forman Crane, ed., *The Diary of Elizabeth Drinker* (Boston: Northeastern University Press, 1991), 2:1127. I have standardized the spelling and punctuation in the quoted passage.

2. Shane White and Graham White, *Stylin': African American Expressive Culture from Its Beginnings to the Zoot Suit* (Ithaca, NY: Cornell University Press, 1998), 88.

3. John Fanning Watson, *Annals of Philadelphia: Being a Collection of Memoirs, Anecdotes, and Incidents of the City and Its Inhabitants* (Philadelphia, 1830), 479. Contrary to Watson's claim, black Philadelphians had not received their "entire exemption from slavery" in 1830, when eleven slaves still resided in the city. See Leonard P. Curry, *The Free Black in Urban America, 1800–1850: The Shadow of a Dream* (Chicago: University of Chicago Press, 1981), 247.

4. Emma Jones Lapsansky, "'Since They Got Those Separate Churches': Afro-Americans and Racism in Jacksonian Philadelphia," *American Quarterly* 32.1 (1980): 58.

5. Gary B. Nash, *Forging Freedom: The Formation of Philadelphia's Black Community, 1720–1840* (Cambridge, MA: Harvard University Press, 1988), 218–19.

6. Douglas A. Jones Jr., *The Captive Stage: Performance and the Proslavery Imagination of the Antebellum North* (Ann Arbor: University of Michigan Press, 2014), 23.

7. David Claypoole Johnston, *A Splendid Procession of Free Masons* (1819), Print Department, Boston Public Library.

8. James Thackera, *A New Mode of Perfuming and Preserveing Clothes from Moths* [sic] (Philadelphia, 1819), Historical Society of Pennsylvania. Thackera's note, which accompanies this etching, is quoted in Phillip Lapsansky, "Graphic Discord: Abolitionist and Antiabolitionist Images," in *The Abolitionist Sisterhood: Women's Political Culture in Antebellum America*, ed. Jean Fagan Yellin and John C. Van Horne (Ithaca, NY: Cornell University Press, 1994), 217–18.

9. Samuel Otter, *Philadelphia Stories: America's Literature of Race and Freedom* (New York: Oxford University Press, 2010), 82–83.

10. Edward Williams Clay, *Life in Philadelphia: "Behold Thou Art Fair, Deborah . . . ,"* plate 2 (Philadelphia, ca. 1830), Library Company of Philadelphia. Although no complete edition of *Life in Philadelphia* exists, the Library Company of Philadelphia has copies of all fourteen prints in the series, some published by William Simpson in 1828–29 and some published by Sarah Hart in 1830. Simpson issued the first edition of prints one through eleven, and Hart issued the first edition of prints twelve through fourteen as well as a reprint of the entire series from the original plates. For a detailed account of *Life in Philadelphia*'s local publication history, see Nancy Reynolds Davison, "E. W. Clay: American Political Caricaturist of the Jacksonian Era" (PhD diss., University of Michigan, 1980), 86–87.

11. Edward Williams Clay, *Life in Philadelphia: Fancy Ball*, plate 1 (Philadelphia, 1829), Library Company of Philadelphia.

12. Martha S. Jones, "Reframing the Color Line," in *Reframing the Color Line: Race and the Visual Culture of the Atlantic World* (Ann Arbor: William L. Clements Library, University of Michigan, 2009), 4.

13. Jenna M. Gibbs, *Performing the Temple of Liberty: Slavery, Theater, and Popular Culture in London and Philadelphia, 1760–1850* (Baltimore: Johns Hopkins University Press, 2014), 137.

14. E. Lapsansky, "Since They Got Those Separate Churches," 57.

15. Edward Williams Clay, *Life in Philadelphia: "Is Miss Dinah at Home?,"* plate 3 (Philadelphia, 1828), Library Company of Philadelphia.

16. Tavia Nyong'o, *The Amalgamation Waltz: Race, Performance, and the Ruses of Memory* (Minneapolis: University of Minnesota Press, 2009), 29.

17. Edward Williams Clay, *The Fruits of Amalgamation* (New York, 1839), American Antiquarian Society; Edward Williams Clay, *An Amalgamation Waltz* (New York, 1839), American Antiquarian Society.

18. Nyong'o, *Amalgamation Waltz*, 83.

19. Elise Lemire, *"Miscegenation": Making Race in America* (Philadelphia: Uni-

versity of Pennsylvania Press, 2002), 94. Descriptions of Francis Johnson quoted from Robert Waln, *The Hermit in America on a Visit to Philadelphia: Containing Some Account of the Beaux and Belles, Dandies and Coquettes, Cotillion Parties, Supper Parties &c. &c. of that Famous City* (Philadelphia, 1819), 202.

20. Lemire, "Miscegenation," 71.

21. On Dixon's premiere performance as Long Tail Blue, see the commentary in S. Foster Damon, *Series of Old American Songs, Reproduced in Facsimile from Original or Early Editions in the Harris Collection of American Poetry and Plays, Brown University* (Providence, RI: Brown University Library, 1936), n.p.

22. Barbara Lewis, "Daddy Blue: The Evolution of the Dark Daddy," in *Inside the Minstrel Mask: Readings in Nineteenth-Century Blackface Minstrelsy*, ed. Annemarie Bean, James V. Hatch, and Brooks McNamara (Hanover, NH: Wesleyan University Press, 1996), 258–59.

23. Monica L. Miller, *Slaves to Fashion: Black Dandyism and the Styling of Black Diasporic Identity* (Durham, NC: Duke University Press, 2009), 98–99.

24. "Long Tail Blue, as Sung at the Theatres" (New York, 1827), Brown University Library.

25. Eric Lott, *Love and Theft: Blackface Minstrelsy and the American Working Class* (New York: Oxford University Press, 1993), 25.

26. Davison, "E. W. Clay," 90.

27. White and White, *Stylin'*, 93–94.

28. Nyong'o, *Amalgamation Waltz*, 30.

29. Davison, "E. W. Clay," 93.

30. "Life in Philadelphia," *New Comic Annual*, 1831, 147–61.

31. Nash, *Forging Freedom*, 259.

32. W. T. Lhamon Jr., introduction to *Jump Jim Crow: Lost Plays, Lyrics, and Street Prose of the First Atlantic Popular Culture* (Cambridge, MA: Harvard University Press, 2003), 55.

33. *New York Courier and Enquirer*, qtd. in Lhamon, *Jump Jim Crow*, 19.

34. Davison, "E. W. Clay," 92.

35. Hosea Easton, *A Treatise on the Intellectual Character, and Civil and Political Position, of the Colored People of the U. States; and the Prejudice Exercised toward Them* (Boston, 1837), 41–42.

36. Julie Winch, ed., *The Elite of Our People: Joseph Willson's Sketches of Black Upper-Class Life in Antebellum Philadelphia* (University Park: Penn State University Press, 2000), 79.

37. P. Lapsansky, "Graphic Discord," 220.

38. Edward Raymond Turner, *The Negro in Pennsylvania: Slavery, Servitude, Freedom, 1639–1861* (New York: Negro Universities Press, 1969), 140–41.

39. Davison, "E. W. Clay," 60.

40. Nathaniel S. Wheaton, *Journal of a Residence during Several Months in London . . . in the Years 1823 and 1824* (Hartford, CT, 1830), 59.

41. M. Jones, "Reframing the Color Line," 5.

42. Pierce Egan, *Life in London; or, The Day and Night Scenes of Jerry Hawthorn, Esq. and His Elegant Friend Corinthian Tom, Accompanied by Bob Logic, the Oxonian, in Their Rambles and Sprees through the Metropolis* (London, 1821).

43. Jane Moody, *Illegitimate Theatre in London, 1770–1840* (Cambridge: Cambridge University Press, 2000), 110–11.

44. Tracy C. Davis, "Acting Black, 1824: Charles Mathews's *Trip to America*," *Theatre Journal* 63.2 (2011): 165.

45. Cowan's Auctions, *Spring Decorative Arts Catalog* (2006), http://www.cowanauctions.com/auctions/catalog.aspx?id=67

46. Edgar Quinet, qtd. in Elizabeth C. Childs, *Daumier and Exoticism: Satirizing the French and the Foreign* (New York: Peter Lang, 2004), 159.

47. Victor Hugo, *Les Orientales* (Paris, 1829), qtd. in ibid. (my translation).

48. W. T. Lhamon Jr., *Raising Cain: Blackface Performance from Jim Crow to Hip Hop* (Cambridge, MA: Harvard University Press, 1998), 1–55.

49. Ibid., 156.

50. Ibid., 207.

51. Lott, *Love and Theft*; Noel Ignatiev, *How the Irish Became White* (New York: Routledge, 1995); David R. Roediger, *The Wages of Whiteness: Race and the Making of the American Working Class*, rev. ed. (London: Verso, 2007).

52. *Irishman in Jim Crow Pose*, in *Specimens of Theatrical Cuts . . . Suitable for Theatrical, Variety, or Circus Business* (Philadelphia, 1869), Winterthur Library.

53. Lhamon, *Raising Cain*, 56.

54. T. D. Rice, *The Original Jim Crow*, qtd. in Lhamon, *Jump Jim Crow*, 98, 101.

55. Clay appears to use *juba* as a generic term for African American dance. According to Marian Hannah Winter, the word *juba* derives from *giouba*, a common West African step dance transported to North America through the Atlantic slave trade. William Henry Lane, the first African American dancer to perform alongside white minstrels in blackface, adopted the stage name Master Juba in the early 1840s, more than a decade after the publication of Clay's *Pat Juba* print. See Winter, "Juba and American Minstrelsy," in Bean, Hatch, and McNamara, *Inside the Minstrel Mask*, 224.

56. James Green identifies several of the figures in *Lessons in Dancing* in an email dated January 24, 2011, and filed in the E. W. Clay research folder at the Library Company of Philadelphia.

57. Miller, *Slaves to Fashion*, 104.

58. *Pennsylvania Gazette*, February 29, 1828, qtd. in *Freedom's Journal*, March 14, 1828, *Accessible Archives*, http://www.accessible.com

59. *Freedom's Journal*, March 14, 1828.

60. *North Star*, July 6, 1849, 2.

61. *Pennsylvania Gazette*, February 29, 1828, qtd. in *Freedom's Journal*, March 14, 1828.

62. White and White, *Stylin'*, 79.

63. Katrin Sieg, *Ethnic Drag: Performing Race, Nation, Sexuality in West Germany* (Ann Arbor: University of Michigan Press, 2002), 32.

64. Coco Fusco, "Framing Whiteness," *e-misférica* 5.2 (2008), www.emisferica.org

65. Dale Cockrell, *Demons of Disorder: Early Blackface Minstrels and Their World* (Cambridge: Cambridge University Press, 1997), 96.

66. Ibid., 56; J. Thomas Scharf and Thompson Westcott, *History of Philadelphia, 1609–1884* (Philadelphia, 1884), 2:1080. T. Allston Brown corroborates Scharf and Westcott's account, though he gives the name of the Philadelphia actor who premiered "Coal Black Rose" as Bill Keller rather than William Kelly. See Brown's "Early History of Negro Minstrelsy," a series of fifty-nine articles

in the *New York Clipper* published between 1912 and 1914 and reprinted in *Burnt Cork and Tambourines: A Sourcebook of Negro Minstrelsy*, ed. William L. Slout (San Bernardino, CA: Borgo Press, 2007), 7.

67. Qtd. in Davison, "E. W. Clay," 92.

68. White Snyder, "The Coal Black Rose" (ca. 1827–29), Brown University Library.

69. Qtd. in Lhamon, *Jump Jim Crow*, 414n78.

70. Ibid., 43.

71. Ibid., 43–44.

72. Ibid., 43.

73. T. D. Rice, *Oh! Hush! Or the Virginny Cupids*, in ibid., 152–53, 156, 158.

74. Edward Williams Clay, *Life in Philadelphia: "How you like de new fashion shirt . . . ,"* plate 9 (Philadelphia, 1830), Library Company of Philadelphia.

75. Miller, *Slaves to Fashion*, 104.

76. Maureen Needham Costonis, "'The Wild Doe': Augusta Maywood in Philadelphia and Paris, 1837–1840," *Dance Chronicle* 17.2 (1994): 125.

77. Ibid., 124–27. Maywood left New York City in May 1838 to study and perform in Europe, where she quickly became a star. See ibid., 129–44.

78. Théophile Gautier, *La Presse*, November 27, 1837, qtd. in Ivor Guest, ed., *Gautier on Dance* (London: Dance Books Ltd., 1986), 30.

79. Gautier, *La Presse*, June 10, 1844, qtd. in ibid., 135. On *ballet blanc*, the second act of a typical romantic ballet, see Sarah Davies Cordova, "Romantic Ballet in France, 1830–1850," in *The Cambridge Companion to Ballet*, ed. Marion Kant (Cambridge: Cambridge University Press, 2007), 113–25.

80. Edward W. Said, *Orientalism* (1978; repr., New York: Penguin Books, 2003), 2.

81. Gautier, *La Presse*, August 20, 1838, qtd. in Guest, *Gautier on Dance*, 41.

82. Said, *Orientalism*, 63.

83. Fabio Ciaramelli, "Levinas's Ethical Discourse between Individuation and Universality," in *Re-reading Levinas*, ed. Robert Bernasconi and Simon Critchley (Bloomington: Indiana University Press, 1991), 90.

84. Homi K. Bhabha, *The Location of Culture* (1991; London: Routledge, 2004), 122.

85. Daniel R. Biddle and Murray Dubin, *Tasting Freedom: Octavius Catto and the Battle for Equality in Civil War America* (Philadelphia: Temple University Press, 2010), 169.

86. For a thorough account of the restriction of black voting rights in 1830s Pennsylvania, see Nick Salvatore, *We All Got History: The Memory Books of Amos Webber* (New York: Times Books, 1996), 13–16.

87. Bhabha, *Location of Culture*, 128.

CHAPTER FOUR

Epigraph: Gertrude Stein, *Gertrude Stein's America*, ed. Gilbert A. Harrison (Washington, DC: Robert B. Luce, 1965), 95.

1. Susan G. Davis, *Parades and Power: Street Theatre in Nineteenth-Century*

Philadelphia (Philadelphia: Temple University Press, 1986); Mary P. Ryan, *Women in Public: Between Banners and Ballots, 1825–1880* (Baltimore: Johns Hopkins University Press, 1990); David Glassberg, *American Historical Pageantry: The Uses of Tradition in the Early Twentieth Century* (Chapel Hill: University of North Carolina Press, 1990); Brooks McNamara, *Day of Jubilee: The Great Age of Public Celebrations in New York, 1788–1909* (New Brunswick, NJ: Rutgers University Press, 1997).

2. Robin Bernstein, *Racial Innocence: Performing American Childhood from Slavery to Civil Rights* (New York: New York University Press, 2011), 129.

3. Michel de Certeau, *The Practice of Everyday Life*, trans. Steven Rendall (Berkeley: University of California Press, 1984), 92. Gertrude Stein, *Picasso* (1938; repr., New York: Dover Publications, 1984), 50.

4. William Penn, *The Papers of William Penn*, vol. 2, 1680–1684, ed. Richard S. Dunn and Mary Maples Dunn (Philadelphia: University of Pennsylvania Press, 1982), 121. Lewis Mumford, *The City in History: Its Origins, its Transformations, and its Prospects* (San Diego: Harcourt, 1961), 279.

5. Nick Salvato, *Obstruction* (Durham, NC: Duke University Press, 2016), 24.

6. Militia Act of 1792, The Constitution Society, http://www.constitution.org/mil/mil_act_1792.htm

7. S. Davis, *Parades and Power*, 81. Throughout this chapter I draw on Davis's detailed account of Pluck's militia career.

8. *Saturday Evening Post*, September 9, 1826, 2. See also *Saturday Evening Post*, September 23, 1826, 2.

9. Francis Preston Blair, John Cook Rives, and Franklin Rives, eds., *The Congressional Globe: Containing Sketches of the Debates and Proceedings of the Twenty-Fifth Congress* [1837–39] (Washington, DC, 1839), 7:397.

10. *Saturday Evening Post*, May 21, 1825, 3.

11. *Niles' Weekly Register*, October 28, 1826, 134.

12. "Colonel Pluck and Landlord, Fill the Flowing Bowl" (Boston, ca. 1837–40), Library Company of Philadelphia. I thank Phillip Lapsansky for bringing this source to my attention.

13. Steven Rosswurm, *Arms, Country, and Class: The Philadelphia Militia and the "Lower Sort" during the American Revolution* (New Brunswick, NJ: Rutgers University Press, 1987), 75. Rosswurm notes that Pennsylvania—unlike Britain's other North American colonies—lacked "an institutional militia system" at the outbreak of the Revolutionary War. "Because Philadelphia began with no militia structure," he argues, "the laboring poor were able more easily to place their imprint on the institution" (49).

14. Samuel Curwen, qtd. in ibid., 50. S. Davis, *Parades and Power*, 51. For a thorough account of burlesque militia parades in Philadelphia and other northern U.S. cities in the early nineteenth century, see S. Davis., 77–103.

15. Ibid., 39–42.

16. *Saturday Evening Post*, May 7, 1825, 3.

17. S. Davis, *Parades and Power*, 80–81.

18. Ibid., 62.

19. *Niles' Weekly Register*, August 12, 1826, 413.

20. *New York Mirror and Ladies' Literary Gazette*, August 12, 1826, 23.

21. *Niles' Weekly Register*, September 16, 1826, 48.

22. Barbara A. Babcock, introduction to *The Reversible World: Symbolic Inversion in Art and Society*, ed. Barbara A. Babcock (Ithaca, NY: Cornell University Press, 1978), 32.

23. Terry Eagleton, *Walter Benjamin; or, Toward a Revolutionary Criticism* (London: New Left Books, 1981), 148.

24. Bernard F. Reilly tentatively dates Johnston's lithograph of Pluck to 1825, but given that Pluck did not tour to Boston until the following year, a date of 1826 for this engraving seems just as likely. See Reilly, *American Political Prints, 1766–1876: A Catalog of the Collections in the Library of Congress* (Boston: G.K. Hall, 1991), 30.

25. J. Thomas Scharf and Thompson Westcott, *History of Philadelphia, 1609–1884* (Philadelphia, 1884), 2:1058.

26. On Johnston's theatrical career, see ibid., 2:1058; and Charles A. Poulson, collector, "Durang's History of the Philadelphia Stage Scrapbook, 1854–1863," 1:18, Library Company of Philadelphia.

27. The relevant lines from *Henry IV, Part I*, are:

> By being seldom seen, I could not stir
> But like a comet I was wond'red at,
> That men would tell their children, "This is he";
> Others would say, "Where, which is Bullingbrook?"
> And then I stole all courtesy from heaven,
> And dress'd myself in such humility
> That I did pluck allegiance from men's hearts.

William Shakespeare, *Henry IV, Part 1*, in *The Riverside Shakespeare*, ed. G. Blakemore Evans (Boston: Houghton Mifflin, 1974), 3.2.46–52. Johnston elides the phrase "By being seldom seen" and adapts the remainder of Shakespeare's lines as follows:

> . . . I could not stir,
> But like a comet, I was wonder'd at;
> Others would tell their children "This is he"
> Others would say—Where? which is the "Colonel?"
> And then I stole all courtesy from heaven,
> And dres'd myself in such humility,
> That I did PLUCK allegience [*sic*] from men's hearts.

28. Mikhail Bakhtin, *Rabelais and His World*, trans. Hélène Iswolsky (Bloomington: Indiana University Press, 1984), 197.

29. S. Davis, *Parades and Power*, 62.

30. Gary B. Nash, *Forging Freedom: The Formation of Philadelphia's Black Community, 1720–1840* (Cambridge, MA: Harvard University Press, 1988), 254–56; Phillip Lapsansky, "Graphic Discord: Abolitionist and Antiabolitionist Images," in *The Abolitionist Sisterhood: Women's Political Culture in Antebellum America*, ed. Jean Fagan Yellin and John C. Van Horne (Ithaca, NY: Cornell University Press, 1994), 217–23; Jennifer A. Greenhill, "Playing the Fool: David

Claypoole Johnston and the Menial Labor of Caricature," *American Art* 17.3 (2003): 43. In *Sound Asleep or Wide Awake*, two native-born white laborers draw a face on the bald pate of a drunk, sleeping Irishman.

31. Peter Stallybrass and Allon White, *The Politics and Poetics of Transgression* (Ithaca, NY: Cornell University Press, 1986), 16, 19, 44–45, 53.

32. Bakhtin, *Rabelais*, 184.

33. Charles Jewett, *A Forty Years' Fight with the Drink Demon; or, A History of the Temperance Reform as I Have Seen It, and of My Labor in Connection Therewith* (New York, 1872), 117–18.

34. Bakhtin, *Rabelais*, 11–12.

35. My approximate count includes the "replies to bobalition," a series of rebuttals to the bobalition broadsides, which retained much of the scurrilous language and imagery that they purported to argue against.

36. Shane White, "'It Was a Proud Day': African Americans, Festivals, and Parades in the North, 1741–1834," *Journal of American History* 81.1 (1994): 35, 38.

37. David Waldstreicher, *In the Midst of Perpetual Fetes: The Making of American Nationalism, 1776–1820* (Chapel Hill: University of North Carolina Press, 1997), 337.

38. E. K. Chambers, *The Medieval Stage* (London: Oxford University Press, 1903), 1:394.

39. Dale Cockrell, *Demons of Disorder: Early Blackface Minstrels and Their World* (Cambridge: Cambridge University Press, 1997), 44.

40. Herbert Halpert, "A Typology of Mumming," in *Christmas Mumming in Newfoundland: Essays in Anthropology, Folklore, and History*, ed. Herbert Halpert and G. M. Story (Toronto: University of Toronto Press, 1990), 35–37.

41. E. K. Chambers, *The English Folk-Play* (Oxford: Oxford University Press, 1933), 9.

42. On male-to-female transvestism in mummers' plays, see Halpert, "Typology of Mumming," 58–59.

43. Chambers, *English Folk-Play*, 212. For further examples and analyses of brooms and sweeping in English mummers' plays, see also 19, 23, 67, 101, 125, 131, 208, 211.

44. George Speaight, *Punch and Judy: A History* (London: Studio Vista, 1970), 28.

45. On the Punch and Judy show in the United States, see Ryan Howard, *Punch and Judy in Nineteenth-Century America* (Jefferson, NC: McFarland, 2013).

46. "Clare de Kitchen" (Baltimore, ca. 1830), qtd. in W. T. Lhamon Jr., *Jump Jim Crow: Lost Plays, Lyrics, and Street Prose of the First Atlantic Popular Culture* (Cambridge, MA: Harvard University Press, 2003), 137.

47. Cockrell, *Demons of Disorder*, 50.

48. "Buy a Broom" (Baltimore, ca. 1827–29), box 1, Sheet Music Collection, Winterthur Library.

49. Corey Capers, "Black Voices/White Print: Race-Making, Print Politics, and the Rhetoric of Disorder in the Early National U.S. North, 1793–1824" (PhD diss., University of California, Santa Cruz, 2004), 128.

50. Waldstreicher, *In the Midst of Perpetual Fetes*, 337; Joanne Pope Melish, *Disowning Slavery: Gradual Emancipation and "Race" in New England, 1780–1860* (Ithaca, NY: Cornell University Press, 1998), 182.

51. Waldstreicher, *In the Midst of Perpetual Fetes*, 337.

52. Phillip Lapsansky, "Afro-Americana: Inventing Black Folks," *Annual Report of the Library Company of Philadelphia for the Year 1997: Presented at the Annual Meeting, May 1998* (Philadelphia: Library Company of Philadelphia, 1998), 33.

53. Douglas A. Jones Jr., *The Captive Stage: Performance and the Proslavery Imagination of the Antebellum North* (Ann Arbor: University of Michigan Press, 2014), 49.

54. *Bobalition of Slavery* (Boston, ca. 1832), Library of Congress.

55. *Pennsylvania Gazette*, May 21, 1833, qtd. in S. Davis, *Parades and Power*, 93.

56. Waldstreicher, *In the Midst of Perpetual Fetes*, 334.

57. White, "It Was a Proud Day," 50.

58. Jones, *Captive Stage*, 31.

59. Eliza Cope Harrison, ed., *Philadelphia Merchant: The Diary of Thomas P. Cope, 1800–1851* (South Bend, IN: Gateway Editions, 1978), 468.

60. Daniel R. Biddle and Murray Dubin, *Tasting Freedom: Octavius Catto and the Battle for Equality in Civil War America* (Philadelphia: Temple University Press, 2010), 252.

61. Nick Salvatore, *We All Got History: The Memory Books of Amos Webber* (New York: Times Books, 1996), 66.

62. Corey Capers, "Black Voices, White Print: Racial Practice, Print Publicity, and Order in the Early American Republic," in *Early African American Print Culture*, ed. Lara Langer Cohen and Jordan Alexander Stein (Philadelphia: University of Pennsylvania Press, 2012), 111.

63. Waldstreicher, *In the Midst of Perpetual Fetes*, 296.

64. Paul Gilroy, *The Black Atlantic: Modernity and Double Consciousness* (Cambridge, MA: Harvard University Press, 1993), 37–38.

65. Sigmund Freud, *Jokes and their Relation to the Unconscious*, trans. and ed. James Strachey (New York: W.W. Norton, 1989), 137–38. I thank John Emigh for suggesting this Freudian intervention.

66. Ibid., 185.

67. Timothy Meagher, *The Columbia Guide to Irish American History* (New York: Columbia University Press, 2005), 43, 52.

68. Ibid., 52–53.

69. David R. Roediger, *The Wages of Whiteness: Race and the Making of the American Working Class*, rev. ed. (London: Verso, 2007), 134.

70. Hugh J. Nolan, qtd. in Carl Wittke, *The Irish in America* (Baton Rouge: Louisiana State University Press, 1956), 125.

71. Roediger, *Wages of Whiteness*, 134.

72. *Philadelphia North American*, December 21, 1913, qtd. in Alfred L. Shoemaker, *Christmas in Pennsylvania: A Folk-Cultural Study* (1959; repr., Mechanicsburg, PA: Stackpole Books, 1999), 6.

73. Bruce Laurie, *Working People of Philadelphia, 1800–1850* (Philadelphia: Temple University Press, 1980), 64.

74. John Runcie, "'Hunting the Nigs' in Philadelphia: The Race Riot of August 1834," *Pennsylvania History* 39.2 (1972): 196.

75. *Pennsylvanian*, August 16, 1834; and *Philadelphia Intelligencer*, August 15, 1834, both qtd. in *Niles' Weekly Register*, August 23, 1834, 435.

76. Runcie, "Hunting the Nigs," 217.

77. According to Runcie, less than 1 percent of black Philadelphians worked in the same skilled trades as the white craftsmen who participated in the Moyamensing riots. Ibid., 201.

78. Emma Jones Lapsansky, "'Since They Got Those Separate Churches': Afro-Americans and Racism in Jacksonian Philadelphia," *American Quarterly* 32.1 (1980): 75–76.

79. For a detailed account of the burning of Pennsylvania Hall, see Samuel Otter, *Philadelphia Stories: America's Literature of Race and Freedom* (New York: Oxford University Press, 2010), 131–57.

80. Sam Bass Warner Jr., *The Private City: Philadelphia in Three Periods of Its Growth* (Philadelphia: University of Pennsylvania Press, 1968), 140–41.

81. "Local Affairs," *Philadelphia Public Ledger*, October 10, 1849, 2.

82. Runcie, "Hunting the Nigs," 62. On anti-German violence in Philadelphia, see S. Davis, *Parades and Power*, 107–8.

83. For a thorough history of the Kensington riots, see Michael Feldberg, *The Philadelphia Riots of 1844: A Study of Ethnic Conflict* (Westport, CT: Greenwood Press, 1975).

84. "De Philadelphia Riots; or, I Guess It Wan't de Niggas Dis Time" (Philadelphia, ca. 1844), Library Company of Philadelphia.

85. Diane Negra, introduction to *The Irish in Us: Irishness, Performativity, and Popular Culture*, ed. Diane Negra (Durham, NC: Duke University Press, 2006), 3.

86. E. S. Abdy, *Journal of a Residence and Tour in the United States of North America, from April 1833 to October 1834* (New York: Negro Universities Press, 1969), 3:325.

87. "Colonel Pluck and Landlord, Fill the Flowing Bowl," Boston, ca. 1837–40, Library Company of Philadelphia.

88. *Philadelphia Gazette*, March 5, 1821, qtd. in Milo M. Naeve, *John Lewis Krimmel: An Artist in Federal America* (Newark: University of Delaware Press, 1987), 116.

89. *Poulson's American Daily Advertiser*, March 13, 1821, qtd. in ibid., 117.

90. Alexander Nemerov, *The Body of Raphaelle Peale: Still Life and Selfhood, 1812–1824* (Berkeley: University of California Press, 2001), 94.

91. For a characterization of "butchers' boys" as dog fighters and "blackguards," see Robert Waln, *The Hermit in America on a Visit to Philadelphia: Containing Some Account of the Beaux and Belles, Dandies and Coquettes, Cotillion Parties, Supper Parties &c. &c. of that Famous City* (Philadelphia, 1819), 202. Harold O. Sprogle blames "firemen and butcher boys" for the nightly brawls outside Philadelphia's Grand Central Theater during the Civil War. See Sprogle, *The Philadelphia Police, Past and Present* (Philadelphia, 1887), 326.

92. Laurie, *Working People of Philadelphia*, 10.

93. Oliver Evans, "Steam Boats and Steam Wagons," *Niles' Weekly Register*, June 27, 1835, 297.

94. Seth Rockman, *Scraping By: Wage Labor, Slavery, and Survival in Early Baltimore* (Baltimore: Johns Hopkins University Press, 2009), 76, 79, 86–87, 99. Unlike in Philadelphia, Baltimore's dredging operation remained horse powered

rather than steam powered for most of the early nineteenth century. See ibid., 76, 81–83.

95. Solon Robinson, *Hot Corn: Life Scenes in New York, Illustrated, Including the Story of Little Katy, Madalina, the Rag-Picker's Daughter, Wild Maggie &c., with Original Designs Engraved by N. Orr* (New York, 1854).

96. Karl Marx, *The Eighteenth Brumaire of Louis Bonaparte*, ed. C. P. Dutt (New York: International Publishers, 1963), 75.

97. W. T. Lhamon Jr., *Raising Cain: Blackface Performance from Jim Crow to Hip Hop* (Cambridge, MA: Harvard University Press, 1998), 75–76, 139, 207.

98. Eric Lott, *Love and Theft: Blackface Minstrelsy and the American Working Class* (New York: Oxford University Press, 1993), 35.

99. W. T. Lhamon Jr., "Ebery Time I Wheel about I Jump Jim Crow: Cycles of Minstrel Transgression from Cool White to Vanilla Ice," in *Inside the Minstrel Mask: Readings in Nineteenth-Century Blackface Minstrelsy*, ed. Annemarie Bean, James V. Hatch, and Brooks McNamara (Hanover, NH: Wesleyan University Press, 1996), 278.

100. *Statutes at Large of the United States of America*, vol. 13 (Boston, 1866), 599.

101. Biddle and Dubin, *Tasting Freedom*, 291–92.

102. "Local Affairs," *Philadelphia Public Ledger*, August 27, 1859, 2.

103. Amos Webber, qtd. in Salvatore, *We All Got History*, 82.

104. Biddle and Dubin, *Tasting Freedom*, 318–19.

105. "The Black Brigade," in *Songs of Yale: A New Collection of College Songs*, ed. Charles S. Elliot (New Haven, CT, 1870), 82.

106. Robert C. Toll, *Blacking Up: The Minstrel Show in Nineteenth-Century America* (New York: Oxford University Press, 1974), 132n28.

107. Ibid., 124.

108. Edward Le Roy Rice, *Monarchs of Minstrelsy from "Daddy" Rice to Date* (New York: Kenny Publishing, 1911), 34, 92.

109. *Our Day*, November 19 and December 17, 1860, Harvard Theatre Collection.

110. Carncross and Dixey's Minstrels Playbill, 1865, qtd. in Toll, *Blacking Up*, 171.

111. Thomas Dilverd Photo Card, n.d., Minstrel Show Collection, box 6, file 7, Harry Ransom Center, University of Texas, Austin.

112. Toll, *Blacking Up*, 197–98; "Japanese Tommy's Funeral," *New York Times*, July 13, 1887, 8.

113. Frank Dumont, "The Old Dressing Room Mirror," *New York Clipper*, December 25, 1915, 42.

114. John Russell Bartlett, *Dictionary of Americanisms*, 4th ed. (Boston, 1877), 304.

115. Eleventh Street Opera House Playbill, May 13, 1911, Minstrel Show Collection, box 44, file 7, Ransom Center.

116. "Frank Dumont Dies as Curtain Rises," *Philadelphia Inquirer*, March 18, 1919, 10.

117. Corey Elizabeth Leighton, "Strutting It up through Histories: A Performance Genealogy of the Philadelphia Mummers Parade" (PhD diss., Louisiana State University, 2009), 45. Cf. John Jay Daly, *A Song in His Heart: The Life and*

Times of James A. Bland (Philadelphia: John C. Winston Co., 1951), 69.

118. Charles E. Welch Jr., *Oh! Dem Golden Slippers: The Story of the Philadelphia Mummers*, rev. ed. (Philadelphia: Book Street Press, 1991), 123.

119. Leighton, "Strutting It up through Histories," 45.

120. On Charles Dumont's first documented appearance in the Mummers Parade, see "Shooters Amaze and Delight with Fantastic Garb," *Philadelphia Inquirer*, January 2, 1912, 1. On the mummers' first documented performance of "Oh! Dem Golden Slippers," see "Shooters Pageant Delights 500,000 Plucky Beholders," *Philadelphia Inquirer*, January 2, 1920, 2.

121. Tracy C. Davis, "Performative Time," in *Representing the Past: Essays in Performance Historiography*, ed. Charlotte M. Canning and Thomas Postlewait (Iowa City: University of Iowa Press, 2010), 149.

CHAPTER FIVE

1. Charles E. Welch Jr., *Oh! Dem Golden Slippers: The Story of the Philadelphia Mummers*, rev. ed. (Philadelphia: Book Street Press, 1991), 154.

2. Frank Dougherty and Ron Goldwyn, "Anatomy of a Mummer: Yo, Wench," *Philadelphia Daily News*, December 30, 1994, M8.

3. Susan G. Davis, "'Making Night Hideous': Christmas Revelry and Public Order in Nineteenth-Century Philadelphia," *American Quarterly* 34.2 (1982): 185.

4. Ron Goldwyn, telephone interview with the author, February 10, 2010.

5. Welch, *Oh! Dem Golden Slippers*, 154.

6. W. T. Lhamon Jr., *Raising Cain: Blackface Performance from Jim Crow to Hip Hop* (Cambridge, MA: Harvard University Press, 1998), 56.

7. Walnut Street Theater Program, June 15, 1842, qtd. in Frank Dumont, "The Golden Days of Minstrelsy: The Musings of an Old Timer," *New York Clipper*, December 19, 1914, ii.

8. Most historians of blackface minstrelsy argue that the Virginia Minstrels—Billy Whitlock, Frank Pelham, Dan Emmett, and Frank Brower—performed North America's "first" minstrel show at the Chatham Theater in New York City in January or February 1843. Lhamon disputes this claim in *Raising Cain*, arguing instead that the minstrel show began in Buffalo, New York, where E. P. Christy formed a band of three blackface musicians in June 1842—the same month that the "Negro Oddities" act appeared at the Walnut Street Theater in Philadelphia. Rather than debate the exact date and location of the "first" minstrel show, I find it more instructive to note that multipart blackface performances by ensembles of three or more musicians and dancers emerged within months of each other in New York, Buffalo, Philadelphia, and other northern U.S. cities between the summer of 1842 and the winter of 1842–43.

9. Robert B. Winans, "Early Minstrel Show Music, 1843–1852," in *Inside the Minstrel Mask: Readings in Nineteenth-Century Blackface Minstrelsy*, ed. Annemarie Bean, James V. Hatch, and Brooks McNamara (Hanover, NH: Wesleyan University Press, 1996), 150.

10. S. Foster Damon, *Series of Old American Songs, Reproduced in Facsimile from Original or Early Editions in the Harris Collection of American Poetry and Plays, Brown University* (Providence: Brown University Library, 1936), n.p.

11. *The Virginia Serenaders Illustrated Songster: Containing All the Songs, as Sung by the Far Famed Band of Original Virginia Serenaders . . . throughout the Principal Cities of the United States* (New York, 1843), 30–31, Brown University Library.

12. Eric Lott, *Love and Theft: Blackface Minstrelsy and the American Working Class* (New York: Oxford University Press, 1993), 160.

13. Christine Stansell, *City of Women: Sex and Class in New York, 1789–1860* (Urbana: University of Illinois Press, 1987), 81.

14. Lott, *Love and Theft*, 161–64.

15. Bruce McConachie, "Cognitive Studies and Epistemic Competence in Cultural History: Moving beyond Freud and Lacan," in *Performance and Cognition: Theatre Studies and the Cognitive Turn*, ed. Bruce McConachie and F. Elizabeth Hart (London: Routledge, 2006), 63–65. *Pace* McConachie, I note that Lott—concerned as he is with the social *unconscious* of the minstrel show—makes no claims regarding the *conscious* intentions of either performers or spectators of the antebellum wench act.

16. Olive Logan, "The Ancestry of Brudder Bones," *Harper's New Monthly Magazine* 58 (1879): 698.

17. Lynne Fauley Emery, *Black Dance from 1619 to Today*, rev. ed. (Princeton, NJ: Princeton Book, 1988), 208.

18. Dougherty and Goldwyn, "Anatomy of a Mummer," M8.

19. Gayle V. Fischer, *Pantaloons and Power: A Nineteenth-Century Dress Reform in the United States* (Kent, OH: Kent State University Press, 2001), 79–80. See also Marjorie Garber, *Vested Interests: Cross-Dressing and Cultural Anxiety* (New York: Routledge, 1992), 311–12.

20. Fischer, *Pantaloons and Power*, 93.

21. Garber, *Vested Interests*, 314.

22. Mary Walker, qtd. in ibid.

23. Dale Cockrell, *Demons of Disorder: Early Blackface Minstrels and Their World* (Cambridge: Cambridge University Press, 1997), 147.

24. Garber, *Vested Interests*, 277.

25. New Orleans Minstrel Show Playbill, n.d., filed in "Uncatalogued Minstrel Program, Sa-Si," Harvard Theatre Collection.

26. According to Goldwyn, "Some guys will bring their young daughters along [with the wench brigades], but you don't see adolescent girls out there marching with their fathers." Goldwyn, telephone interview.

27. Zoe Strauss, *Tattooed Penises* (2008), in *Zoe Strauss: 10 Years*, ed. Peter Barberie (Philadelphia: Philadelphia Museum of Art, 2012), plate 60. I could not obtain permission to reproduce *Tattooed Penises* in this book.

28. Strauss's other photographs of mummers wenches include *Mummer with Bud in Black Face Paint* (2004), *Wench with Cigarette* (2010), and *Wench with Flag in Front of Dolphin* (2010). See Barberie, *Zoe Strauss*, plates 62, 65, 79.

29. Mikhail Bakhtin, *Rabelais and His World*, trans. Hélène Iswolsky (Bloomington: Indiana University Press, 1984), 218.

30. Rich Porco, qtd. in Christian DuComb, "The Wenches of the Philadelphia Mummers Parade: A Performance Genealogy," in *Performing Utopia*, ed. Rachel Bowditch and Pegge Vissicaro (London: Seagull Books, 2017), 167.

31. Ed Smith, telephone interview with the author, November 10, 2010.

32. Goldwyn, telephone interview.

33. Lhamon, *Raising Cain*, 56–115.

34. Charles A. Poulson, collector, "Durang's History of the Philadelphia Stage Scrapbook, 1854–1863," 2:25, Library Company of Philadelphia.

35. Pierce Egan, *Life in London; or, The Day and Night Scenes of Jerry Hawthorn, Esq. and His Elegant Friend Corinthian Tom, Accompanied by Bob Logic, the Oxonian, in Their Rambles and Sprees through the Metropolis* (London, 1821), 286.

36. W. T. Moncrieff, *Tom and Jerry; or, Life in London in 1820: A Drama in Three Acts, from Pierce Egan's Celebrated Work* (London, n.d.), 62.

37. Peter P. Reed, *Rogue Performances: Staging the Underclass in Early American Theatre Culture* (New York: Palgrave Macmillan, 2009), 130. In a notable exception to this pattern, William Brown, an African American theater producer, staged *Tom and Jerry* in New York City in June 1823 with a primarily black cast, retaining the comic dance by Dusty Bob and African Sal and appending a slave market scene to the end of Moncrieff's play. See ibid., 141–44; Marvin McAllister, *White People Do Not Know How to Behave at Entertainments Designed for Ladies and Gentlemen of Color: William Brown's African and American Theater* (Chapel Hill: University of North Carolina Press, 2003), 115–30.

38. Moncrieff, *Tom and Jerry*, 62.

39. Between 1839 and 1843 the Walnut Street Theater offered lower admission prices, more benefit nights for fire companies (a draw for working-class, male audiences), and a more popular repertoire than its main competitor, the "aristocratic" Chestnut Street Theater, or "Old Drury." See Arthur Herman Wilson, *A History of the Philadelphia Theatre, 1835–1855* (Philadelphia: University of Pennsylvania Press, 1935), 12–24.

40. Reed, *Rogue Performances*, 131.

41. Moncrieff, *Tom and Jerry*, 62.

42. Dougherty and Goldwyn, "Anatomy of a Mummer," M8.

43. Ron Goldwyn, "Fancy This: No More Secrets; 26 Parade Judges Strut out of Closet," *Philadelphia Daily News*, December 29, 1988, M2.

44. *Indianapolis Freeman*, March 3, 1897, qtd. in Henry T. Sampson, *Blacks in Blackface: A Sourcebook on Early Black Musical Shows* (Metuchen, NJ: Scarecrow Press, 1980), 78–79.

45. "Vaudeville Correspondence: Philadelphia, PA," *New York Dramatic Mirror*, March 27, 1897: 20.

46. Errol G. Hill and James V. Hatch, *A History of African American Theatre* (Cambridge: Cambridge University Press, 2003), 152–53.

47. W. E. B. Du Bois, *The Philadelphia Negro: A Social Study*, ed. Henry Louis Gates Jr. (New York: Oxford University Press, 2007), 226.

48. Welch, *Oh! Dem Golden Slippers*, 37.

49. Following terminological conventions in minstrelsy scholarship, I use *minstrelsy* and *white minstrelsy* to refer to minstrel performances by white artists. *Blackface minstrelsy* refers specifically to white minstrels performing in

blackface, and *black minstrel* describes African American artists like James Bland, who participated in the production of minstrel shows.

50. Louis Chude-Sokei, *"The Last Darky": Bert Williams, Black-on-Black Minstrelsy, and the African Diaspora* (Durham, NC: Duke University Press, 2006), 20.

51. Henry Louis Gates Jr., *The Signifying Monkey: A Theory of African American Literary Criticism* (New York: Oxford University Press, 1988), 52.

52. William R. Hullfish, "James A. Bland: Pioneer Black Songwriter," *Black Music Research Journal* 7 (1987): 14.

53. James Bland, "Oh! Dem Golden Slippers" (Boston, 1879), 3–4, Brown University Library.

54. Gary B. Nash, *Forging Freedom: The Formation of Philadelphia's Black Community, 1720–1840* (Cambridge, MA: Harvard University Press, 1988), 2.

55. Nick Salvatore, *We All Got History: The Memory Books of Amos Webber* (New York: Times Books, 1996), 71.

56. Robert Waln, *The Hermit in America on a Visit to Philadelphia: Containing Some Account of the Beaux and Belles, Dandies and Coquettes, Cotillion Parties, Supper Parties, Tea Parties, &c. &c. of that Famous City* (Philadelphia, 1819), 155.

57. John F. Szwed and Morton Marks, "The Afro-American Transformation of European Set Dances and Dance Suites," *Dance Research Journal* 20.1 (1988): 32.

58. Eileen Southern, *The Music of Black Americans: A History*, 2nd ed. (New York: W. W. Norton, 1983), 113, 254, 317; "Local Affairs," *Philadelphia Public Ledger*, August 17, 1859, 2.

59. Will Marion Cook, "Clorindy, the Origin of the Cakewalk," in *Readings in Black American Music*, ed. Eileen Southern (New York: W. W. Norton, 1983), 228.

60. Hill and Hatch, *History of African American Theatre*, 152.

61. Jurretta Jordan Heckscher, "Our National Poetry: The Afro-Chesapeake Inventions of American Dance," in *Ballroom, Boogie, Shimmy Sham, Shake: A Social and Popular Dance Reader*, ed. Julie Malnig (Urbana: University of Illinois Press, 2009), 24; Roger D. Abrahams, *Singing the Master: The Emergence of African American Culture in the Plantation South* (New York: Pantheon Books, 1992), 100.

62. Tom Fletcher, *100 Years of the Negro in Show Business* (1954; repr., New York: De Capo Press, 1984), 103.

63. Barbara L. Webb, "Authentic Possibilities: Plantation Performance of the 1890s," *Theatre Journal* 56.1 (2004): 70.

64. Marshall Stearns and Jean Stearns, *Jazz Dance: The Story of American Vernacular Dance* (New York: Macmillan, 1983), 22–23.

65. David Krasner, *Resistance, Parody, and Double Consciousness in African American Theatre, 1895–1910* (New York: St. Martin's Press, 1997), 81.

66. Following Krasner, I borrow the term *mimetic vertigo* from anthropologist Michael Taussig, who uses it to describe the entry of the self into the alterity "against which the self is defined and sustained." See Taussig, *Mimesis and Alterity: A Particular History of the Senses* (New York: Routledge, 1993), 237.

67. Joseph Roach, *Cities of the Dead: Circum-Atlantic Performance* (New York: Columbia University Press, 1996), 286.

68. Patricia Anne Masters, *The Philadelphia Mummers: Building Community through Play* (Philadelphia: Temple University Press, 2007), 70.

69. Ibid., 70.

70. Ibid., 73.

71. Charles Pete T. Banner-Haley, *To Do Good and to Do Well: Middle-Class Blacks and the Depression, Philadelphia, 1929–1941* (New York: Garland, 1993), xvi.

72. Brian Maher, *The Philadelphia Mummers' String Band Record, 1902–2015,* www.stringbandrecord.com.

73. E. A. Kennedy III, *Life, Liberty, and the Mummers* (Philadelphia: Temple University Press, 2007), 10.

74. Elias Myers, qtd. in Masters, *Philadelphia Mummers,* 75.

75. Charles Bowser, qtd. in Welch, *Oh! Dem Golden Slippers,* 153.

76. Matthew J. Countryman, *Up South: Civil Rights and Black Power in Philadelphia* (Philadelphia: University of Pennsylvania Press, 2006), 120.

77. Anonymous informant, qtd. in Masters, *Philadelphia Mummers,* 81–82.

78. Chris Petty, "CORE, 400 Ministers, NAACP Gang Up on Mummers Parade Blackface," *Philadelphia Tribune,* December 31, 1963, 1, 4.

79. Art Peters, "5 Negro Bands Set to March despite Furor: Elks, Musicians from Local 274 Hired for Parade," *Philadelphia Tribune,* January 4, 1964, 1, 3.

80. Masters, *Philadelphia Mummers,* 84.

81. Peters, "5 Negro Bands Set to March," 1, 3.

82. Welch, *Oh! Dem Golden Slippers,* 157–59.

83. "Bummer Parade," editorial, *Philadelphia Daily News,* January 8, 2009, www.philly.com

84. "The 2010 Census by Neighborhood," www.philly.com

85. Jonathan Vatnor, "Beyond the Cheesesteak Wars in Philadelphia," *New York Times,* March 25, 2010, http://travel.nytimes.com

86. B. Love Stutters, "Aliens of an Illegal Kind," Philadelphia Mummers Parade, January 1, 2009, http://www.youtube.com/watch?v=cYmcKrxLspE

87. Venetian New Year's Association, "Indi-Insourcing," Philadelphia Mummers Parade, January 1, 2013, https://www.youtube.com/watch?v=85jzJkYgFKg

88. Danielle Redden, "Love Buzz: The Matriarchal World of Bees," press release, December 29, 2015, 1.

89. Jill Dolan, *Utopia in Performance: Finding Hope at the Theater* (Ann Arbor: University of Michigan Press, 2010), 5–6.

90. Porco, qtd. in DuComb, "Wenches of the Philadelphia Mummers Parade," 183.

91. Tom Spiroploulos, qtd. in Kennedy, *Life, Liberty, and the Mummers,* 24. Kennedy identifies Spiroploulos as a "freelance" Mummer "who went up the street without the sanction of any club on New Year's Day," but Spiroploulos's Murray Club badge, clearly visible over his left breast, suggests that he is either a member of the Murray Club or the recipient of a pilfered badge from a sympathetic club member.

92. Masters, *Philadelphia Mummers,* 86.

93. Natalia Smirnov, qtd. in DuComb, "Wenches of the Philadelphia Mummers Parade," 185.

CONCLUSION

1. Ed Kirlin, qtd. in Max L. Raab, dir., *Strut* (Max L. Raab Productions, 2002), DVD.

2. Paul Gilroy, *The Black Atlantic: Modernity and Double Consciousness* (Cambridge, MA: Harvard University Press, 1993), 38.

3. Michael Warner, *Publics and Counterpublics* (New York: Zone Books, 2005), 56–57.

4. Elizabeth Maddock Dillon, *New World Drama: The Performative Commons in the Atlantic World, 1649–1849* (Durham, NC: Duke University Press, 2014), 17.

5. Joseph A. Ferko String Band, "Bringin' Back those Minstrel Days," Philadelphia Mummers Parade, January 1, 2013, https://www.youtube.com/watch?v=J_EDvOd0nEQ

6. Jürgen Habermas, "Further Reflections of the Public Sphere," in *Habermas and the Public Sphere*, ed. Craig Calhoun (Cambridge, MA: MIT Press, 1992), 427.

7. Tom Avril, "New Route, Same Mummers Attitude," *Philadelphia Inquirer*, January 1, 2015, www.philly.com

8. Maria Panaritis, "With a New Division, Mummers Embrace Diversity," *Philadelphia Inquirer*, December 26, 2015, www.philly.com

9. Ana Gamboa, "Mummers and Carnavaleros: A Tradition of Inclusion?," *Al Día*, April 16, 2015, www.aldianews.com

10. Dan McQuade, "Mummers: We Promise to Clean Up Our Acts Next Year," *Philadelphia Magazine*, January 4, 2016, www.phillymag.com; Dayna Evans, "The New Year Is the Oldest Thing: Inside Philadelphia's Mummers Parade," *Gawker*, January 19, 2015, www.gawker.com

11. "One Mummer's Vulgar Homophobic Slur Caught on Video," *Philadelphia Inquirer*, January 3, 2016, www.philly.com

12. McQuade, "Mummers."

13. Finnegan New Year's Brigade, "Going for the Gold," Philadelphia Mummers Parade, January 1, 2016, https://youtu.be/tLwM5lTFnZo

14. Michael J. Inemer Sr., qtd. in "One Mummer's Vulgar Homophobic Slur."

15. Steve Mann, "Sousveillance: Wearable Computing and Citizen 'Undersight,'" *H+ Magazine*, July 10, 2009, www.hplusmagazine.com

16. Evans, "The New Year Is the Oldest Thing."

17. Kirlin, qtd. in Raab, *Strut*.

18. Charlene Mires, *Independence Hall in American Memory* (Philadelphia: University of Pennsylvania Press, 2002), 56.

19. Charles Willson Peale, qtd. in ibid., 42.

20. Ibid.

21. *Philadelphia Public Ledger*, qtd. in George William Douglas, *The American Book of Days*, rev. ed. (New York: H. W. Wilson, 1948), 6–7.

22. Brian Connolly, "Intimate Atlantics: Toward a Critical History of Transnational Early America," *Common-Place* 11.2 (2011), www.common-place.org

Index

Page numbers in italics indicate figures.